OPEN
A WORLD
OF POSSIBLE

Real Stories About the
Joy and Power of Reading

es

binson

SCHOLASTIC

New York • Toronto • London • Auckland • Sydney
Mexico City • New Delhi • Hong Kong • Buenos Aires

DEDICATION

For all children, and for all who love and inspire them—
a world of possible awaits in the pages of a book.

And for our beloved friend, Walter Dean Myers (1937–2014),
who related reading to life itself:
"Once I began to read, I began to exist."

Cover Designer: Charles Kreloff
Editor: Lois Bridges
Copy/Production Editor: Danny Miller
Interior Designer: Sarah Morrow
Compilation © 2014 Scholastic Inc.
All rights reserved. Published by Scholastic Inc.
Printed in the U.S.A.
ISBN: 978-0-545-79993-5

1 2 3 4 5 6 7 8 9 10 40 21 20 19 18 17 16 15 14

CONTENTS

Imagination

Inspiration

Advocacy

ACKNOWLEDGMENTS

This book exists because of our illustrious contributors; we are deeply grateful to each and every one of you for sharing these seminal and inspiring moments of your reading lives. We thank you for your wisdom, time, and generosity of spirit. To my collaborator, Billy DiMichele, Vice President, Creative Development, you were the heartbeat of the project. Charming Billy, you make all things possible.

To Editorial Director Virginia Dooley, heartfelt thanks for supporting the work in multiple ways, and to our Teaching Resources colleagues Lynne Wilson, Adrienne Downey, and Zach Chang, thank you for always providing the help that's needed at the exact moment of need. Allison Feldman, your gift of time and space enabled the project.

Regarding those who helped connect us with contributors, we are especially grateful to Teresa Mlawer and Andrea Pinkney, both of whom offered invaluable guidance and kind assistance. For welcomed inspiration and more connections, thank you Francie Alexander, Pam Allyn, Carol Jago, Judy Koch, ReLeah Cossett Lent, Bobbi Mason, Judy Newman, Ned Rust, and Halimah Van Tuyl.

Ellie Berger, thank you for your wise counsel. Trent Hanover, Karen Nachbar, Martha Parlitis, and Mark Seidenfeld, we appreciate your legal support. Ann Sandhurst and Marilyn Small, we are indebted to you for your permissions expertise.

For patient and thoroughly professional production and manufacturing help, we are most grateful to our colleagues David Saylor, Meryl Wolfe, Jaime Capifali, Sawatree Green, Adam Mann, Lisa Serra, Elizabeth Krych, and Rachel Hicks. Charles Kreloff, thank you for our luminous cover!

To my brilliant design and production team, Danny Miller and Sarah Morrow, thank you for knowing how to create a beautiful and polished book from a collection of more than 100 diverse voices. Your expert and tireless efforts never fail to produce stellar results.

I thank my cousin Dawn MacKeen who shares a literacy story that's mine, in part, as well. And Gary, Aislinn, Erin, and Brennan, thank you for being the loves of my life.

Finally, to our Chairman, President, and CEO Richard Robinson, who together with his father, Scholastic founder Maurice R. Robinson, has opened a world of possible for millions of children around the globe: Thank you for seeing, shaping, and supporting the world of possible in this book.

—L.B.

Foreword

We know that children who read frequently and well in school are more confident learners, with a broader understanding of the world. They possess the skills that will enable them to be college and career ready and score better on the tests called for by the new standards.

Yet, we are reluctant to give children the time to read in school or the freedom to choose the books *they* want to read. Decades of research show the connection between reading engagement and reading achievement, but we still worry about whether we should devote the time to "free reading."

Perhaps it is counter-intuitive that independent reading—also known as pleasure reading or reading for enjoyment—is the best path for children to improve their skills and become fluent and proficient readers. We may be influenced still by the old-fashioned notion that school must include a certain amount of drudgery or pain in order to be effective, reminding us of the little Puritan readers used in 19th Century one-room schoolhouses which preached that hard work leads to success while pleasure (such as reading for the joy of it) wastes time.

> Giving children time to read for pleasure in school and at home is a strategy that will pay off in greater reading improvement.

But research shows us that choosing the books you want to read (and perhaps recognizing yourself in the main characters) is the surest way to become a curious and motivated reader. Giving children time to read for pleasure in school and at home is a strategy that will pay off in greater reading improvement.

Today, in our schools, there is a rising number of advocates for independent reading, balanced literacy, and guided reading— all instructional components that reflect student-driven learning and the principles of John Dewey. These educators know that children need to understand the basic building blocks of written language and to master decoding and word and sentence recognition by the end of second grade. These foundational language principles need to be taught actively to every child in the early grades. But teachers also see a drop-off in their students' motivation to read unless they find books that truly interest them, and advance quickly from graded readers to early chapter books to full, rich fiction and nonfiction texts.

The success of Scholastic's Book Clubs and Book Fairs, where children choose and buy the books they want to read, also suggests that many teachers and parents understand the importance of independent reading to support their children's learning.

Lois Bridges, the editor of this book, who asked for the "reading story" of each contributor, discovered the wide variety of ways in which people experience and express their love of reading. Yet these literacy experts describe experiences that are remarkably like the thoughts of millions of teachers and parents who see the impact of a book on children's lives.

Most experiences begin when children suddenly become fluent readers, almost magically, because they want to find out what happens to the characters with whom they identify. From Curious George to Harry Potter and Katniss Everdeen, that excitement is experienced over and over again, and we see how the magic of books discovered can transform lives.

Like many boys growing up in the mid-20th century, the catalytic books for me were sports stories by John R. Tunis. These were the books that first propelled me into reading and a life of helping children find the books they can and want to read, enabling them to make reading a central part of their lives.

We invite you to enjoy the wonderful stories here about the joy and power of reading—and to share these stories, together with books you love, with the children you support, helping them discover just how to Open a World of Possible.

—Richard Robinson
Chairman, President, CEO, Scholastic

Introduction

Open a World of Possible

*R*eading is the ultimate paradox. Every time we lose ourselves between the covers of a book and immerse ourselves in the lives of other people, we're more likely to discover our own. And, oh, what we gain—keener insights, deeper understanding and empathy, and a grander grasp of language, ideas, and the world. Every time we open the pages of a book, we open a world of possible.

The remarkable authors in this volume—literacy experts, language researchers, librarians, children's authors, and poets—share the reading moments that enriched and extended the possibilities of their lives and made them who they are today.

Walter Dean Myers, former National Ambassador of Young People's Literature, captures the life-enhancing nature of reading when he writes: "Once I began to read, I began to exist. I am what I read—all the books, all the papers, all the stories. I think that's what I've always been."

Reading gives life; it also defines and refines life. Boundless, it transcends time, culture, and place, so that Diana, a schoolgirl in Nairobi, faced with the challenges of poverty and discrimination, marvels at the strength and resilience shown by Fern in *Charlotte's Web*. LitWorld founder Pam Allyn explains that Diana discovers that she, too, can be strong. She, like Fern, can stand up and "from a very hard place of beginning, her heart and spirit, too, can soar into possibility."

Stories like Diana's remind us of why we fell in love with reading in the first place. Often, it goes back to a single crystallizing moment, when reading became a portal to a different place or a different life. Our contributors reveal that a transformative reading experience can occur anywhere—from Alaska to Maine, from a maximum-security prison to a convent, from a one-room schoolhouse to an elevated train speeding through the South Bronx. Such an experience can inspire us to change our lives, as occurred with the child of migrant workers who became a leading medical researcher, the young man from a working-class family who became a civil rights activist, the dyslexic child who is now one of the foremost authorities in spelling. These people credit reading with helping them dream of a future they hadn't thought possible. Their stories are our stories. No matter our medium—digital screen or printed book, magazine or comic book—reading can impart courage; it teaches us who we are and who we might become.

Open a World of Possible: Real Stories About the Joy and Power of Reading © 2014 Scholastic

Becoming a Reader

The process of becoming a reader seems nothing short of miraculous. Sometimes, all it takes is getting lost in one magical book (the Harry Potter phenomenon) for the world to open up and a life to be transformed. Reading is always something of a mystery that unfolds as we explore: What titles, topics, genres, and authors will delight and fascinate us and keep us up well past our bedtimes?

There's no question that reading makes us smarter. Recent scientific studies reveal the intimate relationship between reading and intelligence. Reading boosts everything from our vocabulary to our communication and writing skills, our analytical ability, memory, and focus. It even enhances our empathy: new research suggests that those who read more fiction tend to be more understanding and compassionate. We need only look to the biographies of statespeople and world leaders, scientists and physicians, engineers and inventors, writers and artists, entrepreneurs and educators throughout history to see the role of books in creating exemplary lives. Renowned astronomer Carl Sagan reminds us, "Books tap the wisdom of our species—the greatest minds, the best teachers—from all over the world and from all our history." "That's the miracle of literature," notes novelist Edward St. Aubyn, "this private communication between one intelligence and another."

Those of us who care deeply about children and who work directly or indirectly with students must understand the joy and power of reading. Yes, on some level reading is about letters, sounds, and words—but let's not become so focused on the mechanics and minutiae that we lose sight of what made us readers. The great sociolinguist Deborah Tannen maintains, "There is no understanding without caring." Skills and drills, exercises, and exams will never create the thrill that's needed to win a child's heart and make him or her a reader.

Exploring the Anthology

Seven primary themes emerged from the collection of essays anthologized here. They serve as our organizing framework. Given the kaleidoscopic nature of reading, it's inevitable that nearly every essay reflects multiple themes. The thematic structure of the book is simply meant to organize our anthology and illuminate our topic—the joy and power of reading.

JOY

Oh, joy! Getting lost in a book is one of life's greatest pleasures.

TRANSFORMATION

Reading challenges us to take risks, to consider new perspectives and possibilities, to outgrow our present circumstances and ourselves.

ILLUMINATION

Reading illuminates our humanity and expands our circle of knowing and caring.

COMMUNION

The intimate conversation between reader and author—and the language they use in all its magnificent variations.

IMAGINATION

Our life's dreams often begin in the pages of a book that sparks our imagination.

INSPIRATION

We honor those who connect us, at just the right moment, with the text we need.

ADVOCACY

We celebrate those who work to help others access books and discover the triumph of reading.

Reading Makes Lives

Our aim is to reveal, through our authors' stories, the moments of discovery when they understood the allure of reading; how they first connected with the passion and power of reading, and when they knew they wanted to spend a lifetime with books.

If we can capture, explore, and come to understand these transcendent moments, we can work together to ensure that our students comprehend the heart of why we read. As the poet Myra Cohn Livingston once wrote: "Books have more than changed my life—they have made it possible."

We are deeply grateful to our contributors; each essay is its own miracle. Together the essays tell a profound story of what reading makes possible: the best of everything that helps us become kind, hopeful, generous, vibrant human beings.

—Lois Bridges

To learn more about our illustrious authors and their work, read the Author Note at the end of each essay—often you'll find information about their research, their published books, and how to contact them.

Joy

Reading makes possible joyful communities full of endless hope and wonder.

~Yaya Yuan

Katherine Paterson

Reading What I Love: My Greatest Joy as a Writer

I once overheard my grandmother proudly telling someone that she had taught me how to read. How could that be true? I was five years old before I ever met my grandmother and I'd *always* known how to read. I realize, of course, that I wasn't born knowing how to read, I just

can't remember a time when I didn't know how. Reading came as naturally to me as talking, and since we lived in China, I was unstoppable in two languages by the time I was two years old—much to my father's quiet bemusement.

The language in which our mother read to us was English, and most of the books she read to us came from England. I remember her wonderful English lavender smell when I cuddled close as she read of James James Morrison's mother who went down to town without consulting James and has never been heard of since. The hairs prickled on my neck. My mother would never do such a thing. Or would she?

My problem with reading occurred when I entered the first grade in Richmond, Virginia. The teacher was hesitant about me. I wouldn't turn six until the end of October. I was too young to be in school, but the Kindergarten teacher in Lynchburg had pronounced me ready, not because I was already reading, no one at school suspected that, but because I was proficient with scissors, a skill that had been forced upon my clumsy fingers in Chinese Kindergarten in Kuling.

I suspect my first-grade teacher thought she was teaching me to read and that I was a slow learner. But how could I imagine that the basal texts with their "Run, Spot, run!" banalities was what was known in school as "reading?" It seemed to me an entirely different activity from poling on the river with

> I still hold that the greatest joy being a writer is that I can read all I want to and call it work.

Mole and Toad and celebrating with Eeyore a belated birthday. Reading, as I had always known it, was a life of high adventure—what they were doing at school could hardly be thought of as life at all, despite the explosion of exclamation marks at the end of nearly every line.

It took me a while to shake off the torpor of Dick and Jane. My first published work, appearing the following year in the Shanghai American School newspaper, read:

> *Pat, pat, pat,*
> *There is the rat,*
> *Where is the cat,*
> *Pat, pat, pat.*

Beside it was an apology from our teacher: "The second graders' work is not up to our usual standards this week . . ." Well, it took my writing many years to escape the deprivations of my early schooling, but my secret reading never suffered. I still hold that the greatest joy being a writer is that I can read all I want to and call it work.

● ● ● ● ●

Katherine Paterson is the author of more than 30 books including 16 novels for children and young people. She has twice won the Newbery Medal, for *Bridge to Terabithia* in 1978 and *Jacob Have I Loved* in 1981. *The Master Puppeteer* won the National Book Award in 1977 and *The Great Gilly Hopkins* won the National Book Award in 1979 and was also a Newbery Honor Book. For the body of her work, she received the Hans Christian Anderson Award in 1998, the Astrid Lindgren Memorial Award in 2006, and in 2000 was named a Living Legend by the Library of Congress. Paterson is a vice-president of the National Children's Book and Literacy Alliance and is a member of the board of trustees for Vermont College of Fine Arts. She is also an honorary lifetime member of the International Board on Books for Young People and an Alida Cutts lifetime member of the U.S. section, USBBY. From 2010–2011, she served as the National Ambassador for Young People's Literature. She and her husband live in Vermont. They have four grown children, seven grandchildren, and a wonderful Golden Retriever named Annie.

Carol Jago

My Life as a Reader

When I was ten years old, I was in the car taking my mother to the hospital to give birth to my youngest brother. The route to the hospital passed the library and I was unreasonably (according to my father) insistent that we stop so that I could take out another book.

That story has passed into family folklore but it illustrates how I read as a child. I read anything: lives of the saints, romantic novels, Tolstoy, Dostoevsky, Huxley, Hemingway, F. Scott Fitzgerald—anything and everything in print without discrimination.

Did I understand all I read? Without doubt, I did not, but a childhood spent among books prepared me for a lifetime as a reader. The thrill of opening a new book has never gone away.

• • • • •

Carol Jago has taught English in middle and high school for 32 years, is past president of the National Council of Teachers of English (NCTE), and serves as an associate director of the California Reading and Literature Project at UCLA. Jago served as AP Literature content advisor for the College Board and has published six books for teachers including *With Rigor for All* and *Classics in the Classroom*. She has also published four books on contemporary multicultural authors for NCTE's High School Literature series. Jago has written a weekly education column for the *Los Angeles Times*, and her essays have appeared in *English Journal, Language Arts, NEA Today,* as well as in newspapers across the nation. She edits *California English*, the journal of the California Association of Teachers of English, and served on the planning committee for the 2009 NAEP Reading Framework and the 2011 NAEP Writing Framework.

> A childhood spent among books prepared me for a lifetime as a reader.

Rudine Sims Bishop

Reading to Affirm, Inform, and Empower

*M*y parents grew up in the South early in the 20th century. Neither of them made it past fourth grade. Recognizing that their lack of schooling limited their life opportunities, they were determined that, through education, I would have a chance at a better life. I was expected—no, required—to do well in school. So when I went off to first grade, I dutifully learned to read—with Dick and Jane, whose bland, repetitive stories were uninspiring to say the least.

It was at the public library that I discovered the joy of reading. There I spent hours browsing the shelves in the children's room, reading whatever caught my imagination. I remember somewhere around third grade devouring the Andrew Lang Fairy Books, and as a pre-teen, reading books such as Emily Brontë's *Wuthering Heights* that I'm sure I did not understand at the time. What I did understand was the pleasure that good stories offer and the power of books to introduce me to lives and experiences beyond my own. I was "hooked on books," as the saying goes.

Even as a youngster, though, I had felt the absence in books of people who looked and lived like me. I went on to become an elementary teacher and later a teacher educator. One of my early research articles featured an interview with a ten-year-old African American girl who loved to read and told me she was searching in books for "strong black girls" like herself. She confirmed for me the capacity of reading to affirm, to inform, and to empower.

I consider it a blessing that reading, an activity that brings such great pleasure, was also at the heart of what I did for a living.

• • • • •

Rudine Sims Bishop is professor emerita at Ohio State University, where she specialized in children's literature with a particular interest in the literatures of underrepresented groups, especially African Americans. She served on the 1992 American Library Association's Newbery Award Committee, the 1999 Caldecott Award Committee, and is currently on the Coretta Scott King Awards jury. She is the author of multiple journal articles, professional book chapters, and several books including *Shadow and Substance: Afro-American Experience in Contemporary Children's Fiction, Presenting Walter Dean Myers,* and *Free Within Ourselves: The Development of African American Children's Literature.* For children, she has published *Wonders: The Best Children's Poems of Effie Lee Newsome* and *Daniel Alexander Payne: Great Black Leader.* Dr. Bishop was the recipient of the 1996 Arbuthnot Award, given by the International Reading Association to an outstanding college or university teacher of children's literature. She has also received the National Council of Teachers of English Distinguished Service Award, the NCTE Outstanding Elementary Language Arts Educator Award, and the 2013 NCTE James Squire Award. Additionally, she is a member of the Reading Hall of Fame.

Jim Trelease

What Reading Is Really All About: My View from the Mountain Top

I learned to read in first grade, St. Michael's School, Union, New Jersey. My teacher was Sister Elizabeth Francis. There were 94 children in one classroom and the only aide Sister Elizabeth Francis had was the one hanging on the cross

in the front of the room. We practiced phonics drills, read from a Dick and Jane reader, and did myriads of worksheet pages. Those covered the mechanics of reading. But the motivation to read, a far more important ingredient, came from elsewhere.

Like Scout and her father in *To Kill a Mockingbird*, my father would pull me onto his lap each night in our four-room apartment and read aloud the comics page from the *Newark Evening News,* explaining as best he could the strange relationships in "Li'l Abner" and "Rex Morgan, M.D.," or the boss-employee contests between Dagwood and Mr. Dithers. He also read serialized novels from the week's *Saturday Evening Post*. Added to that were the daily readings at 1 pm when Sister Elizabeth Francis stilled 94 hearts and lips with her chapter book readings of *Wopsy*—the story of a fledgling, and often inept, guardian angel.

The classroom mechanical drills were painfully boring for an active six-year-old but the read-alouds had given me a reason to endure the drudgery. I'd been to the mountain top, enjoyed the view, and therefore knew what reading was really all about. Not long-As or short-Es. It was Nancy and Sluggo, Dick Tracy, and the Phantom. While most of my classmates were focused on Dick and Jane, I was looking ahead to *Superman* and *Batman* comics, *Mad Magazine*, and *Classics Illustrated*.

• • • • •

Since writing his million-copy bestseller, *The Read-Aloud Handbook*, in 1982, Jim Trelease has traveled to all 50 states and abroad, advocating the benefits of reading aloud to children. In doing so, he's won the applause of both teachers and parents for his pleas on behalf of literacy efforts that contain less "pain" and more focus on turning books into friends, not enemies. While more than 60 colleges use his book as a text for education students, Korean, Chinese, Japanese, Indonesian, and Spanish editions now reach parents and teachers worldwide, even inspiring the successful "All of Poland Reads to Kids" campaign. *The Read-Aloud Handbook, 7th Edition,* is complete with new children's titles and recommendations, as well as old favorites. This new edition has the latest news on reading aloud, SSR, libraries in the e-book age, boys' learning habits, and the latest findings on digital learning (good news and bad). This is Trelease's "retirement" edition. (Photograph of Jim Trelease by Connor W. Reynolds.)

Colby Sharp

A Place to Fall in Love with Reading

I'm not one of those reading teachers who loved reading when I was a small child. I didn't enter Kindergarten a reader and I was never really one of those kids that you would call "above grade level." Every day, I did what the teacher asked: I followed along in our basal, read aloud when called

on, and flipped pages during independent reading, pretending to be engaged with my book. I read, but I wasn't a reader.

It took me until fourth grade to finally discover the magic of books. My teacher read Gary Paulsen's *Hatchet* to the class and, for the first time in my life, I became truly absorbed in a book. I thought about *Hatchet* all the time and completely identified with the main character, 13-year-old Brian Robeson.

For the rest of the school year, I was obsessed with Brian and his fight for survival in the Canadian wilderness. I even convinced my parents to buy me my very own hatchet. (I still have it!)

Every day after school, I would run home, grab my hatchet, and head over to the woods behind the school. Once I got there, I became Brian: I built shelters, hunted for food (I never killed anything), and I searched for ways to be rescued.

Today, I am teaching in the very elementary school where I fell in love with *Hatchet* as a boy. My classroom is a mere 30 feet from the woods where I spent all those afternoons pretending that I was that Gary Paulsen character. As I enter my classroom every day and see those woods through the window, I can't help but get excited about my 28 third graders who are looking for their own place to fall in love with reading.

● ● ● ● ●

Colby Sharp is a husband, father, and a third-grade teacher in Parma, Michigan. He blogs at Sharpread, and is the co-founder of the Nerdy Book Club.

Helen Oxenbury

Saved by the Library

I had asthma as a child. There were no inhalers in those days, which would have enabled me to carry on normally. Instead, I was confined to bed and missed a lot of school days. No television and no computer games to keep me amused—just piles and piles of old envelopes and

wrapping paper to draw on, lots of crayons, and, of course, books. I was left (quite happily) to myself for hours. My father was at work and my mother was busy around the house. During the war years, my father was an architect, and most of the books in our home were technical books—plumbing and drainage manuals and such—not very inspiring for a small child. My parents were not great readers, although, late in life, my mother took to reading in a big way.

So as a child, I had to rely on the local library. Every Friday morning my father would collect my previous week's books and take them back to the library. I could hardly bear the waiting for him to come home. In the evening when he returned from work, he would come into my bedroom with a fresh pile of books under his arm. I still recall the excitement of looking through each one to see what was going to be in store for me that week. These treasured books were, I see now, quite dreadful and boring and badly printed by today's standards, but they inspired my love of books. One, especially, I read over and over again and I remember it vividly to this day. It was called *The Good Master* by Kate Seredy.

> What would I have done without that library when I was growing up? And how many people must feel the same today? I hope libraries never cease to exist.

Kate, a wild and undisciplined young girl, is sent by her father to stay with his brother. Kate's uncle lives on a ranch on the Hungarian Plains. Horses play a large part in the story as does Kate's cousin, Jancsi, who has been brought up with horses and rides like a dream. He somehow manages to teach the willful Kate to ride and they have great adventures together.

Only after a great deal of wonderfully funny and outrageous behavior does Kate settle down and become one of the family, loved by them all, and guided by the hand of the kind and wise father, the good master. Finally, joy oh joy, Kate is given her own beautiful white horse.

What would I have done without that library when I was growing up? And how many people must feel the same today? I hope libraries never cease to exist.

● ● ● ● ●

One of the world's most acclaimed children's illustrators and twice winner of the Kate Greenaway Medal, Helen Oxenbury grew up in Suffolk and attended the Ipswich School of Art. During vacations, she helped out at the Ipswich Repertory Theatre Workshop and went on to study Theatre Design at the Central School of Art in London. Over a three-year period, she worked at the Habimah Theatre in Tel Aviv, returning to England to work in repertory, theatre, film, and television. Oxenbury's numerous books for children include the *Quangle Wangle's Hat* by Edward Lear which won the Kate Greenaway Medal; her classic Board Books for Babies; *We're Going on a Bear Hunt*, probably her best known picture book, re-told by Michael Rosen; *Farmer Duck* by Martin Waddell which won the Smarties Book Prize; *So Much* by Trish Cooke, which won the Kurt Maschler Award; and *Alice's Adventures in Wonderland* and its companion, *Alice through the Looking Glass*, both by Lewis Carroll. *Alice's Adventures in Wonderland* won both the Kate Greenaway Medal and the Kurt Maschler Award. She also illustrated *King Jack and the Dragon* by Peter Bentley, which was short-listed for the Kate Greenaway Medal in 2013 and *When Charley Met Grampa* by Amy Hest, which was published by Walker Books in 2013. Oxenbury and her husband, John Burningham, live in London where Helen works in a nearby studio.

John Burningham

Nothing Like a Good Book

I was very lucky to have been a child when there was no television or digital games, apart from the few radio programmes that were for children. The great luxury was being read to by my mother before I went to sleep. The stories were a mixture of the classics and lavishly illustrated works, which we call picture books today.

Growing up during World War II, there were times when my family and I had to live in a caravan (trailer). I vividly remember hearing the rain thundering on the roof of the caravan and, if the story that I was hearing read aloud got a bit scary such as the rather frightening sequences in *Treasure Island* by Robert Louis Stevenson, it didn't matter because my parents were never far away.

I learned to read quite late and got great pleasure from books. Today it pleases me a lot that I have managed to write stories for children that have been around for more than 50 years, have been heard over and over again, and are now going head-to-head with addictive computer games. I must be doing something right!

● ● ● ● ●

John Burningham studied illustration and graphic design at the Central School of Art, graduating with distinction in 1959. Many illustration commissions followed, including iconic posters for London Transport, before the publication of *Borka: The Adventures of a Goose with No Feathers*, Burningham's first book for children from Jonathon Cape in 1963, which won the prestigious Kate Greenaway Medal for illustration and heralded the beginning of an extraordinary career. Burningham has since written and/or illustrated over 30 picture books that have been translated and distributed all over the world. These include his classic and much loved children's books and various books for adults including *Chitty Chitty Bang Bang* by Ian Fleming; *Mr Gumpy's Outing*, also awarded the Kate Greenaway Medal; *Around the World in Eighty Days* by Jules Verne; *The Wind in the Willows* by Kenneth Grahame; *Granpa*, later made into an animated film; *Oi! Get Off Our Train*, *The Time of Your Life*, and *When We Were Young*. *Tug of War* was republished in 2012, and a special edition of *Borka*, celebrating 50 years in print, was published in June 2013. *Picnic* appeared in the autumn of 2013 and *The Way to the Zoo* was published in the UK in 2014. Burningham is married to illustrator Helen Oxenbury. They have three children, three grandchildren, and a dog named Miles. They live in London.

Susan B. Neuman

Love at First Sight

For me, it was love at first sight. One of my first literary memories is reading a big picture book of Bible stories about David and Goliath, Samson and the lion, and all the wonderful heroes and villains in the Bible. The stories were a bit scary, but so vivid and compelling that I would want to read them again and again.

My love of books obviously took me to the library. And in those days, the librarian was formidable and quite stern. There were rules, she would say, that needed to be respected: No talking, hardly any whispering, a very strict check-out policy, and library fines galore. You were only allowed to take 10 books out each week—no more, so I devised a strategy. Each week I would take a shelf of books at a time from the biography section, starting with *A*. Week by week, I would strategically go through the alphabet, reading everything I could grab, satisfying my hunger for learning.

Carrying so many books home, some would inevitably fall out of my young hands and hit the ground. This put me into a panic, wondering what the stern librarian would think. Was the binding damaged? Did I get mud on the pages? Still, if she looked more closely, I trust she would have seen what probably had convinced her to become a librarian in the first place—the sheer joy and delight of a young child learning through books. That early excitement transformed me into a lifelong reader.

● ● ● ● ●

Susan B. Neuman is a professor and chair of teaching and learning at New York University, specializing in early literacy development. Previously, she served as a professor at the University of Michigan and the U.S. Assistant Secretary for Elementary and Secondary Education. In her role as Assistant Secretary, she established the Early Reading First program, developed the Early Childhood Educator Professional Development Program, and was responsible for all activities in Title I of the Elementary and Secondary Act. Neuman has served on the IRA Board of Directors and other boards of nonprofit organizations. She is currently the editor of *Reading Research Quarterly*. Her research and teaching interests include early childhood policy, curriculum, and early reading instruction, PreK–Grade 3 for children who live in poverty. She has written over 100 articles and authored and edited 11 books, including the *Handbook of Early Literacy Research* (Volumes I, II, III) with David Dickinson, *Changing the Odds for Children at Risk*, *Educating the Other America*, and *Multimedia and Literacy Development*. Her most recent book is *Giving Our Children a Fighting Chance: Poverty, Literacy, and the Development of Information Capital*.

Janet S. Wong

Reading Made Me Useful

*L*ast month I was outside the vehicle registration office at my local DMV when I heard a desperate young mother pleading with her Kindergarten-age son on the phone. Over and over she asked him to read the car's VIN number to her. After she ended her call, she told me that she needed to renew the registration in the next 15 minutes, before the office closed, but her five-year-old son kept giving her the wrong number.

Poor kid. I know how it is to grow up in a family where reading is something that you need to know to be useful. It's a lot of pressure.

Four years old: I learned to read and write in a hurry because my mother needed help at her tiny beauty shop. When someone needed to book an appointment, I turned to the right page (or sometimes the wrong page) and they'd spell their names and recite their phone numbers. (Many thanks to the ladies who were incorrectly booked for their shampoos-and-sets and always said it was fine.)

Seven years old: While my friends were reading Nancy Drew, I was reading letters from Medicare and the IRS. This is how it is when your grandparents cannot read English, your parents and uncles work long hours, and government offices stop answering phones at 5 pm.

Twelve years old: My father wanted to start a company and needed someone to edit his business plan. What did "procurement" mean? Reading helped me figure it out.

In many working-class immigrant families, the oldest child acts as social worker, translator, interpreter, and scribe for parents and grandparents. You get no praise for it because there is rarely good news from the government. You never tell

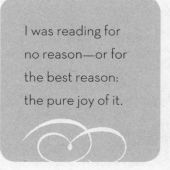

I was reading for no reason—or for the best reason: the pure joy of it.

Open a World of Possible: Real Stories About the Joy and Power of Reading © 2014 Scholastic

your teachers about this "extra stuff" that you need to do, but you carry this responsibility everywhere you go. At the library, you skip stories and look for nonfiction because you're reading to build real-world knowledge. Poetry? Definitely not useful. If only there were books on VIN numbers and practice sheets for medical forms!

This is the kind of thinking that led me to my job as a lawyer. But then, in a bookstore one day with my two-year-old cousin, I found myself sitting on the floor and reading picture books. What fun! I was four years old again—but this time, the reading was totally purposeless. I was reading for no reason—or for the best reason: the pure joy of it.

Now, as a children's author, I have found the perfect balance. When I read for joy, I am simultaneously keeping current in my profession. Poetry? It's not only useful, it is essential. Poetry is a multivitamin for the soul. Read a poem today to a child. It might be the most useful thing you can do.

● ● ● ● ●

Janet S. Wong is the author of 30 books for children, as well as a co-editor (with Sylvia Vardell) of The Poetry Friday Anthology series of professional resource books (learn more about this series at PomeloBooks.com). A graduate of Yale Law School, Wong's dramatic switch from lawyer to children's poet has been featured in *O Magazine* and on *The Oprah Winfrey Show, The Paula Zahn Show*, and *Radical Sabbatical.* She has been honored with her appointment to the NCTE Commission on Literature, the Excellence in Poetry Award Committee, and the IRA Notable Books for a Global Society Committee. A frequent speaker at schools and conferences, Wong travels two weeks each month—but "home" is her very useful kitchen counter in Princeton, New Jersey, where she makes her appointments, pays medical bills, and calculates taxes. See more about Wong at janetwong.com.

Bill McBride

My Life as a Reader: A "Classic" Journey

My first ride was emerald green with lots of chrome that shimmered in the hot Southern sun. It had dual front headlights and an angry hornet of a horn that got people's attention. It was pretty cool until my Dad attached the oversized basket to the front bars, giving my Schwinn Speedster the look of a Corvette with a luggage rack. But with over 100 homes on my afternoon paper route, the bulky basket was a necessity.

Each afternoon, a group of us 12-year-old paperboys congregated down at Mrs. Wiltshire's General Store, staring through the Merita Bread screen door, watching for the *Richmond Times Dispatch* truck to pull over across the street and deposit bound loads of newspapers on the ground. Mrs. Wiltshire didn't mind us hanging out in her store. We paced the old wooden floors and always bought cookies and candy to last us through our arduous routes. Perhaps our favorite treat was to reach our sweaty little hands into the ice cold water circulating in the long Pepsi cooler, pulling out sodas, searching for our favorite. A 16-ounce Pepsi could get me through my entire route in the suburbs under construction outside Richmond.

In the 1960s aluminum cans didn't exist—only bottles. Construction sites were often littered with empty soda pop bottles. Cleaned bottles could be turned into the grocery store for two cents, so as I threw out each rolled newspaper, I tried to replace it with a bottle. I'd spend Friday night cleaning my loot with the garden hose and on Saturday morning take them to Colonial Supermarket to reap my profits.

As soon as the cashier at Colonial handed me my coins, I headed straight to Ben Franklin—a Five and Dime. I went there for three reasons. One—it was air-conditioned. Two—I could get a hot dog, a bag of chips, and a coke made from syrup and carbonated water for less than a dollar. And three—they had a comic book stand.

Now comics are pure genius. Each one always ends in a cliffhanger, so you *have* to go back around the first of the next month to find out if Spiderman fell to his death, or the Fantastic Four had been reduced to the Not-So-Terrific Three. Because only two or three copies of the next sequel would suddenly appear in the rack, you had to go early and often. If some other kid got your favorite, you lived a month of torture. Is he dead? Were they evaporated?

As soon as I got to the comic book rack, I spotted the newest *Flash* (my favorite). Then I'd stand there and read as many other comics as I could before my legs gave way. You see, I was cheap. These things cost 12 cents—that was six bottles! I was only going to buy one, so I had to read, and remember, all the other stories of Superman, Batman, Aquaman, Superwoman, Green Lantern, and so on.

On one particular Saturday, I noticed a Classic Comic with a country boy on the cover, a white fence and paint brush, and a kite. Having flown kites, I was curious and reached for it. Uh-oh! It was thicker, had more words, and worst of all, cost 7½ bottles, i.e., 15 cents! But I started reading and soon was transported to Hannibal, Missouri, and the world of Tom Sawyer.

That journey would take me, a decade later, to the University of North Carolina at Chapel Hill where I majored in Literature. Of all my purchases made from that comic book rack, I have only one *Flash* left, but I still have every Classic Comic I ever bought—from *Tom Sawyer* to *The Iliad*.

Why am I a reader? Well, I was lucky enough to grow up with only three TV channels in black and white. I was lucky enough to grow up without video games or Facebook to isolate me. I was lucky enough to grow up when testing hadn't taken over schooling, and the most wonderful thing a teacher might say was, "Go to the library and pick out a book." And I was lucky enough to grow up without the Internet that seems to have turned many of our children into skimmers and scanners rather than real readers. Don't get me wrong—I appreciate the amazing technological world we live in, but I am so thankful for dirty Pepsi bottles, Ben Franklins with comic book racks, and reading simply for the sheer joy of it.

> I was lucky enough to grow up when . . . the most wonderful thing a teacher might say was, "Go to the library and pick out a book."

● ● ● ● ●

Bill McBride, Ph.D., is a well-known international speaker and educator. He is presently Author-in-Residence for Houghton Mifflin Harcourt. McBride is best known for his heartwarming novel *Entertaining an Elephant*. He has also published *Carrying a Load of Feathers, Building Literacy in Social Studies, Reading Toolkits for Social Studies,* and *If They Can Argue Well, They Can Write Well* which shows teachers how to use classroom debate to teach Internet research, critical thinking, and argumentative writing. His book *What's Happening?* is a Tier 2 reading program for secondary struggling readers. McBride's latest book is the graphic novel version of *Entertaining an Elephant* that comes with a Common Core Teacher's Guide and can be bought in class sets at www.entertaininganelephant.com.

Chris Loker

Picture Books Across the Ages

Strong narratives, unforgettable characters, illustrations that stir the imagination, and insights that engage the mind and heart—these are the forces that drive children's picture books.

I remember the first time this power became apparent to me, at least in simple terms. I was a small girl, and I had picked out a book from our much-used family book basket, handing it to my mother who read to me daily. We snuggled up together on our couch, cross-legged on my father's old college letterman blanket, and my mother read these wonderful words aloud as I savored the pictures in the book she held:

We looked!/Then we saw him step in on the mat.
We looked! And we saw him!
The Cat in the Hat!

That picture book, Dr. Seuss' immortal *The Cat in the Hat*, lived with me daily during my early childhood—at one point I had heard it so many times I could recite it from memory. It followed me through primary and secondary school, and then off to college where I read it to Kindergartners as part of my English Literature major. Later, it followed me to business school, where it brought me respite between economics and finance exams. And then it accompanied me throughout my career in Human Resources as the memento I would give colleagues, and later my staff, when there were heartfelt events to celebrate.

I never guessed that book would stay with me as long as it has. After a 25-year career in the corporate world, and the untimely death of my first husband, this picture book helped carry me over the bridge into a new career as a rare book dealer, specializing in antique children's books. And that's where Dr. Seuss' iconic picture book finds me today—sitting at my desk in my bookshop in San Francisco, its bright blue cover residing near me as I locate antiquarian children's books for collectors, and exercise my hand at writing my own children's picture books.

What I've learned from my love of reading, and from reading *The Cat in the Hat* in particular, is that there is always a shimmer of pure joy in a fine picture book. Picture books have this impact across the ages, regardless of their century, starting in 1658 with the short illustrated encyclopedia *Orbis Sensualium Pictus*, one of the earliest efforts to integrate pictures and words for young readers. Even though the picture book is primarily considered a 20th century development, there are precursor books that show how magic can happen through the interdependence of illustration and text, such as *Alice's Adventures in Wonderland*, *The Wonderful Wizard of Oz*, *The Tale of Peter Rabbit*, and *Just So Stories*.

> What I've learned from my love of reading, and from reading *The Cat in the Hat* in particular, is that there is always a shimmer of pure joy in a fine picture book.

The books that have changed my life are those picture books fully illustrated in glorious color, the ones that "hinge . . . on the drama of the turning of the page" as children's picture book authority Barbara Bader has written. Think of the groundbreaking picture books of the first half of the 20th century that present color-saturated, enticing worlds to explore: *The Velveteen Rabbit*, *Millions of Cats*, *The Story of Babar*, *The Story of Ferdinand*, *Madeline*, *Curious George*, *Make Way for Ducklings*, *Le Petit Prince*, *Eloise*, and perhaps the most colorful of all, *Goodnight Moon*. And then think of the equally glorious picture books of the second half of the 20th century that celebrate color, texture, and message: *The Snowy Day*, *Where the Wild Things Are*, and *The Very Hungry Caterpillar*, to name just a few.

It's a joyous world that picture books create, and a world that has inspired me since I was small. You can imagine the joy in my heart when my young son brought a book over to read, sitting with me in our big "reading chair"—a book that he learned to recite from memory before he began school. I'm sure you can guess what that book was: *The Cat in the Hat*.

● ● ● ● ●

Chris Loker is the proprietor of Children's Book Gallery, an antiquarian children's bookshop in San Francisco, specializing in children's books and original book art from 1750 to 1950. She is also the curator of "One Hundred Books Famous in Children's Literature," an exhibition of landmark children's books at the Grolier Club in New York City. She has written the (colorful) picture books *In Awhile, Crocodile; Sapphire Starfish;* and *Alastair Acorn*. Loker is married to an antiquarian bookseller, has one son, two cats, and not nearly enough picture books.

Yaya Yuan

I Am a Reader

*I*f I were asked to make a list of words to describe myself today, *reader* would be right there at the top. But I have not always identified as a reader. I was born in China, and if we did do read-alouds in Chinese preschool, it did not leave much of an impression as I can't remember a single one. When I moved to the United States, I struggled to communicate and only managed to piece together what I wanted to say in a confusing mix of Chinese and English. Speaking was difficult for me and reading was even harder.

Then, when I was seven or eight, my father read to me from *The Boxcar Children* by Gertrude Chandler Warner. I consider this my first reading memory. Finally fluent in my new language, I fell in love with the story of the four mystery-solving brothers and sisters, and I rejoiced with them when they found their grandfather and a place to call home.

From then on, I was unstoppable. I read everything from *The Baby-sitter's Club* by Ann M. Martin to *Little House on the Prairie* by Laura Ingalls Wilder. And if I loved a story, I read it again. I read before I went to bed and first thing when I woke up. Series were my favorites because I could spend just a little more time with the places I loved and the people I considered to be my friends.

In my work, I find there are many children who do not think of themselves as readers. Usually, they live in slums (or worse) and do not have the resources to explore what it means to be a reader. Sometimes they have been told that they are bad readers, and so, they write themselves off at an early age and give up on reading entirely.

But, gather any of these children together, read a book to them, and just like that, a lifelong love of reading is sparked, new worlds are discovered, and new friends are made.

In the Philippines, I was part of a LitWorld team that worked with a group of teenagers who seemed far older than their 16 years, many of them already acting as parents for their younger siblings. As mature and grown-up as they had to be, when I read aloud *Bill and Pete* by Tomie dePaola, they shrieked and guffawed when the crocodile-hunting Bad Guy runs for his life, naked, down the banks of the Nile.

In India, I was trying to wrangle a raucous group of six-year-old boys, doing everything I could think of to get all 20 of them to sit down quietly at the same time, when I decided to read them *Where the Wild Things Are* by Maurice Sendak. You have never heard a quieter pack of wild things—until we got to the wild rumpus, of course.

In Haiti, we ran a camp for 30 young girls, ages six to eighteen, and despite the rather large age range, the minute they entered the LitWorld library where we hosted camp, each and every one of them would grab a book and huddle close together, reading in groups of two or three, the room buzzing with the sounds of shared stories.

Reading makes possible joyful communities full of endless hope and wonder.

In New York, I have spent the last three years mentoring a group of girls who will soon graduate high school and fulfill their dreams of attending college. Each one of them has grown into her own reading identity during our time together, deciding what she likes, what she does not like, and debating plot twists and character traits with her friends—practicing the habits of lifelong readers.

These moments stand out to me as testimonials and they bear witness to the power of reading. Most of these children did not think of themselves as readers. But by falling in love with a story, they, too, can say, "Yes, I am a reader!" They will continue to take books into their hands and explore new worlds, make new friends, and cultivate a brighter future. To me, reading makes possible joyful communities full of endless hope and wonder.

● ● ● ● ●

Yaya Yuan is Advocacy and U.S. Program Director for the nonprofit organization LitWorld (www.litworld.org). LitWorld empowers children to create lives of independence, hope, and joy through its LitClub and LitCamp programs and its World Read Aloud Day campaign.

Maria Walther

Reading: Experience It!

*R*aised by a mother who believed in the power of real-life experiences, we regularly hopped on the subway to travel to downtown Chicago so that my sister and I could peer into the miniature Thorne Rooms at the Art Institute. My parents, sister, and I participated in an exchange program where we lived with a farm family in Iowa to gain

a firsthand look at life on a farm. In our basement, we performed plays, hatched chicks, painted rocks, made sand candles, and much, much more. You might ask, "What does all of that have to do with reading?" I would say, "Everything!" My mom gave me the greatest gift—a wealth of background knowledge on which to build.

As I "read" the illustrations in *The Little House* by Virginia Lee Burton, I could understand the house's sadness as she was moved to the city. Why? I had seen the open countryside from the back of our station wagon and walked through the cramped city streets. Later, when I read *Charlotte's Web,* I could empathize with Fern because I had held a baby pig in my own arms. I could picture the Clock family from *The Borrowers* living in the Thorne Rooms at the museum. With the help of my mom's constant quest for unique experiences, the books I read came alive.

Fortunately for me, my early school experiences continued to nurture my love of the written word and from the time I was a first-grade student, I set my sights on being a first-grade teacher. In 1986, fresh out of college, I found myself in my own first-grade classroom surrounded by 24 enthusiastic learners. I wanted to recreate for them the magic that I experienced when I read a book. And while I knew I couldn't take all of my students to live on a farm, I could tell them stories from my own childhood as I read them *Charlotte's Web.*

I started on that first day of teaching sharing my passion for books and the joyful bond that is formed during read-aloud experiences, and I haven't stopped since. Nowadays, my students and I read aloud about 800 books a year! I carve out time each day to read at least four books, balancing fiction and nonfiction, that build my students' background knowledge about topics of interest, various genres, favorite authors, and their world.

The experiences I shared with my family shaped who I am as a reader and as an educator. I encourage the parents of my first graders to do the same for their children. They know that each Monday, my students and I will sit in a circle and have "weekend share," a time for the first graders to show their friends the cool rock they found at the park or the map they brought home from the zoo. It is my hope that the read-aloud experiences I share with my first graders will help shape the kind of people they will become. After nearly three decades of gathering first graders around me to read a story, I believe that a wealth of experiences plus a love of reading are the keys to a happy life.

> After nearly three decades of gathering first graders around me to read a story, I believe that a wealth of experiences plus a love of reading are the keys to a happy life.

• • • • •

Maria Walther, who earned a doctorate in elementary education from Northern Illinois University, has taught first grade since 1986. She is a National Board Certified educator and currently teaches in Aurora, Illinois. Along with teaching young learners, Walther inspires other professionals by sharing her knowledge through customized professional development experiences and by serving as an adjunct professor in Judson University's Masters in Literacy program. The ideas she shares reflect her continued commitment to teaching, researching, writing, and collaborating with her colleagues. Walther was honored as Illinois Reading Educator of the Year and earned the ICARE for Reading Award for fostering the love of reading in children. With Carol Fuhler, she co-authored *Literature Is Back!* and *Teaching Struggling Readers With Poetry.* She and Katherine Phillips co-wrote *Month-by-Month Trait-Based Writing Instruction* and *Month-by-Month Reading Instruction for the Differentiated Classroom.* She collaborated with Jan Richardson to create *The Next Step Guided Reading Assessment.* Her latest publication is *Transforming Literacy: Teaching in the Era of Higher Standards.* Learn more about her books at mariawalther.com and follow her on Twitter @mariapwalther.

Alan Lawrence Sitomer

Books, I Love You!

When I was a teen drowning in a sea of troubles, the waves of adolescent life crashing over my head, I cried to the heavens, "Someone, please throw me a life preserver!" A life preserver never came but the universe did toss me a book. It was heavy but it hoisted me up.

When I was a first-year teacher in the inner city—lost, brought to tears, brought to my knees, brought to the breaking point—I cried to the heavens, "Someone, please give me a tool!"

A tool never came but the universe did toss me a book. It wasn't made of steel but it empowered me to forge ahead.

When I've had crises of faith, when I've had ignorance to squash, when I've had a need to fill my soul with joy and laughs and humor and hope, I would call to the heavens, "Someone, please deliver to me the stuff for which my spirit aches."

And each time the offering was the same: the universe tossed me a book. The books came in many shapes. They came in many sizes. They came with different jackets, perspectives, and voices, yet they came and they came and they came.

And they still keep comin'.

Our universe is filled with a medicine that cannot be found in bottles, hypodermic needles, or pills. Indeed, the remedy for many of life's maladies can be found in books.

Our universe is filled with magic, the stuff of dragons and wands and sorcerers. Indeed, the secret to all that cannot be readily seen can be readily experienced in books.

Sometimes, I dine on movies. Other times, I'll nibble at TV. Indubitably, I'll gobble down the Internet. But when it

> When it comes time for a true banquet, a feast for my mind and spirit, there is no other nourishment quite like a book.

comes time for a true banquet, a feast for my mind and spirit, there is no other nourishment quite like a book.

The only real disappointment I've ever had with books is that there aren't enough years on this planet for me to read all the ones I'd like to. Yet from my "glass is half full" perspective, this means books will be with me to my dying day.

And how many things in life can we really say that about? Books, I love you!

● ● ● ● ●

Alan Lawrence Sitomer is a California Teacher of the Year award winner and the founder of the Writer's Success Academy. In addition to having been an inner-city high school English teacher and former professor in the Graduate School of Education at Loyola Marymount University, Sitomer is a nationally renowned keynote speaker who specializes in engaging underperforming students. To date, he has authored 16 books ranging from hard-hitting YA novels like *Homeboyz, The Hoopster,* and *Hip-Hop High School* to humorous children's picture books such as *Daddies Do It Different* and *Daddy and the Zigzagging Bedtime Story.* Additionally, he is the author of two teacher methodology books and a classroom curriculum series for secondary English Language Arts instruction called the Alan Sitomer BookJam.

Franki Sibberson

Knowing Yourself as a Reader

I am working with our fourth and fifth graders about really knowing themselves as readers. I gave them a basic reading interview to help them begin to look at their reading lives. Then I asked them to turn it over to write 100 things about themselves as readers. I tried to do the same.

None of us got to 100, but we might by the end of the year if we keep noticing and adding. Here is my list so far:

1. I read almost every Nancy Drew book when I was in sixth grade. My grandmother had the collection in her attic.

2. I loved the Betsy books by Carolyn Hayward when I was in elementary school.

3. Realistic fiction is my favorite genre.

4. No one is allowed to talk to me or bother me during the last ten pages of a book. Endings are key for me.

5. I have to love the main character in a book to enjoy the book.

6. I occasionally enjoy science fiction and fantasy.

7. When I was younger, I loved the Bookmobile that parked right down the street from our home every two weeks.

8. *Walk Two Moons* is one of my favorite books of all time.

9. I have a shelf of books that I haven't yet read. I like to have back-ups in case of a snowstorm or for some other reason that would give time to read.

10. I often skip parts in books when scenery or nature is described.

11. I am not so good at listening to books on tape. I get distracted. I like to see the print.

12. I almost never like the movie better than the book.

13. I never read a book after I've seen the movie.

14. I like to read books that are brand new—hot off the press!

15. I don't get excited about having authors autograph my books.

16. I don't really like to share my favorite books. I want my friends to read them, but I really like to keep favorites after I am finished with them.

17. I like to alternate between long and short books.
18. I like to read children's fiction on airplane trips.
19. I can't read in the car. I get carsick.
20. I rely on blogs and other reviews to choose children's books.
21. I have many favorite authors.
22. I love to hear authors speak and share their work.
23. I love Young Adult books but never have time (or give myself time) to read them.
24. Many graphic novels are hard for me to read and understand.
25. My mother read me *The Secret Garden* and *A Little Princess* when I was little; they are still two of my favorite books.
26. Most of my nonfiction reading is connected to my work.
27. I have very little patience for reading how-to books or directions.
28. I love, love, love to hang out in any bookstore.
29. I buy too many books.
30. I love to visit new bookstores when I travel.
31. I am convinced that Cover to Cover in Columbus, Ohio, is the best children's bookstore in the country.

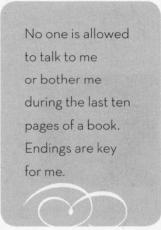

No one is allowed to talk to me or bother me during the last ten pages of a book. Endings are key for me.

This is a really fun thing to do—I know as the year progresses, I will notice more aspects about myself as a reader and I will add them to my list. Who knows if I will get to 100. It is just an entertaining and informative way to think about my reading life—what works for me as a reader and what doesn't. If you try this, let me know how it goes. When I hear other people's lists, they remind me of things I hadn't thought about myself.

● ● ● ● ●

Franki Sibberson, K–5 school librarian, now teaches third grade. She is the author of *Beyond Leveled Books*, *Still Learning to Read, Day-to-Day Assessment in the Reading Workshop,* and *The Joy of Planning.* She is also a regular contributor to *Choice Literacy.* You can reach her on Twitter @frankisibberson or through her blog, A Year of Reading (readingyear.blogspot.com).

Linda Alston

Love and Literacy

*M*ama drove off into the balmy summer night with Lil' Alice and me in the back seat, heads, shoulders, and thighs stuck together like old family photos, reading *Soul Confessions*. It was a two-hour drive back to Natchitoches from Shreveport. Lil' Alice and I waited patiently between highway lights. In the brief time the light shone on the printed page, we read frantically of love, passion, romance, and broken hearts only to have the page fade to black again at the juiciest passages.

My parents were members of many different religious faiths through the years. The common thread that ran through them all was a Puritan view of sexuality. The silence of my parents about sex launched me into a kind of literacy cycle where my number one genre was adolescence.

I subscribed to *Teen* magazine. I read about other teenagers and the trials and tribulations they were having with their parents, teachers, boyfriends, and younger siblings.

The desire, the *need* to read had taken on a practical purpose. Reading was opening up a world of information that I desperately wanted even while all the adults around me were determined to keep it from me.

The Farmer's Almanac said that I was born under the sign of Cancer. I liked rich foods, home, art, and would suffer from gastritis. But the important morsel was that I was compatible with boys born under the sign of Pisces. Pop Monroe was a Pisces.

The era was the '60s and it was a great time to be in love with Pop. The lyrics of the popular songs during that time are what sparked my interest in reading poetry. This was the era of the Supremes, Smokey Robinson, the Miracles, and the Four Tops. I listened to words like:

> *As pretty as you are*
> *You know you could have been a flower . . .*

> —The Temptations

This music inspired me to write love poetry of my own to Pop Monroe. During this time, I started reading all kinds of poetry. I read

Robert Frost, Langston Hughes, James Weldon Johnson, Edna St. Vincent Millay, and, of course, Elizabeth Barrett Browning. Pop was always very proud of my writings. He would show my poems to all his friends and they were always impressed.

This literacy cycle, my quest for adolescent understanding, continued through high school. Ninth grade I remember as the year of D. H. Lawrence's *Lady Chatterley's Lover*. Until this day I don't know where the illicit book came from, I never found out who brought it to school. It circulated around to all my classmates under a brown paper grocery bag cover.

I was still reading to try and understand these tinglings and new sensations I was feeling that I called love.

During this time, we attended a fundamentalist Pentecostal church. At a revival one summer night, I took one look at Joe Green and Pop Monroe was history. Joe's grandmother was the Church Mother. This was the highest office a woman could hold in our church—it was the female equivalent to the pastor. I taught Sunday school to a group of young children. I was probably the most well-read teenaged Sunday school teacher in Louisiana. Why? Because I had to impress Joe Green. After all, I was in love with him.

> Today, reading is an exquisite joy in my life . . . a sweet, rich indulgence that feeds me at a deep, soul-ular level.

At the end of Sunday school, all the groups would review their lessons for the entire church. The pastor, Elder Feltus, always commented on how well my group did in the review. I would smile and glance over at Joe and his grandmother, Mother Norman, for their approval. And it was a good thing they approved. Little did they know that I had read all week to prepare for that Sunday's lesson.

We were encouraged to read the Bible every day. I enjoyed reading the Psalms of David in the Old Testament. I liked the sound and flow of the words.

There was a time during Elder Feltus' sermon when he would request that someone from the audience stand up and read a scripture aloud to support what he was preaching. He would say, "Someone get me the second chapter of *Acts*." Then he would continue to preach, giving the member time to find the passage. This practice helped me read with speed and learn the organizational layout of the Bible so I could find the scripture first. When I found it, I would stand up quickly. This let everyone else know that I would be the reader. It was competitive. Then Elder Feltus would say, "Okay, read, girl!" I always felt good going home from church when I had read a scripture for Elder Feltus.

Today, reading is an exquisite joy in my life . . . a sweet, rich indulgence that feeds me at a deep, soul–ular level. As a Master Life Coach, I still read religious and spiritual books to continue my own personal evolution and to empower others. And I'm head over heels in love—with Edward! He sings old skool Temptations songs with a tribute group so the music will not die. He writes poetry and songs about how much he loves me. One of our favorite pastimes is reading and discussing books together while snuggled up on the sofa and sharing a bowl of popcorn. Edward is a Taurus, not a Pisces. But I haven't laid eyes on a *Farmer's Almanac* since I left Louisiana many years ago.

As an avid reader, I know how to pick through books and choose passages that I feel embrace my truth. Somewhere, in all those forbidden texts, a protagonist must have told me to never give up on true love . . . maybe it was Lady Chatterley!

● ● ● ● ●

Linda Alston, a peer teacher evaluator for Denver Public Schools, is also a master teacher of young children. She has won numerous awards, including the Milken National Educator Award, the Walt Disney American Teacher Award, and the first $100,000 Kinder Excellence in Teaching Award, focusing on outstanding work by K–12 public-school educators in low-income communities. Alston has traveled to Sierra Leone as a Fulbright Scholar, organized six inner-city Montessori Child Development Centers, and is an educational consultant, motivational speaker, and Master Life Coach. She is the author of the bestselling *Why We Teach: Learning, Laughter, Love, and the Power to Transform Lives.*

Transformation

*Reading energizes my heart with a dream
for a better life.*

~Jimmy Santiago Baca

Charles M. Blow

Reading Books Is Fundamental

*T*he first thing I can remember buying for myself, aside from candy, of course, was not a toy. It was a book. It was a religious picture book about Job from the Bible, bought at Kmart.

It was on one of the rare occasions when my mother had enough money to give my brothers and me each a few dollars so that we could buy whatever we wanted.

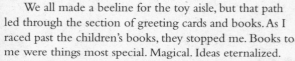

We all made a beeline for the toy aisle, but that path led through the section of greeting cards and books. As I raced past the children's books, they stopped me. Books to me were things most special. Magical. Ideas eternalized.

Books were the things my brothers brought home from school before I was old enough to attend, the things that engrossed them late into the night as they did their homework. They were the things my mother brought home from her evening classes, which she attended after work, to earn her degree and teaching certificate.

Books, to me, were powerful and transformational.

So there, in the greeting card section of the store, I flipped through children's books until I found the one that I wanted, the one about Job. I thought the book fascinating in part because it was a tale of hardship, to which I could closely relate, and in part because it contained the first drawing I'd even seen of God, who in those pages was a white man with a white beard and a long robe that looked like one of my mother's nightgowns. I picked up the book, held it close to my chest, and walked proudly to the checkout. I never made it to the toy aisle.

That was the beginning of a lifelong journey in which books would shape and change me, making me who I was to become.

We couldn't afford many books. We had a small collection. They were kept on a homemade, rough-hewn bookcase about three feet tall with three shelves. One shelf held the encyclopedia, a gift from our uncle, books that provided my brothers and me a chance to see the world without leaving home.

The other shelves held a hodgepodge of books, most of which were giveaways my mother picked when school librarians thinned their collections at the end of the year. I read what we had and cherished the days that our class at school was allowed to go to the library—a space I approached the way most people approach religious buildings—and the days when the bookmobile came to our school from the regional library. It is no exaggeration to say that those books saved me: from a life of poverty, stress, depression, and isolation.

James Baldwin, one of the authors who most spoke to my spirit, once put it this way: "You think your pain and your heartbreak are unprecedented in the history of the world, but then you read. It was books that taught me that the things that tormented me the most were the very things that connected me with all the people who were alive, who had ever been alive."

That is the inimitable power of literature, to give context and meaning to the trials and triumphs of living. That is why it was particularly distressing that *The Atlantic*'s Jordan Weissmann recently pointed out that according to The Pew Research Center, "nearly a quarter of American adults had not read a single book in the past year. As in, they hadn't cracked a paperback, fired up a Kindle, or even hit play on an audiobook while in the car. The number of non-book-readers has nearly tripled since 1978."

> That was the beginning of a lifelong journey in which books would shape and change me, making me who I was to become.

The details of the Pew report are quite interesting and somewhat counterintuitive. Among American adults, women were more likely to have read at least one book in the last 12 months than men. Blacks were more likely to have read a book than whites or Hispanics. People aged 18–29 were more likely to have read a book than those in any other age group. And there was little difference in readership among urban, suburban, and rural populations.

I understand that we are now inundated with information, and people's reading habits have become fragmented to some degree by bite-size nuggets of text messages and social media, and that takes up much of the time that could otherwise be devoted to long-form reading. I get it. And I don't take a troglodytic view of social media. I participate and enjoy it.

But reading texts is not the same as reading a *text*.

There is no intellectual equivalent to allowing oneself the time and space to get lost in another person's mind, because in so doing we find ourselves.

Take it from me, the little boy walking to the Kmart checkout with the picture book pressed to his chest.

●　●　●　●　●

Charles M. Blow is the *New York Times*' visual Op-Ed columnist. Blow joined the *New York Times* in 1994 as a graphics editor and quickly became the paper's graphics director, a position he held for nine years. He graduated *magna cum laude* from Grambling State University in Louisiana where he received a B.A. in mass communications. He lives in Brooklyn with his three children.

Sonia Manzano

Turn the Page and Know Yourself

*D*on't turn the page when you get to the end of the passage," the teacher warned. "We all have to read from the same page at the same time."

I read, "Go, Spot, go," in my Dick and Jane book and stopped to wait for the rest of the class to catch up.

So was reading in the South Bronx, 1956.

Until I found myself on the Third Avenue elevated train with my older sister. Curious about what the ads above our heads said, I asked her, and she, sick of having to babysit me, rolled her eyes answering, "Why don't you just try reading it?" I thought she had lost her mind. That I should try to put letters together, to figure out words, without a teacher, had never occurred to me. But I tried anyway, and before we reached our station I read, "More doctors smoke Camels than any other cigarette," "Meet Miss Subways," "I dreamed I was wanted in my Maidenform bra," and all sorts of other confusing misinformation people were getting in the mid-fifties.

But my mind was in a whirl—who knew that combinations of letters made words and that reading was not confined to my Dick and Jane reader at school? Walking the rest of the way home in a stupor, I wondered how long this reading business had been going on, for I hadn't perceived what we did at school as reading—I experienced it as exercises in memorization. Suddenly I became irritated that I hadn't been allowed to turn the page.

From then on, I metaphorically "turned the page" every chance I got. Nothing escaped me. My stressed-out parents didn't see the value of reading when you could be doing something useful like washing the dishes or mopping the floor, so books were not available in our home. But no matter—I found the print on cereal boxes, jars of Bosco, and toothpaste tubes fascinating. Not only that, I whiled away the time finding letter shapes in the cracks of our ceiling and in the formation of clouds.

I was even presumptuous enough to think that all the Bar and Grill signs I spied from my father's '57 Chevy as he sped up Third Avenue were incorrect, because based on the nightclub scenes I watched on television, I was sure the signs meant to say Bar and *Girls*—tsk, tsk.

Eventually, I was able to get my hands on romance magazines and comic books. On weekly visits to the school library, where we could look at but not take out books, I managed to read whole books by remembering where I had left off so I could return to them.

Fast-forward to college days in 1969 when I happened upon *Sesame Street*. There, on a television in the student union of Carnegie-Mellon University, I saw this remarkable show that authorized the recognition of letters and words everywhere. Films that illustrated that a manhole cover was an *o* shape, that the letter *m* looked very much like mountains, that a broken-down muffler sounded like an *r*, and that, with careful viewing, one might find a *t* shape in a park bench. Was that so very different from my experiences with letters on the train, the cracks in my ceiling, and the clouds?

A few years later, because of perseverance, timing, and good luck, I got cast as Maria and found myself in the midst of this innovative program. Once I saw the inner workings of the show, I vowed to play a greater part in it. The way to do that was to metaphorically turn a page on my career and become a writer as well as a performer.

I used my experiences with letters and reading as a little girl to get started, then let my love for the show's zany characters carry me the rest of the way. The possibilities were endless: Cookie Monster finds all the items that begin with the letter *c* on the menu in Hooper's store but then can't resist eating the menu. Big Bird gets bonked on the head and forgets the alphabet, giving me the opportunity to teach it again and again; the Tooth Fairy needs help reading the names on his list of toothless children he plans to visit.

And then I did the same thing in Spanish— writing a song so everyone would know that "Hola" meant "Hello." I saw myself in every single kid in our vast audience and was happy to provide them with the happy news. Find letters and words everywhere and read them!

Writing for television was just the beginning, because there were more pages to turn. Eventually, adult literature authors who wrote humorously about trying childhoods intrigued me. I had both requisites—a trying childhood and a sense of humor. Could I share those stories with

> Who knew that combinations of letters made words and that reading was not confined to my Dick and Jane reader at school?

children? Absolutely—and not only was I able to share, I personally took great pleasure in giving myself a more sensible childhood.

But were there more pages to turn? Yes—when I got the opportunity to write for an older audience. Now the challenge was to tell a story without benefit of illustrations or Muppets. Could I do that? There was no way of knowing but to try, so I did, and managed to carve a fictitious story out of a historical event that was close to my heart.

And then it was time to look within and chart how it was that I went from recognizing words on a subway train to writing books. That gave birth to a memoir that has allowed me to put painful experiences where they cannot hurt me anymore and where those experiences belong—in the past.

So, if asked to describe what reading has done for me, I'd say I've learned to keep turning pages. I have done that, and, as a great poet said, "it has made all the difference."

● ● ● ● ●

Sonia Manzano has affected the lives of millions since the early 1970s as the actress who defined the role of Maria on the acclaimed television series *Sesame Street*. Manzano was twice nominated for an Emmy Award as best performer in a children series and has won 15 Emmy Awards for her television writing. She is also the author of the picture books *No Dogs Allowed* and *A Box Full of Kittens* published by Simon and Schuster. Manzano's first YA novel, *The Revolution of Evelyn Serrano*, published by Scholastic, was a Pura Belpré honor book, winner of the CLASP Américas Book Award, and acclaimed by Kirkus as a "stunning debut." Manzano's Christmas picture book with Simon and Schuster and a memoir with Scholastic will both be published in 2015. Manzano enjoys traveling the country on the lecture circuit. She lives in New York City with her husband Richard. Visit her website at www.TheRevolutionOfEvelynSerrano.com.

Shirley Brice Heath

Gifted Seeds

*T*hroughout my early childhood, I never knew books. I lived with my grandmother until I had to go live with foster parents. My grandmother had only a few years of schooling, but she learned how to "fake" reading. She would take me on her lap and "read" books of the Old Testament that had

what she thought of as the most adventurous stories: those of Job, Jonah, Daniel, and the like. My foster family had books but no time to read, for the farm and household chores had to be done. I learned to work hard and fast to save time for exploring the books of the household.

As the years rolled by, my love of literature remained with me, but I never forgot that reading children's books did not find a way into many households, including my own. Stories told, sung, and re-lived in the imagination during chores, boring moments of classes, and on long car rides drew me into research on language, culture, and literacy. I never forgot how growing up poor, isolated, or disadvantaged affects access to reading and writing. Of special interest to me was the matter of how even small seeds of reading at some point in early life can sprout later in life and will often have the staying power of the toughest of plants.

When I had my own two children, a boy and a girl, I immersed them in children's books, reading, and storytelling. We worked together in the garden, and doing household chores and community work, but we always had a story going and books in nearby knapsacks. We did so because of the pleasure, the joy, and the fun of reading. Only when my daughter, at age 18, suffered a serious head injury in an accident did I learn that stories and reading meant much more than I had thought possible.

In the first eight years of her recovery, she did learn again to walk, sit, talk, and, yes, to read and write. She defied what medical caregivers thought possible. My daughter's brain injuries had not taken away the intense will and determination that had led her, before the accident, to become a national champion swimmer as well as a national scholar in mathematics and science. As the years have passed, however, the injuries to her brain increasingly take their toll on her abilities. As her brain has atrophied and her memory and tolerance for social interactions that involve conversation have declined, she has turned once again to childhood reading habits. Though she has no memory of her life before the accident, somewhere deep inside her very being, the seed of reading lives and has brought forth sprouts that will not go down easily.

My daughter has become a well-known figure in her community. Never having been able to drive, she walks everywhere—through rain, snow, sleet, or sunshine. On her back at all times is a knapsack full of books—those she has bought and those she has checked out from the library. She moves from schools to eldercare facilities to homeless shelters. She reads and reads and reads, for the words from the pages replace those she has trouble producing and comprehending in lively multi-party conversations.

Children on the playground see her coming and know that on rainy days, or when they feel ostracized by others, her knapsack of books will be open to them. They go through her selection and read for themselves or they ask her to read aloud. When she writes about what she sees in the children, she shows her surprise that somehow the power of stories stretches far. She writes:

> I walked into a second-grade portable today and one of the girls was in tears. None of her friends seemed to know what was wrong. I was armed with a big book of fairy tales. So I asked the mournful child if she would help me pick out a story to read to some of the kids. And so I read Sleeping Beauty. Amazingly enough, there were no more tears. Ah, to be seven again, when all the world's problems could be solved with just a fairy tale.
>
> Yesterday as I was helping supervise Kindergarten recess, some of the kids asked me to read to them. I started reading to just a few, but when I looked up there were 20 kids seated in front of me, listening. I've been reading to kids at recess for several years now and I am still astonished at the number of kids who want to spend part or all of their recess listening to me read to them.
>
> Today I read to listeners from age five to 90 (Kindergartners at a local elementary school all the way up to residents at a local group home for the elderly). The fifth graders prefer to raid my bag for books to read instead of being read to. I do not mind. I consider it the highest compliment to be considered a portable library.
>
> When I was reading to kids at the middle school, an adult asked me what my expectations were. I responded by telling him what a fifth grader told me—as a bus patrol boy, he had started reading to the Kindergartners he is responsible for while they wait for their bus. He has become their favorite patrol boy. He told me that now he understands why I love to read to kids so much.

I am supposed to be the literacy expert in the family. Yet over the years, as I have watched my daughter's ways of adapting to life with her disabilities, I marvel again and again at the staying power of books. She has become the Johnny Appleseed of reading in her neighborhood, affecting the lives of many individuals for whom others cannot take the time or may think reading unlikely to be desired or appreciated.

My daughter has taught me that each of us embodies innumerable aspects of human potential. She certainly does not experience today the literate life either she or I imagined for her before her accident. But now her world revolves around reading to others the books she knew so well as a child and those she relishes getting to know today. I know of no one more informed than she about which books children most enjoy or the stories that will hold enraptured a group of elderly residents diagnosed with severe dementia.

> I marvel again and again at the staying power of books.

With her gift of time spent reading, she can bring young and old into memory, affect, and engagement with both the future and the past. It is wise for all of us to remember that reading is a seed that may lie dormant but yet holds on for dear life and may someday give forth beautiful lasting plants that keep growing and growing for ourselves and others.

● ● ● ● ●

Shirley Brice Heath has a Ph.D. from Columbia University where she studied linguistics and anthropology. She has done groundbreaking research on the impact of community organizations and voluntary learning settings that draw young people from under-resourced communities into learning. She is best-known for her long-term studies of families (begun in the 1980s with her book, *Ways with Words: Language, Life, and Work in Communities and Classrooms* and followed up 30 years later with *Words at Work and Play: Three Decades in Family and Community Life*). Her work has taken her into township theaters and reading centers in South Africa, economically devastated towns in Great Britain, communities in Mexico, and, most recently, museums and other major cultural centers. She has influenced numerous museums in modern economies to shift their emphasis on learning for young people from one-time visits through school field trips to open enrollment for old and young in ongoing laboratories, studios, and curating sessions. She has lectured around the world and served on the faculties of the University of Pennsylvania, Stanford University, and Brown University.

Jimmy Santiago Baca

Reading Energizes My Heart

My first experience with reading was at the rural school where my Grandpa was the janitor. While he dust-mopped hallways and emptied trashcans, I roamed classrooms, spinning the Atlas globes, touching pencils on students' desks, and sounding out the large alphabet cards that ran above the blackboard from wall to wall. The wadded paper in the trashcan smelled like dry prairie rose; the wooden floors smelled like tree bark. And I felt like a bear cub waking up to his first magnificent spring.

With the same joy I felt while picking wild raspberries, I traced the letters on frosty panes; in the tortilla flour on the cutting board; with my spit beading on the hot woodstove top; when I peed outside in the dirt. "Don't do that!" Grandma cried, "Stop writing letters everywhere!"

I saw myself as an alchemist, with chalice in hand, gathering magic in my play, using sounds to conjure spells and blessings, to chase evil away, and to invoke forest fairies.

Taken from Grandma's to St. Anthony's Orphanage, the nuns made us memorize religious hymns and I competed against my friends to sing the loudest so I could hear my voice filled with feeling (if the Lord heard me, I'm sure He covered His ears). Though I could barely read, I enjoyed the Dick and Jane illustrations in class and memorized catechism prayers.

Fifteen years passed before another book was in my hands, one I stole in the county jail from the receptionist. Reading Wordsworth changed my life. My sister brought me a dictionary and at 18, I learned grammar. From county jail to prison for possession of drugs—here, reading triggers images in my mind; a catalyst that pops them up with such exciting force it makes me catch my breath—images with voices and scents and features recharge and energize my heart with a dream for a better

Reading energizes my heart with a dream for a better life.

life, moving in a metaphorical rainbow that metabolized their life-force through my DNA.

Owning a book was a grievous crime in my outlaw world. A gang, in league with the prison administration, warned my friend Charles Green not to go to the library. He ignored their warning and, as he entered the library door, they stabbed him to death. This brutal act made me read even more to defy those who would stop us from reading.

And now, some five decades later, I read every day; my rooms are filled with books, my children read every night, as does my wife. I can see my Grandma. I whisper to her, "Grandmother, I can write now; I even wrote you some poems." She leans over my shoulder to observe, and smiles."

● ● ● ● ●

As an abandoned child and a runaway, Jimmy Santiago Baca's childhood was spent on the margins of society. In early adulthood he reverted again and again to a life of crime, eventually being sentenced to five years in a maximum-security prison. After years of hellish suffering in isolation, he emerged from prison a voracious reader and a skilled, self-taught writer. He discovered a deep attachment to poetry that became his saving grace. Now an accomplished and celebrated author, Baca is the recipient of many honors including the Pushcart Prize, the American Book Award, and the Hispanic Heritage Award. For his memoir, *A Place to Stand*, he received the prestigious International Prize. In 2006, Baca won the Cornelius P. Turner Award, a national award that annually recognizes one GED graduate who has made outstanding contributions to society in education, justice, health, public service, and social welfare. Devoting his post-prison life to writing and teaching others who are overcoming hardship, Baca has conducted hundreds of writing workshops in prisons, community centers, libraries, and universities. In 2005, he created Cedar Tree, Inc., a nonprofit foundation dedicated to helping others improve their lives through education. Baca is the published author of multiple books and professional resources for educators with co-author ReLeah Cossett Lent; additionally, he is featured in several films. See www.jimmysantiagobaca.com.

Elfrieda (Freddy) H. Hiebert

A to Anno: The Gift That Changed My Life

I grew up in a Mennonite community. My dad was the first full-time minister in our Mennonite group's conference in Canada. He made all of $150 a month—about what I now casually pay for yet another pair of shoes from Zappos.

My parents worked hard to make ends meet, with a huge garden to plant and harvest in the short summers of the Canadian prairies, a coop filled with chickens for eggs and fryers for Sunday dinner, and a cow for milk and cream that my mom skimmed and sold for a little extra cash. And the list of chores goes on, including melting snow in winter to fill the washtub on Mondays and the bathtub on Saturday nights.

My Opa had read stories to my siblings and me in German but my formal introduction to reading began as a first grader in a four-room schoolhouse in the hinterlands of Saskatchewan. On the first day of first grade, I was introduced to Dick and Jane and, simultaneously, to reading as a potentially subversive activity. Miss Braun, the teacher of the first through third graders, required that each child bring a rubber ring, the kind that was used to seal canning jars, to school. We stretched the rubber ring over the part of the Dick and Jane reader that we hadn't yet covered in our lessons with Miss Braun. We had to promise that we would not release the rubber ring, either in the classroom or when we took our books home.

This prohibition was all I needed to race through the reader (of course, I had to wait until the others caught up, but I was an early adopter of repeated reading). What I encountered in the Dick and Jane readers confused and perplexed me. These books were not just my introduction to reading, but also to the world of *die Engländer*—the English—the label the Mennonites gave to everyone outside the group.

I was intrigued to find out more about the world beyond, but there was no library in our school or hamlet. Other than the adventures of Dick and Jane, my reading consisted primarily of the Simpson Sears catalog (which also served an important function in the privy), a book of Bible stories, and another about missionary families.

But one day when I was almost eight, things changed. It was the day that the first installment of the *Encyclopedia Britannica* arrived. I was absolutely gobsmacked. In Volume 1 (A to Anno) alone, I could learn about abbeys, aerial navigation, Africa, and angling—these were all of the topics with pictures. My life was to change even more the next year. That's when we moved to Vancouver, where my father became the minister of a church that served the many Mennonites who were making the migration from farm to city. After that, I would be immersed in the culture of *die Engländer*, including their public and school libraries. But it was that encyclopedia that opened up the possibility of the world for me.

For years, my parents paid for that encyclopedia—$2 a month. I have the yearbooks for the span of years during which those payments were made: 1956 to 1963. The yearbooks with the encyclopedia are on a bookcase in a visible and central place in my home. A few years ago, my spouse arranged for an artist to create a custom bookcase for it. As valuable as the bookcase is, I don't believe its value will ever equal the $168 my parents paid for that encyclopedia.

> I was absolutely gobsmacked. In Volume 1 (A to Anno) alone, I could learn about abbeys, aerial navigation, Africa, and angling.

• • • • •

Elfrieda (Freddy) H. Hiebert, Ph.D., is president and CEO of TextProject, a nonprofit that provides open-access resources for teachers to help students who depend on schools to become highly literate. Hiebert has worked as a literacy educator for 45 years—first, as a teacher's aide and teacher of primary-level students in California and, after getting her Ph.D. at the University of Wisconsin, as a professor at the universities of Kentucky, Colorado-Boulder, Michigan, and California-Berkeley. Hiebert's research on effective literacy practices has been published in many scholarly journals and she has also authored or edited 11 books. Hiebert spends part of every day working on projects to support the reading opportunities of low-income students. In addition, she loves her life as a wife, daughter, sister, aunt, friend, and neighbor. The birthday parties Hiebert throws to mark each new decade of her life are legendary. Become part of her community at textproject.org.

F. Isabel Campoy

Liberation Through Reading

$\int$itting in the lap of a parent or grandparent, wrapped within their arms, and sharing the wonders of imagination through a book was one privilege I did not enjoy as a child. The rhythm of family life in postwar Spain focused on the basic essentials. Adults had to wait in endless lines to buy milk, bread,

or potatoes to improvise a meal and the coal needed to cook it. Children concentrated on being minimally invasive while doing their multiple chores of daily life. Our Civil War had ended seven years before I was born and I was one year old when World War II ended. But the 40–year grip that dictator Francisco Franco had on the country lasted until 1975.

My privilege instead was the uniqueness of a family that valued education and was able to supplant the void of meaningful books in libraries and bookshops, as well as contradict in our home the Nazi propaganda of our textbooks. Having a mother who knew every traditional song, limerick, saying, and tale from our country's folklore enriched my childhood. Having a father who taught me not only to read, but also to understand the silence between the lines, made me curious about the hidden messages in books. As soon as I learned to read, my teachers chose me to read out loud while my classmates did art or sewing. I had a good voice and I couldn't hold a thread and needle for more than two seconds, so it was a perfect match and kept everyone busy.

Because censorship was imposed both by the government and the Catholic Church until I was 29 years old, reading was an act of rebellion. Books were smuggled through the border with France or hidden in luggage from trips abroad. On those pages, I understood that history belongs to those who write it, and that truth must be viewed through more than one perspective. Books gave me that freedom.

As a professor of English, my father had many contacts with the outside world. One day when I was six, he brought home a picture book. He had glued his Spanish translation over the English text, and he said that it was a wonderful book for all ages that we would all enjoy. The book was *Goodnight Moon*. The author, Margaret Wise Brown, had died some days before in a town not too far from the Spanish border. Father told us she had died dancing the Can-Can, which I found truly fascinating. Ten years later, I was a 16–year-old AFS exchange student in Trenton, Michigan, when I discovered in the public library the other books Margaret Wise Brown had written. Books didn't travel into Spain, but I travelled outside in search of books.

Reading in two languages allowed me to fall in love with a different symphony of sounds and rhythms, landscapes, characters, and behaviors. When I began to read in English, I noticed not only a different grammar order, but different life perspectives, too.

Reading also allowed me to know about scholarships that made it possible to leave the country and pursue a career abroad; to learn about my identity and enjoy innocence way past my years of innocence; and to compare and contrast the world I lived in with other worlds while traveling through the pages of Federico García Lorca, Walt Whitman, or Langston Hughes. I am who I am because in each book I read I found the humor, the pain, knowledge, and laughter of which the fabric of life is made.

There are no arms wrapped around many of the children in our schools and no laps of parents or grandparents to sit in while sharing the wonders of imagination through a book, yet these children also deserve that privilege. Neither poverty nor a thousand misfortunes should deprive any child of a book, because books DO change lives. They did mine.

> Neither poverty nor a thousand misfortunes should deprive any child of a book, because books DO change lives. They did mine.

• • • • •

F. Isabel Campoy could be described in her own words as an adventurous, international, multilingual, multicultural, *mestiza*. She obtained her degree in Philology from University Complutense of Madrid. For her post-graduate work, she was a Ford Scholar at Reading University in England, and a Fulbright Scholar at UCLA. She is the author of over 150 titles in Spanish and English, including children's books in the areas of poetry, theatre, fiction, biography, and art, as well as books for educators that address Transformative Education, Second Language Acquisition, and Authentic Writing. Her work aims at providing children keys to interpret the world in a fun, challenging, and affirmative way. CABE (The California Association for Bilingual Education) has established an endowment in her name to provide scholarships for future teachers. She has been recognized with the Laureate Award from the San Francisco Public Library and the 2005 Reading the World Award from the University of San Francisco. Her books have been honored with the ALA Notable Book Award and have been cited by Kirkus Best Books and as the Nick Jr. Best Book of the Year as well as being six times a Junior Library Guild selection. Campoy is a contributing member of the North American Academy of the Spanish Language and member of the American Academy of Poets. She also belongs to several organizations for the advancement of multicultural awareness and world peace.

Phyllis C. Hunter

Reading Grows High Cotton

I grew up on the south side of Chicago. Not the Chicago of *Good Times* and the Evans Family. No, not at all! I went to Catholic School in a crisp uniform and walked home by way of my grandfather's grocery store. We owned everything on the corner and all the houses across the street. Money wasn't an issue, but

health was. My grandmother was bedridden, dying of bladder cancer and the doctors had done all they could. So my job at eight years old was to come straight home from Holy Name of Mary School and sit by my Mamoo's bedside and read to her.

In those weeks and months, I read everything: the Bible, my textbooks, the pocket-size *Daily Word* magazine, and hundreds of Hallmark get well cards. I became a fluent reader at eight years old with phenomenal comprehension skills because I had to be ready to answer Mamoo's questions. She made me promise to go to college and always be smart. And I've done, and still try to do that. Being told I was smart by everyone because I was such a good reader changed my life and made me believe that anything is possible—except going against my mother's hopes and dreams for me.

Several years later, when I was planning my high school course schedule, my mother reviewed my choices: "No! No, you cannot take typing or a home economics class at the Academy of Our Lady!" she declared. "I'm not paying all that money for you to become a cook or a seamstress."

I pleaded that those two classes were the only electives I was taking. I had signed up for Geometry and Spanish and all the others were college prep classes. But she still said "No!" So I read cookbooks like novels and McCall's

As a family we discovered that— thanks to reading— we grow our own high cotton!

Sewing Encyclopedia into the night. I taught myself to sew and cook (gourmet!), hobbies I still enjoy today at age 67. Yes, reading has enriched and emboldened and changed my life!

Being an educator, speech therapist, principal, and international reading consultant, however, is not being in "high cotton," as we sometimes say in the south. High cotton was attending Parents' Weekend at Groton Prep School in Groton, Massachusetts, where many parents arrived in their private planes. Reading made it possible for our only son Drew to score in the 99th percentile of the PSAT and attend Groton and, from there, enter Ivy League Dartmouth. As a black male, the odds were against Drew, but from the age of four he has been, like me, an avid reader and he beat the oddsmakers. In 2005, Drew graduated from Georgetown Medical School. As a family we discovered that—thanks to reading—we grow our own high cotton!

● ● ● ● ●

Phyllis C. Hunter, internationally renowned, award-winning educational consultant and author, is a sought-after motivational speaker and reading advisor for many educational stakeholders. She is a veteran educator, having worked as a district reading manager, principal, and speech and language therapist. She is the author of *It's Not Complicated: What I Know for Sure About Helping Our Students of Color Become Successful Readers.* Hunter serves on the advisory board for the Broad Prize in Urban Education which awards the nation's largest yearly K–12 public education prize, and she is on the advisory board of several national literacy organizations, including Scholastic's Family and Community Engagement (FACE), Consortium for Reading Excellence (CORE), the Neuhaus Education Center, and the National Center for Family Literacy. In 2002, she was named the Marcus Garvey Educator of the Year by the National Alliance of Black School Educators; in 2009, Scholastic Education presented Hunter with its inaugural Heroes Award for her contributions to the field of children's literacy.

JoAnn Trejo

Imagining Possibilities

I grew up in a family of migrant farm workers in California's Central Valley. My mother raised me and my four older siblings. Throughout my childhood, I was surrounded by strong women; my grandmother, mother, aunts, and older sister. Everyone in my family worked hard. When

my mom got home from a day's work in the fields or the cannery, she got right to work cooking homemade beans, rice, and tortillas. Every night she made sure there was a warm meal for us. By the time we ate and cleaned up, it was time for bed. In my home, there was neither time nor energy to read. I did not grow up in a household with books.

In elementary school, I was mostly bored. I usually finished my schoolwork by 10:00 am. By fifth grade I was spending a lot of my time in the office with the principal, Mrs. Astorga, helping her with various tasks and tutoring Kindergartners. That year, Mrs. Astorga talked to my mom, encouraging her to send me to the local Catholic School. My family qualified for a scholarship, and in sixth grade I put on my uniform and entered San Joaquin Middle School. It wasn't long before I organized the other Mexican girls into a "society." We made membership cards and became card-carrying members of the "Brown Sensations." We mostly kept each other company and helped each other feel comfortable; we did not spend time reading.

One day my sixth-grade teacher, Mrs. Cort, put a book on my desk. It was a biography of actress Greta Garbo. I picked it up, went to the convent, and began to read. By then I had established the pattern of staying at school until my mom got home from work. Feeling safe in the silence of the convent, the words I read captivated me and soon I was enthralled. Through Greta Garbo's story, I realized that there were other women who had struggled, persevered, and transformed their lives. I recognized myself in her: a leader and immigrant who did not find solace at school. It was the first time I had read anything other than SRA cards and I couldn't stop. I devoured it in one sitting.

From then on, Mrs. Cort had a hard time keeping me supplied with books. She dug up all the biographies of women that she could find. I

Open a World of Possible: Real Stories About the Joy and Power of Reading © 2014 Scholastic

remember reading about the lives of Judy Garland, Katharine Hepburn, Helen Keller, and many other spirited, gutsy women. I began to realize that the stories of their lives could help me transform my life. These biographies are the first books I remember reading. They were words given to me by someone who knew me and cared about my future. They comprised stories that ignited my imagination and hope. They were the road maps that allowed me to see where I could go with my life.

It has been a long road. I am now a tenured professor in the school of medicine at the University of California, San Diego. As a scientist, most of my time is spent reading scientific literature. However, recently my partner, someone who knows me and cares about my future, gave me *My Beloved World*, Justice Sonia Sotomayor's autobiography. I sat down and read it from cover to cover. Once again, I am inspired and am envisioning new possibilities for my life.

> These biographies comprised stories that ignited my imagination and hope. They were the road maps that allowed me to see where I could go with my life.

● ● ● ● ●

JoAnn Trejo, Ph.D., is a professor at the University of California, San Diego. Dr. Trejo is Mexican-American and the youngest of five children raised by a single mother in the central valley of California. She credits her success to the influence of her mother, older sister, and teacher mentors. Dr. Trejo conducts research on cardiovascular disease and breast cancer. She has received numerous grants from the National Institutes of Health (NIH), the Komen Foundation, UC Tobacco-related Disease Research Program, and the American Heart Association (AHA) including the prestigious AHA Established Investigator Award. Dr. Trejo is a leader in the scientific community. She was elected to serve on the Council of the American Society for Cell Biology (ASCB). She is a life member of the Society for the Advancement of Chicanos and Native Americans in Science (SACNAS), a member of the ASCB Women in Cell Biology Committee, ASCB Minority Affairs Committee, and the Keystone Symposia Diversity Advisory Committee. Dr. Trejo is currently the director of the San Diego Institutional Research and Academic Career Development Award (IRACDA), a NIH-sponsored program for postdoctoral fellows that aims to develop a diverse group of highly trained biomedical and behavioral scientists.

Robert E. Probst

What I Did on My Summer Vacation

*I*t wasn't much of a store. A very narrow aisle, not even wide enough to accommodate two people standing side-by-side, led to a counter at which you could buy soft drinks, then back down the other side of the shelves that divided the store to the cash register and the exit. It was a "sundries"

store, as I recall, not that I had the faintest idea at the time what a sundry was (though I was fairly sure that I didn't need one), and I have no idea what my mother and my aunt were looking for. We were on the Boardwalk at Ocean City, Maryland, and I was eager to get out to the beach, so it may have been something like sunscreen, if sunscreen had been invented at the time—this was about 1955 as I recall, long before our national obsession with safety had led to such developments as sunscreen, seat belts, and bicycle helmets. I wasn't fascinated with whatever the store had to offer and can remember almost nothing about its selection of sundries.

Except for the wire-rack book stand right at the U-turn in the aisle.

My two guardians must have paused to find something, giving me time to look over the colorful paperbacks arrayed there, covers facing out, in a display two books wide and about six books high. It was a rack that rotated and it mostly displayed the sort of books whose graphic covers my mother did not want me, at age 12, looking at. But as I slowly spun the rack—searching, I'm sure, for some work of great literature or weighty volume of scholarship and wisdom—I spotted, in the bottom right corner of one of the panels, a cover with a photograph of a man wearing some odd equipment. His eyes were hidden behind a mask, he had a metal tube clutched in his teeth, corrugated rubber hoses ran from that tube to tanks he was wearing on his back, and he was obviously underwater, exploring what I would come to learn was a coral reef.

I picked it up, glanced through the photographs clustered in a section in the middle of the book, grew fascinated at the idea of men swimming free, deep under the surface of the sea, and asked my aunt to buy it for me. I suspect that she thought the book would be far above my head but, relieved that I hadn't chosen one of the more lurid (and I have to admit, intriguing) covers, bought it for me. It was Jacques Cousteau's *The Silent World*, the story of his fascination with the world beneath the waters and his invention of the Aqua-Lung, the first self-contained-underwater-breathing-apparatus (SCUBA).

Details grow vague at this point. I'd like to report that I read the book that afternoon sitting on the beach, but I doubt that's true—there was, after all, the ocean in all its mystery calling me down to its depths. But I'm certain that I started reading it that night, back in the motel room. And then I read it again, almost every year, until other demands pushed it aside. I still have that copy, or most of its more than 60-year-old tattered pages, now held together with a rubber band. But I hold on tightly to what's left of it because that one little volume has had such an impact on my life.

As a result of reading that book, I've spent as much of my life as possible 30-130 feet underwater, and I've come to love the ocean and its creatures. I ended up studying French in school, just in case Cousteau might need my help on board *The Calypso*. He never did call. But this encounter, perhaps more than any other, convinced me that reading mattered. If one book, discovered at age 12, could exert such influence on me, then there was the grand potential that some other book, discovered by some other reader at age 10, 20, or 90 could transform that reader's life.

> If one book, discovered at age 12, could exert such influence on me, then there was the grand potential that some other book, discovered by some other reader at age 10, 20, or 90 could transform that reader's life.

A book offers possibility. And a library of books offers a world of possibilities. This is one of the things that makes teaching so worthwhile—as teachers, we can help our students find the books that will open their worlds of possibility.

For me, it led to a lifelong fascination with the sea—though I occasionally wonder what course my life might have taken if I had made it out of the store with one of those other paperbacks with the more . . . colorful . . . covers.

● ● ● ● ●

Robert E. Probst, professor emeritus of English Education at Georgia State University, has spent most of his career working on the teaching of literature and reading. He is the author of *Response and Analysis;* co-editor of *Adolescent Literacy: Turning Promise into Practice;* co-author, with Kylene Beers of *Notice and Note: Strategies for Close Reading.* Probst has presented frequently at conventions, both national and international, and has served the National Council of Teachers of English in various roles, including membership on the Commission on Reading, on the board of directors of the Conference on English Leadership, and as column editor for *Voices in the Middle.* In 2004, he was awarded the NCTE's Exemplary Leadership Award, presented by the Conference on English Leadership.

Kylene Beers

Lost and Found

*I*t wasn't until I was a teacher that I came to understand the power of books. A third-year teacher to be exact. In the spring of that third year to get specific.

That's not to say that prior to that moment I didn't love reading and

didn't understand that a life spent in the company of books would be enriched. I did. Of course I did. I grew up reading—everything. As a child, I loved the adventures of Mike Mulligan and his steam shovel, of the man in a yellow hat and his oh-so-curious monkey; I wanted to be like Madeline who saw the fun in stepping out of those two straight lines. I became a track star running with Babe Didrikson, a nurse helping Florence Nightingale, a statesman standing beside Patrick Henry, an inventor working alongside Ben Franklin. I was an intrepid explorer with Tom Sawyer, a Swiss family named Robinson, a doll named Hitty, and a girl in the Limberlost. I felt confusion and fear and anger and sadness and ultimately hope all from one girl named Anne. I was a Bobbsey twin, a Hardy boy, and a Nancy Drew wanna-be. I ran away to a museum, hid on a ship, walked up a road slowly, and journeyed to the center of the Earth. I sat halfway up a stair (because "there isn't any other stair quite like it"), tesseracted across the universe, and journeyed a yellow-brick road to discover that there is no place like home.

Yes, I loved getting lost in a book. And so it was no great surprise that I went on to become an English teacher. I walked into teaching eager to encourage a love of reading in all my students. My students and I survived my first couple of years, and then I hit that third year. That was the year that a colleague in the middle school where I taught suggested that I was ready to help chaperone the annual voluntary spring break trip for our seventh and eighth graders to Washington, D.C. I had never been to our nation's capital, and I didn't yet have my own children to be with during this break. Though students who wanted to go paid a fee, the trip was free for the teachers who agreed to give up their vacation and travel with students. I was in and began talking to my seventh graders about this trip.

Though every veteran teacher had warned me about not having a favorite student, that wasn't possible that third year. This was the year I taught Gary, a small seventh grader with an impish smile, uncombed hair, wild freckles, and an optimism that was contagious. We began to talk about this trip and one day he happily announced that he'd get to go. He, too, had never visited D.C. On and off over the next few months, we talked about what it would be like to visit the Tomb of the Unknown Soldier, to walk through the Capitol, to go to the Pentagon, to actually stand in the shadow of the Lincoln Memorial. On Monday of the final week to make the payment, Gary came into my classroom at the end of the day. "I need to talk to you about our trip to Washington," I can still hear him say.

"Sure," I said. "Do you need another payment form?"

"No," he said, slowly. Then he took a deep breath and continued, "I can't go." Before I could say anything, he explained, "My mom says we don't have enough money for one of us kids in the family to get to take a trip like this and the others not. So I can't go."

> Yes, getting lost in a book is a magical thing. But finding your way because of a book is better.

I sat at my desk, trying to figure out how I could pay Gary's way but not pay for all the others. I started to say something—though I don't know what—and again he stopped me short. "But it's ok. My mom says that we'll go to the library and check out books about all the places you will go while you are there. So, on the day you are at the White House, we'll read about the White House. And when you are at the Smithsonian, we'll read about that. We'll read about everything that you will see. And then Mom says when you get back you should come over for dinner and we'll both talk about our trips because Mom says that the only difference is that you'll take a trip on a plane and I'll take a trip in my mind. So, will you give me a copy of the itinerary?"

I would have given him anything.

Spring break came. I headed off to the airport and Gary headed to the library. When I returned, sure enough, his mother invited me to dinner. The night I visited we had one of my favorite meals: meat loaf, English peas with carrots, mashed potatoes and gravy, and lettuce leafs topped with peach slices and a dollop of mayonnaise. (Those of you from the South recognize this as Sunday dinner best.) Later, we moved to the living room where I took out my photos and Gary opened up his books. We began talking about our respective trips and it was soon evident that Gary had had a better trip than I—but that's a different story. Eventually it was time for me to go.

I stood at the door and told his mother how much the evening had meant to me. I told her that I thought the world would be a better place if every kid had a mom just like her. I told her what a difference she had made, not only in Gary's life but in mine. This woman, weary from a job that paid too little for hours that went on too long, smiled, turned away, and picked up her purse that sat on a small table by the front door. She went through it and took out her wallet. She opened that up and pulled out a small blue card. She handed it to me. "See this?" she said.

I held it and nodded.

"This is our library card," she told me. "There are many things I will never be able to buy my children, but because we have a library card there is nothing they can't have. They can travel anywhere, learn anything, meet anyone, and ultimately become whatever they dream to be because we have this card that gives us access to a world of books. And it's those books that will help Gary find his place in the world."

Yes, getting lost in a book is a magical thing. But finding your way because of a book is better.

● ● ● ● ●

Kylene Beers is a former middle-school teacher turned teacher educator who spends her time focusing on the needs of struggling readers. She is author of *When Kids Can't Read/What Teachers Can Do;* the co-author with Robert E. Probst of *Notice and Note: Strategies for Close Reading;* and co-editor with Linda Rief and Robert E. Probst of *Adolescent Literacy: Turning Promise into Practice.* In 2008–2009, she served as president of the National Council of Teachers of English (NCTE) and in 2011, she received the NCTE Exemplary Leader Award given by the Conference on English Leadership. She has served as a consultant to the National Governor's Association Education Committee, was the editor of the national literacy journal *Voices from the Middle,* taught in the College of Education at the University of Houston, was senior reading researcher for the Comer School Development Program at Yale University, and has most recently served as the senior reading advisor to the Reading and Writing Project at Teachers College, Columbia University. You can follow Beers on Twitter or on her blog at KyleneBeers.com.

Peter H. Johnston

Reading Changes Me

L indsay, an eighth grader in one of our research projects, made the
following observation after reading *Hate List* by Jennifer Brown:

> *That book is really good, and it changes my mind about how people
> feel about things. And even, like, a little comment can change someone's*

> *life. And, like, the other day, I saw people on
> Facebook picking on this one girl, saying nobody
> liked her because she was ugly and had no
> friends. And I kind of put a stop to it. I told them
> it was wrong and that people commit suicide for
> it all the time. So, it changed my way of seeing
> things. Normally I wouldn't have said anything
> to stop. But now, if I see anything, I stop it.*

Reading transforms us in many, many ways, and when we are transformed,
our relationships with others change, transforming them as well. This has been
my experience in research, and in life.

I lived with my grandparents when I was very young and my reading
began with them. Scottish immigrants to New Zealand, they read with
strong Scots accents, which I appropriated. I remember two favorite books
(since money was very tight, they might actually have been the only books—
except for the Robbie Burns collection). One was Gertrude Crampton's
Scuffy the Tugboat, about a toy tugboat who longed for bigger things, the
pursuit of which led to being lost and alone, to overcoming challenges, and
to being found again and brought back into a loving family. The second
book, inappropriate by today's standards, was *Little Black Sambo* by Helen
Bannerman. Over and over, as Little Black Sambo, I cleverly triumphed over
the terrifying tiger.

In elementary school, I recall my father reading us Rudyard Kipling's *The
Jungle Book*. To this day I remember "the great grey-green, greasy Limpopo
River all set about with fever trees," a memory refreshed by my reading
the book with my own children. A fourth-grade substitute teacher read us
Cargoes by John Masefield, savoring the mouth feel of "Quinquireme of
Nineveh from distant Ophir" and the "Stately Spanish galleon coming from
the Isthmus, Dipping through the Tropics by the palm-green shores." She also

regaled us with Banjo Patterson's bush poetry. Her efforts doubtless explain the occasional recitation parties we hold at our house.

My high school years, alas, were a reading wasteland. I failed to find the requisite Shakespearean plays and poems and related classics more engaging than my other life pursuits to which they bore no relevance. I lost the thread. Fortunately, my love of science continued, right through college.

Then it was my first year teaching. A four-teacher country school miles from anywhere in New Zealand, reading children's books every day to an appreciative audience, but I made no time for my own reading (and I didn't even have television). One cold wet winter day, I had nothing to do—except read the only book on my shelf, *The French Lieutenant's Woman* by John Fowles, given to me by a friend for Christmas. When at last I put it down, I wrote a letter of appreciation to my friend, who thought I might also like *Siddhartha* by Herman Hesse. I did. Over the years many such books and the people who put them in my path have proven transformative, each in their own way. Last night it was John Green's *The Fault in Our Stars*.

When I returned to graduate school, my mentor extended my love of science into critical reading of research on teaching and literacy. Theory, evidence, and critical analysis: exhilarating!

> Reading has changed who I've become (over and over), how I make sense of others and the world, and how I live my life.

Reading with my own children subsequently made wonderful memories, and many children's authors (such as William Steig, Margaret Mahy, and Russell Hoban) put more playful language flavors, melodies, and textures on my tongue. In Margaret Mahy's *The Man Whose Mother Was a Pirate*, the Little Man's first experience with the sea so overwhelmed him that "the drift and the dream of it, the weave and the wave of it, the fume and the foam of it, never left him again." So it is with me and language. This joyful, relational experience of reading with my children performed an additional service. It inoculated me against overzealous scientific pronouncements about the process of teaching reading.

The outcome of this history has been a career spent researching literacy in the lives of teachers and children, most recently the transformative power of young adults' deep engagement in reading (my own missing years). I wish my teachers had known, as we have learned, that when young adults can choose among personally meaningful books, and are not bound by controlling assignments, they become deeply engaged, prolific readers and personally, relationally, and morally healthier human beings.

Reading has changed who I've become (over and over), how I make sense of others and the world, and how I live my life. Above all, I met my wife of 36 years in the library. I won her over by telling her stories that made her laugh—stories and language that had roots in my reading life.

● ● ● ● ●

Peter H. Johnston, Ph.D., researches the consequences of teachers' classroom talk and its effect on how children learn and experience themselves and each other. Now professor emeritus at the University at Albany, State University of New York, he has published over 80 articles and a dozen books (some in multiple languages), the most recent being *Opening Minds: Using Language to Change Lives.* His election to the Reading Hall of Fame established his Old Fart status beyond reasonable doubt—a fact, he notes, that is not lost on his three grown children or his wonderful wife of 35 years. Most recently, the Literacy Research Association honored him with the P. David Pearson Scholarly Influence Award, citing his book *Choice Words: How Our Language Affects Children's Learning* as having "demonstrably and positively influenced literacy teaching in classrooms and districts nationally."

Kendall Hailey

"V" Is for Victory

Why was I reading Flaubert? Why not Nancy Mitford? Or Evelyn Waugh? Or P.G. Wodehouse? I suppose I knew the wit I adored would be wasted on me now, and so I sat by my baby boy's incubator reading Flaubert, so numbed by despair that I had chosen this small book of three novellas, thinking that reading it would at least put me one book closer to reading all the books in our home. There was no comfort for me in the good Monsieur, but surely there would be no harm in reading him aloud. Maybe, even in translation, I would finally appreciate his dedication to "le mot juste," perhaps there would be a word so damn "juste" it would stun me back into life.

I began to read softly, so only Charlie and I could hear. Of course, though I talked to him constantly, I had no idea if my son could hear at all. A much-longed for pregnancy had ended without warning at 24 weeks and 5 days. Charlie had been born right after his twin Oliver, who had died in my arms after living only 12 hours. Oliver had weighed more (one pound nine ounces compared to Charlie's one pound four) and he had suffered no brain bleeds (technically, intraventricular hemorrhages, common to extremely premature babies). Charlie's were catastrophic.

Did he really need the minor works of Flaubert on top of all this? Sitting by his incubator all day long, holding his tiny hand, I had run out of conversation and Flaubert was all I had left to give. The older I get, the less I believe that we have the power to make ourselves well or sick. I have seen those longing to live die and those who care so little for life go on and on. I can certainly take no credit for Charlie's miraculous progress nor would I have let myself assume the blame had the doctors' hopeless predictions all come true.

It is said that hearing is the last sense to leave when a person dies, so perhaps it is also the first to take hold. We cannot be sure when Charlie began to hear, but when he did, either my husband or I were probably mid-sentence, talking, singing, or reading to him. We were lucky enough to be able to be by his incubator for most of the hours of the five months he spent in the hospital. My husband is better at being still than I am. He can actually just sit and be present. I could not face life without a book. There is always one either in my hand, in my purse, or in the trunk of my car. (More than once has my husband tried to excuse himself to go to the bathroom during a dinner out only to hear my plaintive cry, "But I didn't bring a book!") From the moment he could see, Charlie saw me with a book in my hand. He heard the turning of pages, he heard the words, perhaps somewhere deep inside he began to know that the world was so much more than a plastic box and terrified parents.

A less discreet doctor told us that when Charlie's brain surgeon first opened his skull to place the ventriculo–peritoneal (VP) shunt that he would need for the rest of his life, he said, "It looks like a bomb went off in there." Was it all those words that led Charlie's brain to rebuild itself so perfectly? Certainly, his relationship with words has become one of the most important and emotional of his life. Charlie has never had to be told "Use your words" because he always has, even before he could form a sentence. When he was less than two, he would express anger by rhyming. "Dog, cog, wog, nog!" he would cry. "Sit, nit, kit, wit!" Now he finds an outlet for his four-year-old frustration in the misuse of words. Is his early exposure to Monsieur Mot Juste himself the cause? All I know is you better not say "in" when "on" would be the better choice if Charlie Miller is hungry or tired. "Why did you say 'in'? It's not 'in'! It's 'on'!" he howls as he hurls himself to the floor. A little rest or food soon solves the problem, but your mistake is not forgotten. Fed, rested, and calm again, he will say in a level voice, "Why did you say 'in'? You know you should have said 'on'."

> We cannot be sure when Charlie began to hear, but when he did, either my husband or I were probably mid-sentence, talking, singing, or reading to him.

Charlie discovered books with a wonder that would have made any author weep for joy. As a baby, you could not read him a book with a car, truck, or train pictured without his pushing the book to the floor so that he could crawl onto the illustration and ride on it himself! Just as my dearest loves are the English wits of the 1930s, Charlie has a favorite genre as well—

garbage truck literature—fiction, nonfiction, and memoir. His favorites cannot be heard often enough—from *Trashy Town,* which sounds like a 1950s film noir starring Gloria Grahame, to *Grandma Drove the Garbage Truck,* which could have been the title for a heartwarming 1970s TV movie starring Loretta Young.

Charlie could read books all day long. I certainly never thought I would say to my child, "Please, no more books right now!" but parenting is rife with humiliating surprises. However, I will say we rarely ever miss his bedtime reading. Of course, unless we are reading a previously unheard work, this has become what I like to think of as a soothing shared charade since Charlie knows every single word of the books his Daddy or I are reading to him and will correct us over the slightest mistake.

After we finish his books, I turn off the bedside light, turn on my booklight, and start to read my book while he cuddles next to me and falls asleep. I always tell him who I'm reading and he loves to ask the name of the author rhetorically every night. "Are you reading P.G. Wodehouse?" He likes to look at the words on the page as he falls asleep and just a few nights ago offered this literary criticism, "This book has a lot of *b*'s in it." When he is feeling wide awake, he asks me to read to him from my book. I always thought the words were going right over his sleepy head until one night I came to a sentence with "truck" in it and he suddenly popped up, "Truck? What?" My literary taste rose in his estimation that night.

I forget what denial or change of plans caused Charlie's most articulate tantrum to date, but soon tears were followed by a new declaration, "I don't love you, I don't love garbage trucks, I don't love books." Charlie may have been declaring war, but to see books so high on the list of everything he suddenly didn't love spelled victory to me.

● ● ● ● ●

Kendall Hailey published *The Day I Became an Autodidact and the Advice, Adventures, and Acrimonies That Befell Me Thereafter* when she was 21 years old. A memoir of educating herself without going to college, it was voted one of the Best Books of the Year by the American Library Association.

Jeffrey D. Wilhelm

To Read, to Love, and to Stand Up

*T*he major impulses of my life have been to love and to be loved, to know and to be known, and to take a stance when necessary, which means knowing where to stand. These three impulses are informed by my reading life and have led to my primary professional goal: to read and to help others read—not only books, but the world.

My life is continuously shaped and changed by reading. Reading is part of my perpetual act of becoming more fully myself and placing myself in the world. Reading is a thrilling and "dangerous" game, a way of surfing on the crest of the future's breaking wave, of questioning the status quo, of becoming something new.

I trace my earliest memory of reading back to our evenings together as a family in our small Ohio house. After dinner, my father, a science teacher, sat in an upholstered green recliner and my brother Jon and I would sit on opposite armrests as he read the evening newspaper or a magazine. He would read an article or excerpt he thought we might find interesting, as well as some of our favorite comics, which he would patiently explain to us until we got the jokes. Then we would leave our father in peace and migrate to our mother, in a brown upholstered swivel chair, and sit on her lap as she read us picture book versions of *The Odyssey*, the Greek myths, the King Arthur stories (how I loved and still love Parsifal!), *The Arabian Nights*, stories from the Bible, the Frances books (*Best Friends for Frances* still holds a place in my heart), and so much more.

How glad I am that Mom and Dad both treated us like real readers from the start: they read all manner of texts, and they read not *to* us, but *with* us. I'm grateful they also let us choose our own books and forge our own reading lives.

My parents related to me, in part, through reading. I learned that reading was essential to learning how to love and relate to others. My parents taught me that reading is a conversation, a way of listening to others and the world—of listening new ideas into existence. Harold Brodkey asserts: "Reading is an intimate act, perhaps more intimate than any other human act. I say this because it provides the most prolonged and intense exposure of one mind to another." Through reading, I related to my parents, to characters, and to authors, many of whom were distant from me in time, space, and experience, and whose ideas differed greatly from mine. I learned to listen, to consider others' ideas, and decide whether I wished to affirm, adapt, or resist.

> Reading is a thrilling and "dangerous" game, a way of surfing on the crest of the future's breaking wave, of questioning the status quo, of becoming something new.

Reading was always essential to my dating and love life: I only dated girls who were readers, and I used reading to pursue my romantic relationships: "Read one of mine; I'll read one of yours. Then let's talk. Let's explore each other's inner geography. Let us see what we have in common as well as what we can learn from each other." Sharing reading is a way of knowing and a way to be known. It has enriched my marriage, my parenthood, and my friendships.

Resistance—knowing when to take a stand—has likewise always been essential to my life. It is through resistance, as well as alignment, that we stake our identities and explore the boundaries of the self. Whenever we align with an idea or with a group, we are resisting something else. Conscious resistance, as well as alignment, is energizing. Roger Soder offers a nifty explanation:

"Compliance is never edifying, it never rings with human dignity, and it never pulses with excitement and curiosity and wonder. You'd never come running home from school telling your parents how much you complied that day and how much you liked it!"

Reading has taught me the terms of many a debate and the excitement and joy of participating in those debates.

I love Stephen Spender's wonderful poem of heroism:

"I think continually of those who were truly great.
Who, from the womb, remembered the soul's history . . .
Whose lovely ambition / Was that their lips, still touched with fire,
Should tell of the Spirit clothed from head to foot in song . . ."

For me, the heroes are authors. They sing, lips touched with fire, of the Spirit and of the soul's history. I am grateful to them. They have given me great gifts . . . gifts of transition to new ways of thinking, understanding, and being.

How do I return these great favors? As my daughters (the incomparable Fiona and Jasmine) were growing up, I'd carry them to bed, one in each arm (which I did until they were 9 and 11), and then I'd read to them. We read the newspaper, the Old and New Testaments, *The Odyssey*, the Greek myths, *The Arabian Nights*, and, every night, numerous picture books—I must have read *Madeline* 4,000 times, and when I finally hid the book, my girls found it and insisted on another reading. They are adults now, but they still know I will always reimburse them for the price of a book. A book: what an investment in the future, what a legacy to pass on!

Like my father and mother, I became a teacher. I have dedicated my life to promoting reading and to helping teachers create nurturing environments and interventions that assist student reading. I have argued that students need to be helped to do what expert readers do—not only to learn their stances and strategies, but to make choices, to read what they need, to contend with issues in the world, and to forge their own reading lives in ways that help them become their best possible selves.

I teach reading. The gift is one of possibility and transformation; the capacity to imagine what has not yet come to be—for oneself, for others, for the world. And with imagination—with reading—all things are possible.

● ● ● ● ●

Jeffrey D. Wilhelm, Ph.D., has been a teacher for 32 years. He is the author of 32 books about literacy and teaching. His latest book, co-authored with Michael W. Smith, is *Reading Unbound: Why Kids Need to Read What They Want—and Why We Should Let Them*. He is the editor of three series of issues-oriented books for adolescents: The Ten, XBooks, and Issues 21.

Anne E. Cunningham

Friends for Life

As a young girl, I found solace in books. Each night before bed, listening to my mother read *Winnie the Pooh* or *When We Were Very Young* by A.A. Milne entertained me and made me feel safe. I loved hearing her tell stories about the adventures Pooh and his friends had in the Hundred Acre Wood and I would imagine myself getting into similar predicaments, all the while knowing that I was tucked in for the night and had nothing to worry about.

I also found sitting in a comfy chair at the Baldwin Public Library in Birmingham, Michigan, where my mother would take me and my three siblings every few weeks to be a soothing and calming routine. These were spaces and places where I could immerse myself in a new world. Discovering a new story or book series on a topic I enjoyed was exhilarating, and each new book made me feel as if I had found a new friend. Nancy Drew was so confident, sophisticated, and clever. Her adventures around the world and the danger she experienced were extraordinary to a shy, awkward Midwestern girl. I also loved discovering characters who were more like me. The protagonist of *A Tree Grows In Brooklyn*, Francie Nolan, shared my sense of imagination and idealism in the face of adversity and life's many challenges. We were both Irish and even though I was from Michigan, my parents were from Brooklyn, and both Francie and I were young when our fathers died. In spite of our sadness, we were sustained by the wonder of a tree returning to life—a reflection of our own hope and resilience. Reading about these girls made me feel understood and helped me see the possibilities beyond my doorstep.

Yet each week I faced a dilemma. As a young girl who spent some of her best years caught up with a book, how could I choose from among my favorite friends? *Anne of Green Gables* was another with whom I loved to spend time. The library book limit of 8-12 books forced me to choose and created much consternation.

During these early years, books gave me an opportunity to think about situations I had never considered on my own. And as I got older, reading books offered me a chance to vicariously experience the activities I longed to explore even when the experience itself was beyond the resources or time I had available. As an aspiring young equestrian, with *My Friend Flicka* by my side, I felt the thrill of galloping on a horse across the lush fields and sailing over a hedge. I could smell the alfalfa as it was pitched over the grill and into the stall. Books remained my close friends and, like all good friends, pushed me to think in new ways and see how exciting the world could be.

Years later, books provided an opportunity for me to explore the inner psychological landscape of my maturing mind. As an adolescent in high school searching for the meaning of life outside of her Catholic upbringing, Herman Hesse offered me an alternative viewpoint. Siddhartha listens to the river and learns what it taught his friend: as the river flows into the ocean and is returned as rain, all life is connected in an endless cycle. I felt deeply captivated by the ideas contained within the philosophical works I consumed during this time and I rarely regretted the sleepless nights necessary to finish the books. While a literacy theorist might value Siddhartha over Nancy Drew, I have always felt lucky that I collected many and varied book "friends," because each provided the nourishment I needed to understand the world around me.

> Books remained my close friends and, like all good friends, pushed me to think in new ways and see how exciting the world could be.

As an adult who can get around the library's rule by splurging at the bookstore when I can't wait to get my hands on a new book, I am no longer limited by the number of books I can bring home—only the time I can allocate to reading. Even so, I can imagine no better nighttime ritual than the one my mother taught me many years ago—to tuck myself into bed with a book and, from the comfort of my own home, explore new worlds with new friends who nurture and expand my mind and spirit.

● ● ● ● ●

Anne E. Cunningham, a former preschool and elementary teacher, received her Ph.D. in Developmental Psychology from the University of Michigan, and is a professor of cognition and development in the Graduate School of Education at University of California, Berkeley. She is a Fellow of the American Educational Research Association and the American Psychological Association. A recipient of multiple awards and fellowships, Cunningham has been awarded the International Reading Association's Dissertation of the Year Award, the George Graham Award, the National Academy of Education: Spencer Fellowship, and the McDonnell Foundation Cognitive Studies for Educational Practice Fellowship. Known for her research on reading acquisition and development, Cunningham examines the cognitive and motivational processes underlying reading ability and the interplay of context, development, and literacy instruction. Her research with mentor Keith E. Stanovich demonstrated the rich cognitive consequences of reading volume and engagement, illustrating that reading really does make you smarter. Her new book, co-authored with Dr. Jamie Zibulsky, written for parents and teachers, entitled *Book Smart: How to Develop and Support Successful Motivated Readers,* illustrates how children learn to read, as well as what parents and teachers can do to promote children's reading development and love of reading. Cunningham can be reached at Booksmartfamily.com and acunning@berkeley.edu.

Glenna Sloan

Literacy Begins in the Heart

*M*y mother moved from cupboard to table to stove preparing the family's weekly supply of bread and cinnamon buns. As she moved about, my mother talked, telling a story to keep me safely occupied, having warned me of the dangers of being "underfoot." Some stories were difficult to understand, I remember, but she patiently answered my many questions. Over time I developed favorites, begging to hear again and again about the baby Moses, adrift alone on the river in a bulrush basket until a kind lady rescued him, and of brave David, a young man who saved his people from Goliath, a giant enemy twice his size. Once I asked her where the stories came from. "I read them in a book," she told me.

Money was scarce during the Great Depression. We owned few books besides the Bible. In our Ontario hamlet, population 300, there was no library. But I knew what reading was because my father sat in his high-backed chair by the window most days after work, staring at a large paper covered in black marks. Often he invited me to sit on his lap "to read the funnies together." Weary from a long day's labor, my father would nod off, leaving me to figure out what Blondie and Dagwood or the Katzenjammer Kids were saying as they acted out their stories. The comics taught me to read.

At six, I was a first grader in the local one-room school, where I remained until I graduated from eighth grade at age 13. There was no library beyond a bookcase that contained dictionaries and other reference material. Stacked on one shelf were *National Geographic* magazines someone had donated. In the early grades, we read from a primer starring Mary, John, and Peter which, like its American counterpart featuring Dick and Jane, was utterly bereft of good stories and fine poems. But all was not lost. I knew what stories were and that they came from books. Every month a box of books was delivered from the county library to our school. Whoever selected them seemed unaware that they were to be read by children. I remember *King Lear* appearing when I was 10 or 11 and my valiant, but frustrating, efforts to read his story. Books by Daphne Du Maurier and Lloyd C. Douglas, intended for adults, were easier. I read every one.

My sister, 15 years older, was a teacher in a faraway town. She tried to fill the literary gaps in my life by bringing books and an occasional magazine when she visited. By age 13, I had read the Hardy Boys mysteries; a series that chronicled the adventures of Canadian schoolgirl, Ruth Fielding, a literary cousin of America's Nancy Drew; and *Anne of Green Gables*, plus many of its sequels, setting each book aside before reaching the end, postponing the time I had to leave the friends inside. I read every book she brought as well as the stories, both factual and fictional, in *Liberty* magazine.

One of our elementary school teachers was with us for several years. She was an expert knitter. That skill, together with her ability to choose fine books and read them aloud effectively, made her memorable. Each day after lunch, she would sit on a desktop facing the entire school, a smattering of pupils, Grades 1 through 8, reading aloud as she knit. Some days, having a self-imposed knitting quota to meet, she read on and on from her personal store of books, valuables she kept locked away— allowing only senior students with washed hands to occasionally examine them at their desks. I listened, enthralled at the exploits of Pooh and Piglet; I happily chanted the refrain of *Millions of Cats*; became a friend of Heidi and Tom Sawyer; and delighted in *The Hobbit*.

> My early reading revealed to me a world outside my village, a world of possibilities.

From my earliest days, I was hooked on stories for a lifetime. My early reading revealed to me a world outside my village, a world of possibilities. Love of stories helped me decide to become a teacher. What could be a better life than sharing with children what you love? I wanted to study the best ways to help students develop literacy, always keeping in mind that anyone who has never thrilled to words is likely to remain indifferent to reading and writing them. From experience, I understood that literacy begins in the heart, not the head.

● ● ● ● ●

Glenna Sloan, Ph.D., taught graduate courses in literacy development and children's literature for several decades in the Department of Elementary Education at Queens College of the City University of New York, where she also served five years as department chair. Besides the classics, *The Child as Critic: Developing Literacy Through Literature, K–8; Give Them Poetry! A Guide for Sharing Poetry with Children;* and *Tales Out of School: Reflections on Teaching and Learning*, she has published three novels for teens, numerous articles in professional journals, a series on reading and study skills for junior high school students, and a sixth-grade language arts text. She was an author and consultant for the Harcourt Brace Jovanovich series, *Literature: Uses of the Imagination*. In 2001, Sloan was the recipient of the International Reading Association's Arbuthnot Award for an Outstanding Teacher of Children's and Young Adult Literature. Visit her website at www.glennasloan.com.

Jim Burke

A New Orientation

I sat at a large, elegant writing table made of dark wood looking at the yellow Star of David inscribed with the word *Jude* my host's father was made to wear many years ago during the war. The star was now encased in glass and as I looked at it, I thought of my father. The walls around me were

made of books; there was no wall to see—just books, the spines of which spoke in many languages, came in many colors, and stood at different heights in the sanctity of the study of the small apartment my wife Susan and I were renting that summer. This was the summer when our first son Evan was two; the summer when his younger brother was entering his sixth month in the womb; and the summer my father and Susan's father were both dying. My father was then the age I

am now as I write this. It was also the summer that I received a fellowship to study the Book of Psalms as poetry at the University of Wisconsin.

But let me back up a bit to explain where I was and how I got there. I read nothing as a kid except *Serpico* (many times throughout my teens) and *Bless the Beasts and the Children*. As soon as I entered the local junior college, however, something stirred, woke, and left me changed forever: I discovered reading.

I remember one day around that time, I was maybe 18: I sat in my dark bedroom, in a rocking chair, reading Homer's *Odyssey* for the first time. I was beginning my own odyssey, my only light coming in through the window which suddenly darkened. It was my father, shirtless, tapping the bedroom window with an empty beer can, asking if I could get him another. I remember feeling frustrated, agitated, imagining he thought I was doing nothing—only reading. But I was not just reading, I was *reaching* for that next self, doing for myself what Telemachus had accomplished in *The Odyssey*: going out on my own, moving from who I was to what I would become years later when I sat down in that room to study the psalms the summer that both my father and father-in-law were entering the last months of their lives.

In Wisconsin that summer, we discussed the psalms all day in a small circle, 15 teachers gathered together around texts, words, and ideas which rose up through my eyes to enter my life. There at that desk, the sun lighting the yellow badge encased in glass, I read the psalms and the ideas of those scholars who had devoted their lives to the study of those sacred texts.

Throughout the summer, we discussed one idea in particular: that the psalms fell into three types. Psalms of Orientation, in which we give thanks for all we have. Psalms of Disorientation, which sing of loss, their ink-dark words like a forest through which we wander, the way forward lost to us. And Psalms of New Orientation, which celebrate all that we endured as we crossed over to the other side of our pain where a new self, a second chance, awaits us, one pointing a way forward we could not imagine in the midst of our troubles.

These are the songs I read every day that summer while my young son laughed and the other one grew towards life, while my wife and I were as happy as the day was long, and our mothers back home prepared to enter those new lives that would begin for them that September.

It was the psalms and their scholars that kept me company that summer, as I moved from one page to the next, from one age to the next, from my orientation as a happy new father through the disorientation of a son who would soon lose his own, to the new orientation of being a man who would have to make his own way through the years ahead, through those recurring cycles of orientation-disorientation-new orientation. In the psalms I found comfort and wisdom, and a conversation that kept me company there in Wisconsin as it had kept all who read them company for the last two millennia.

At summer's end, I returned home a changed man, transformed in that way we are when we come in contact with the perfect book at just the right moment. Throughout our lives we face such moments as Psalm 23 describes: "Yea, though I walk through the valley of the shadow of death, I will fear no evil: for thou art with me; thy rod and thy staff they comfort me."

That summer and all those since, the sons from those years having grown and gone into their own lives, it is the psalms that have helped to

> But I was not just reading, I was *reaching* for that next self, doing for myself what Telemachus had to do for himself in *The Odyssey*: going out on my own, moving from who I was to what I would become.

orient me, and the poetry of Seamus Heaney, whose words became so dear to me around the time of my father's death. Sons of fathers we both respected for their rugged integrity, Heaney spoke often of the Bible and his love of its language, of men such as our fathers whom it was not our destiny to follow into the fields.

In my own way, though, I honor my father, who spent 38 years in the publishing industry, every time I teach a book, every time I write one, every time I read those texts that allowed me to endure his loss and better understand the lessons his life offered for my own.

● ● ● ● ●

Jim Burke teaches English at Burlingame High School in Burlingame, California, where he has worked since 1992. He is the author of more than 20 books, including The Common Core Companion series and *The English Teacher's Companion*. He is currently working with Gerald Graff and Cathy Birkenstein on a high school edition of *They Say/I Say: The Moves That Matter in Academic Writing* for W. W. Norton. He has received numerous awards, including the Distinguished Service Award from CATE, Exemplary Leader Award from the Conference on English Leadership, Best Social Network for Educators as moderator of the English Companion Ning, and the Intellectual Freedom Award from NCTE. He currently serves on various committees at PARCC, the Advanced Placement program, and the College Board 6–12 English Language Arts Advisory Committee. He lives in San Francisco with his wife, three children, dog, and two tortoises.

Illumination

Books can often show us who we are and how we, the people of the world, regardless of race, color, or creed, are all connected at the core of humanity.

~Marva Allen

Naomi Shihab Nye

I Will Float Through This Day

*I*f the big people fight. If there is no money. If the grandfather forgets how to smile and sits on the couch in the living room, hours on end, staring straight ahead. And then has a heart attack, right before the tornado. When the car slides into a ditch, smashing its headlights. When the mother cries and cries. For small things as well as large. Milk souring. Birds nipping all the cherries on the trees before she can pick the high ones. Daddy coming home late. It's okay. The books stacked by the bed will still be holding their calm sentences, their fruitful phrases . . . nothing can erase them. You can take those words into your own head and heart and mouth, turning them over under the tongue like refreshing drops that soothe the throat. But they will soothe everything, not just the throat. There are other worlds. You could have been someone else. You might have lived in the white house on Tiffin Street with the brick steps and the pointed gable. That could be your room. You are not stuck. Emily, Carl, Langston, Rabindranath, Cristina, Margaret Wise, Louisa May, Walt, E.B. You belong to me. People survived many worse things. People you don't know might like you better than anyone you can see. And that keeps you going.

● ● ● ● ●

Naomi Shihab Nye's forthcoming book is *The Turtle of Oman*, a chapter book from Greenwillow. She won the NSK Neustadt Award for Children's Literature in 2013 and has written or edited around 34 books. (Photo of Naomi Shihab Nye by Ha Lam.)

Georgia Heard

Books Are the Thread We Follow

*C*hirp . . . *chirp* . . . *chirp* squeaked the very quiet cricket sounding more like a very tired cricket. Where is that sound coming from? I searched through a pile of books on my study floor, after having moved to our new house the week before, and spotted a tattered copy of *The*

Very Quiet Cricket still chirping after 15 years. As I stood there holding the book, I remember reading these words dozens of times as I rocked my son to sleep, "One warm day, from a tiny egg a little cricket was born . . ."

There in my study with hundreds of my books around me, *The Very Quiet Cricket* in my hands, the words from William Stafford's poem *The Way It Is* came to mind:

There's a thread you follow. It goes among
things that change. But it doesn't change . . .
Nothing you can do can stop time's unfolding.
You don't ever let go of the thread.

Words stay with us, marinated in meaning and sound, if it's a memorable book, no matter how long ago we read it. We remember how the book made us feel—how it tugged at our heart, and still tugs, as we grow older and change. Books are our constant, our North Star that connects us no matter how many years have passed. Books are the threads we follow, that lead us home, to our own voices—to ourselves.

● ● ● ● ●

Georgia Heard received her M.F.A. in Poetry from Columbia University and is a founding member of the Teachers College Reading and Writing Project in New York City. She is the author or editor of 14 books, and is currently working on an anthology of poetry for women entitled *On the Porch*.

Pedro Noguera

Reading Saved My Life

Reading saved my life at an early age. Actually, to be honest, I must admit that at first it just saved me from having to do extra chores. When I was a boy growing up in the Brownsville section of Brooklyn (a neighborhood better known for producing rap stars like Biggie Smalls and boxers like Mike

Tyson than for producing college professors like me), my mother would make us take the bus to the public library after we finished our chores every Saturday morning. At first I didn't want to go. I would much rather have stayed at home watching my favorite cartoons. However, my mother made it clear that if I chose not to go to the library, the alternative would be extra chores, not cartoons. Reluctantly, I took the bus along with other kids in my neighborhood to this strange place with lots of books.

When I got there, I was greeted by an extremely warm and friendly Panamanian woman named Ms. McDonald. Though she didn't know me or the other children, she told us how happy she was to see us and she seemed to really mean it. She proceeded to wrap her arms around us as she led us to long tables where books were displayed. She took time to get to know each of us and to find out what we were interested in. When she came to me, I explained that I was interested in action and adventure. Up to that point I hadn't been much of a reader. I was eight years old and though I could read, it wasn't something I did on my own time, much less for pleasure. Ms. McDonald seized upon my stated interest and exclaimed that she had just the book for me. She handed me a copy of Madeline L'Engle's *A Wrinkle in Time*. I looked at it not knowing what to make of it because the cover wasn't particularly inviting. Nonetheless, I accepted her recommendation and, even before boarding the bus to go home, I commenced with reading the book.

From that moment, I couldn't put the book down. Although it was not the kind of book I would have been drawn to on my own—I didn't particularly like science fiction—I read it almost non-stop. By the next Saturday I had finished the book and wanted to talk about it with Ms. McDonald. She took great pleasure in seeing that I had enjoyed the book and proceeded to give me another. This happened every Saturday when I visited the library. I would finish a book during the week and be ready for another by the time I saw her again. I soon found that reading was the best thing to do whenever I was bored: riding in the car or on the bus, on days when we were stuck inside due to bad weather, or before I went to sleep.

I began to realize that reading had truly saved my life because it had opened my imagination and freed me from the limitations of my environment. I was no longer merely a little boy growing up in the projects of Brooklyn. I was visiting far-off lands, traveling through history, and grappling with world events. Biographies of interesting and important people became my favorite genre and through them I developed an appreciation and love for history and politics. My identity changed and I began to see myself as a person who could accomplish great things. I began challenging my teachers when I thought that the information they presented in class, especially on topics related to American history, was skewed or biased, and I began sharing what I learned with my friends, even when they weren't interested.

> Reading changed my life by saving me from a narrow world of parochial ideas and by allowing me to see beyond the confines of the world I knew.

Reading changed my life by saving me from a narrow world of parochial ideas and by allowing me to see beyond the confines of the world I knew. I am forever grateful to Ms. McDonald, and to my mother for making me take the bus to the library.

● ● ● ● ●

Pedro Noguera, Ph.D., is the Peter L. Agnew Professor of Education and the executive director of the Metropolitan Center for Urban Education at New York University. He is the author of nine books and over 150 articles and monographs. Dr. Noguera serves on the boards of numerous national and local organizations including the Economic Policy Institute, the Young Women's Leadership Institute, the After School Corporation, and *The Nation*. He is also a member of the National Academy of Education.

Marva Allen

Caribbean Sky and My Home With Books

Friday nights were always a scurry of excitement. We couldn't wait until the twinkling stars (brighter than I have ever seen elsewhere) lit the Caribbean sky because that was when Daddy would start story time. My sisters and I would be ready with pots, pans, and ladles to create exquisite (only in

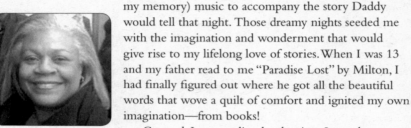

my memory) music to accompany the story Daddy would tell that night. Those dreamy nights seeded me with the imagination and wonderment that would give rise to my lifelong love of stories. When I was 13 and my father read to me "Paradise Lost" by Milton, I had finally figured out where he got all the beautiful words that wove a quilt of comfort and ignited my own imagination—from books!

Granted, I was reading by the time I was three years old, which is not uncommon for kids in Jamaica. By the age of nine I was in boarding school in the capital of Jamaica, Kingston, which is also not uncommon for Jamaican children. Away from home and Daddy's stories, reading became my lifeline. Reading for me is like DNA woven into the strands of my life.

I was always the first to arrive in literature class, securing my seat right up front, eager for the words that would transport me into other worlds. By the time I was in the third form (being a British Colony at the time, Jamaica had adopted the English learning system), I had read almost all the Shakespeare plays, could recite Longfellow, Wordsworth, and Byron by heart, and I had further developed my musical talent by moving from pots and pans to the piano. In fourth form when I got to Orwell's *1984*, I had already figured out that my very strict Catholic School, Convent of Mercy Alpha, was indeed molding us into "citizens."

I have always understood the world through books, but, as you can glean, my love for words also included the songs and ditties that held such great stories: "By Yon Bonnie Banks and by Yon Bonnie Braes" taught me that many paths lead to the same place—something I would come to appreciate even more as time went on. The words of Johann Strauss's "Gentle Breezes" painted such a vivid picture of "the wind that touches us with grace, offering unseen companionship" that it made having faith easy.

The cross-pollination of words that gives rise to stories, expressed in various artistic ways, had me at hello.

By the time I got to college in America, my world opened up to literature to which I had never been privy. My understanding of the struggle of America's blacks came through Ralph Ellison's *Black Boy*, Toni Morrison's *The Bluest Eyes,* and Maya Angelou's *I Know Why the Caged Bird Sings*. In my world lit classes, I was introduced to international writers and my world opened up like a flower.

Reading is a basic building block of life and can lead to a very satisfying and well-built house inside our minds and hearts. Words made into sentences made into paragraphs, pages, and books hold a wealth of information for the mind, the soul, and the spirit. Simply put, reading changes lives. It did mine. Books can often show us who we are and how we, the people of the world, regardless of race, color, or creed, are all connected at the core of humanity. Art, in any form, can do that, as it is part of the universal language. I certainly understood that.

I have had many professional lives, as a technologist, writer, lecturer, nurse, but little did I know then that I would spend many years of my later life making books accessible to all by becoming a bookstore owner. The best part of it all was not just reading the books but being able to give a book to someone who couldn't afford it but who would love to read it. Why? Because I know that books open the door to worlds before unimagined.

> Reading for me is like DNA woven into the strands of my life.

● ● ● ● ●

Marva Allen was president and co-owner of USI, a multi-million dollar technology firm in Southfield, Michigan, that was nominated three times for the Ernst & Young Entrepreneurship Award. After retiring from the world of technology, she became the CEO of Hue-Man Bookstore, the largest and best-known independent African American bookstore in the country. Allen is the author of two acclaimed books—*Protegee* and *Camouflage*, the sequel. Her latest novel, *If I Should Die Tonight*, will be published by Simon and Schuster in 2015. Allen is also a partner in the imprint Open Lens. She holds a B.S.N. from SGI, England, a B.S. in Biology from the University of Michigan, and an M.S. in Health and Business Administration.

Yvonne Siu-Runyan

Hope, Breath, and Light

"Hula is the language of the heart and therefore the heartbeat of the Hawaiian people."—David Kalākaua (1836–1891), Hawaii's last reigning king

"...it's hard to transmit feelings, but it's our obligation. Don't do empty movements. Do a piece of your heart. People need to feel the beauty of your dance."
—Auntie Nona Beamer (1923–2008) at the World
    Conference on Hula, 2005

*W*hen anyone asks me, "What is dear to you?" my response is, "Dancing hula. It takes me away to another place. Hula is my culture—it's in my blood, in my soul, and it makes me happy."

Hula is the art of storytelling through dance and every part of the body is involved. For any hula to be done well, one must interpret the story and its layers of meaning—to look beyond the literal meaning of the poetic words and dance from the heart. To *be the hula*, one must read deeply and metaphorically in order to interpret both the literal translation as well as the multiple metaphors in the story. The essence of hula is to go inward, to touch one's center—to feel the words and their layers of meaning. Then, and only then, can hula be truly danced with *mana,* the light and power within.

I take heed from my Auntie Winona Kapuailohiamanonokalani Desha Beamer (1923–2008), who we affectionately called Auntie Nona. She constantly reminded us to "Dance from the heart!" It is a hula dancer's obligation to dance hula with *ha* (breath) so that others feel the beauty and understand the multiple layers of meaning of the dance. So I read and re-read both the Hawaiian words and the English translation to remember the *mo'olelo* (story) as well as to understand the deeper meanings of the *oli* (chant) or *mele* (song): the poetic layers of the Hawaiian language. Without this kind of understanding, it is difficult to dance hula from the heart with expression and meaning.

When dancing hula, I *live* the dance and remember not to do empty motions. Similarly, when I read, be it fiction or nonfiction, I *live* the book.

Without reading, my soul would die. Ever stay up all night reading a book because you are so enthralled and lost track of time? I have. My father would tell me, "*Moe moe* time. Go to sleep. Stop reading under the covers or you will damage your eyes and be tired tomorrow." Usually I heeded my father's words, but there were some books that I just couldn't put down. It was worth being tired the next day.

My self-selected reading diet during my K–12 years comprised books mostly related to the Hawaiian Islands and its many cultures. I was sick of Dick, Jane, Sally, and their dog, Spot. I really disliked reading the basal texts. The assigned readings in grades K–12 just didn't excite me.

Fortunately, while in elementary school, once a month parents would drive the students to the only public library on O'ahu. The elementary school I attended didn't have classroom or school libraries. Going to the only public library on O'ahu was a real treat and it fostered my love for libraries and the many books they housed. Just walking up the cement stairs and passing the stone lions guarding the entrance made me feel as though I was entering another world, one filled with wonder and joy. To this day, I still love the smell and feel of a library—with all its books and other media housing so much knowledge and so many adventures.

Anticipation and bliss washed over me as I counted down the days until the next library visit. Once there, I plopped myself in the folk literature section. I loved reading tales from China, Japan, the Philippine Islands, India, and those written by Hans Christian Andersen and the Brothers Grimm. And I adored reading stories about the Hawaiian deities such as Maui, ancient hero and chief; Pele, Goddess of Fire; Ku, God of War; and Lono, God of Agriculture. Reading about these Hawaiian deities grounded me in dancing the hula and knowing my roots. Through reading Hawaiian folklore, I learned the importance of *pono* (goodness, uprightness, morality) as well as what is valued in my culture.

Every book I read changes me in some way. Like everyone else, I am a work in progress, and reading helps me become more insightful, and, I hope, a better person. We all need to reach back to learn about our heritage in order to reach out to others, and move forward with hope, breath, and light.

● ● ● ● ●

Yvonne Siu-Runyan, Ph.D., is professor emerita at the University of Northern Colorado and past president of the National Council of Teachers of English. Dr. Siu-Runyan has taught Grades K–12 in the states of Hawaii, Michigan, Ohio, Colorado, and California. In addition, she has worked as a District Reading Specialist and Language Arts Coordinator for Boulder Valley Schools, and has taught undergraduates, post-baccalaureate students earning their teaching certificates, master's degree candidates, and doctoral students. She is published in refereed journals and books, has presented workshops and papers at local, state, national, and international venues, and has served on and chaired local, statewide, national, and international committees. Dr. Siu-Runyan has been involved in education for over 45 years.

Deborah J. Stipek

The Light in My Hands

I was about eight when my grandmother (and partner in crime) gave me a little light that attached to the back cover of a book. The gift enabled me to read under the covers and thus escape my mother's watchful eye at bedtime. I was a reader as long as I can remember—willing to sacrifice

more sleep than my mother believed was healthy. We didn't have books at home, but I was a regular at the Tacoma Public Library. I stuck with an author to the end. I remember sobbing (and being shushed by the librarian) when I found out that I had read the last Beverly Cleary book and that Henry Huggins, Ramona, and Ribsy would no longer be an active part of my life. Since my childhood, I have run through many authors—Tolstoy, Dickens, Dreiser,

Stendhal, and others; Isabelle Allende is my current favorite. To this day, I get a warm fuzzy feeling when I enter a library or bookstore. I panic when I am close to the end of a book and don't have a new one at hand to start.

The first book I owned was Louisa May Alcott's *Little Women*, a gift from my aunt. I read it over and over, in part because it was my only book, but also because I felt the need to live through the sorrow of Beth's death many times. My adult daughter (who also had her head buried in a book throughout her childhood) recently gave me the same edition that I had as a child; I learned that being 63 years old does not diminish the need for a good cry when Beth dies (again).

How did reading change my life? I don't know what kind of a person I would have been if I hadn't spent a great deal of time immersed in other people's lives and cultures.

> How did reading change my life? I don't know what kind of a person I would have been if I hadn't spent a great deal of time immersed in other people's lives and cultures.

I know that books have exposed me to a world I would never be able to (or in many cases want to) experience directly. I have been introduced to despots and humanitarians, oppressors and the oppressed. I have been exposed to social conventions and hierarchies that have cruel effects on humans, even those in privileged stations, but also to individuals who have cured diseases and achieved extraordinary deeds. I have encountered human suffering beyond my imagination. (I was so distressed by Harriet Beecher Stowe's *Uncle Tom's Cabin* as an elementary school child that I had to stay home from school the day after I finished it.) I have learned history through the eyes of people who lived it and I have lived different cultures and religions through characters in books.

I imagine that all of these experiences have taught me empathy, compassion, and some measure of humility. They have definitely broadened my horizons, piqued my curiosity, entertained me, and brought great joy. I cannot imagine a world or a life without books.

● ● ● ● ●

Deborah J. Stipek, Ph.D., is the dean and the Judy Koch Professor of Education at Stanford University. Her doctorate is from Yale University in developmental psychology. Dr. Stipek's scholarship concerns instructional effects on children's achievement and motivation, early childhood education, elementary education, and school reform. She served for five years on the Board on Children, Youth, and Families of the National Academy of Sciences and is a member of the National Academy of Education. She also chaired the National Academy of Sciences Committee on Increasing High School Students' Engagement & Motivation to Learn and the MacArthur Foundation Network on Teaching and Learning. Dr. Stipek served 10 of her 23 years at UCLA as director of the Corinne Seeds University Elementary School and the Urban Education Studies Center. She joined the Stanford School of Education as dean and professor of education in January 2001.

Alfred W. Tatum

Defined by Books

As a young rambunctious boy who loved sports and the outdoors, books made the indoors equally pleasant. I could easily shift from the baseball field to a cozy spot on my mother's couch. My boyhood years were often balanced with a basketball game and a good piece of literature. As I reflect on my reading experiences, I am sure that I did not get the recommended amount of sleep for a growing boy. Who needs sleep anyway when there is a crisis in the school gymnasium or when you are so close to solving a mystery that you would toss and turn all night if you did not spend the additional 30 minutes deep inside the detective story to put your mind at ease?

How I loved having my very own library card! It allowed me to indulge in the lives and stories of others. I am glad the librarian recognized me, encouraged my frequent visits, and invited me to check out more books than the standard limit. It is difficult to imagine how my life would be different if I had only been allowed to read one book at a time—for me that would be like attending a party with only one other guest!

It was in the sixth grade when I realized that I loved every new word that I met. It was great to be greeted by both small and big words. My eyes would caress these new words—as well as my "old friends," the words that were already a part of me.

I often felt the need to read multiple books at the same time. Part of me was afraid that if I spent too much time with one book, the others would become jealous! Therefore, I often found myself

> Many of the texts I read as a child have been like roadmap markers, showing me a range of life options, suggesting the advantages of one direction over another, helping me define myself not only as a reader but also as a human being.

stretched across my bed with two or three books. I could be with Laura Ingalls Wilder on the prairie one hour and solving a mystery in the garage of a boy detective the next. The next evening I would find myself reading Lincoln's words in the Gettysburg Address after having spent the morning reading short stories in an anthology of African American writers.

Many of the texts I read as a child have been like roadmap markers, showing me a range of life options, suggesting the advantages of one direction over another, helping me define myself not only as a reader but also as a human being. The books' imprints in my life have been lasting, creating a textual lineage that has shaped me, making me who I am today.

As a father, I now quietly celebrate when I see my sons alternate their time among multiple books during the evening hours. I see them sampling various texts, searching for those that resonate, abandoning those that don't. They are building their own textual lineages, finding the books they need at each point in their own personal development, the books that they find engaging, that prompt them to ask essential questions about who they are and who they might want to become. I occasionally step in and suggest titles, but I also trust them to find the books that may ultimately define them and help point the way toward their own promising and productive lives.

● ● ● ● ●

Alfred W. Tatum, Ph.D., serves as Dean of the Department of Curriculum & Instruction at the University of Illinois at Chicago where he also directs the UIC Reading Clinic. He has served on the board of directors for both the International Reading Association and the Literacy Research Association, and written widely on the development of young African American males for such publications as the *Harvard Educational Review*, *Urban Education*, and *Reading & Writing Quarterly*. Tatum is the author of *Fearless Voices: Engaging a New Generation of African American Adolescent Writers*, *Teaching Reading to Black Adolescent Males*, and *Reading for Their Life*, as well as the Scholastic reading-writing resource, *ID: Voice, Vision, and Identity*. He is the proud father of two sons.

Kelly Gallagher

From Aquaman to Shakespeare

*E*very Saturday, immediately after I finished mowing the lawn, my father handed over my weekly allowance: two bucks. With this embarrassment of riches jammed in my front pocket, I would jump on my Schwinn Stingray and pedal the long ride to 7-Eleven, where I couldn't

wait to acquire my weekly bounty: a Slurpee, a box of Lemonhead candy, and a new comic book.

Sometimes, I couldn't wait to get home to catch up with the latest exploits of Aquaman, so I would sit on the sidewalk in front of the store and dive into the adventure right there. Thirty minutes later, when Aquaman had finally defeated the evil forces of Aquabeast, I would jump back on my bike and ride home, the story still swimming in my head.

All these years later, things haven't changed much. I am still using my "allowance" to purchase books. I don't sit and read in front of 7-Eleven anymore; instead, I read on the subway, in the park, and on airplanes. I still have stories swirling in my head—tales and thoughts that have helped me live a richer life.

As a high school English teacher, I now experience that richness every day. I long ago traded Aquaman for William Shakespeare, but when you come to think of it, the world of Aquaman and the world of Hamlet are not that far apart. Both fight against injustice. Both rebel against power struggles. Both are embroiled in dysfunctional family issues. And both help me to better understand the dynamics of the world we live in today.

> Stories help me make connections to both unique and shared experiences and to other points of view.

That's what reading has made possible for me. Reading stories—both fictional and real—has made me wiser. Because I have read Anne Frank's diary, I have a deeper understanding of what is happening today in Syria. Because I have read *1984*, I am less susceptible to the language manipulation and propaganda found in advertising and politics. Because I have read *All Quiet on the Western Front,* I have a greater empathy for the men and women serving our country. Because I have read Nelson Mandela's *Long Walk to Freedom*, I have a deeper understanding of oppression.

Stories help me make connections to both unique and shared experiences and to other points of view. They help me gather insight to the nuances and subtleties of the world. This is why I became an English teacher—because reading stories can play a central role in building meaningful lives. I want my students to make these same connections, to read and to understand the world at a deeper level, and to develop empathy. I want reading to give their lives context. In short, I want reading to make possible for them what it has made possible for me.

● ● ● ● ●

Kelly Gallagher is in his 30th year as a high school teacher in Anaheim, California, and is president of the Secondary Reading Group of the International Reading Association. He is the author of numerous books for teachers including *Readicide: How Schools Are Killing Reading and What You Can Do About It* and his latest book, *Write Like This: Teaching Real-World Writing Through Modeling and Mentor Texts.* Gallagher can be reached at kellygallagher.org or on Twitter @KellyGToGo.

Farin Houk

Fundamental Truths

*A*t 15, I read *One Hundred Years of Solitude* by the brilliant Colombian master Gabriel García Márquez. Although great stories always change us as human beings, this book was different. It's as if this story somehow bonded to the cells of my body, altering my life and my path in ways that were only beginning to be revealed, slowly, undeniably, and fundamentally.

As it did for millions of readers around the world, the story captured my imagination and drew me into a mystical world where tiny yellow flowers rain down from the sky and a child is born with the tail of a pig. As captivated as I was reading the English translation, I made a vow then and there to read the story in its original language. I began what has become a lifelong journey to learn the language of *Cien Años de Soledad*, and to understand the psyche from which it was born.

When the book *Cien Años de Soledad* and I finally came together, many, many years later, we were both different. I was a mother of three young bilingual children, I lived between two cultures, and the world was a much more nuanced and complicated place. Maybe because I was reading it in the original language, maybe because I had lived, loved, suffered, and grown so much in the intervening decades, maybe the original seeds had just matured; in any case, it was a different story, I was a different person, and the connection I felt to the story was more intimate and intense than ever.

Rather than simply whirling through the fantastic landscape of Macondo and the Buendías, this later reading illuminated more about the nature of our relationships with the world, with each other, and most importantly with ourselves. As I turned each page, what became clearer, in pure García Márquez fashion, was the lack of clarity. The essence of this masterpiece was the rejection of binary thinking, the ability of two seemingly opposite realities to exist together in one space, in one family, in one self. Past and future, nobility and humility, science and the divine, memory and amnesia, love and conflict, fantasy and realism, all co-exist easily within the pages of García Márquez's novel. Indeed, by embracing the presence of seemingly exclusive realities, a new reality emerges. It is *Cien Años de Soledad*. It is my own life.

In a world that exacts allegiances, we are trained to believe in absolutes. We love our country or we're traitors. We're Republican or Democrat. We're pro-life or anti-choice or anti-woman or pro-abortion. We're Caucasian or Hispanic or Other. Except that we're not. We're complicated. We're mysterious. We're magical. We're real.

Today, with my own children and with my students, my work is to not only challenge this either-or thinking and the many ways we are limited by it, but to absolutely relish our new, real lives "in the hyphen." We are not just English-speakers or Spanish-speakers, we are bilingual, and each of those realities informs our lives in an irreplaceable way. We take care of our grandparents, and we create new community on Facebook. We master codes of power and access, and we connect our inner voices through art and music. We learn about history, and we speak our own truths.

> Great stories are not only measured by how compelling the characters or dilemmas are; the true test is how they help us understand our deepest selves and our relationship to the world and others around us.

Great stories are not only measured by how compelling the characters or dilemmas are; the true test is how they help us understand our deepest selves and our relationship to the world and others around us. *One Hundred Years of Solitude*, through its meandering storyline and its intricate language, continues to bring me back to the simplest, most fundamental truths of my life.

And by the way, I named my first son Gabriel.

● ● ● ● ●

Farin Houk is the founder and head of Seattle Amistad School, a two-way dual-immersion school dedicated to providing a bilingual, bicultural education to native Spanish and native English speakers. Houk has been a teacher for almost 20 years, working in early childhood settings, Head Start, dual-immersion programs, and with children of homeless families. She did graduate work in bilingual/bicultural studies at Pacific Oaks College NW, and is a graduate of the Danforth Educational Leadership Program for Education Administration at the University of Washington. She is also the author of *Supporting English Language Learners: A Guide for Teachers and Administrators*. Houk lives in Seattle with her three beautiful, bilingual, bicultural children.

Christopher Lehman

Reading Is Dumb. There, I Said It.

A cross my middle and high school years, I learned an important fact of life: reading is a dumb waste of time. Who gives half a darn what Tom Sawyer did with the fence. I'd rather be kissing girls.

While *Treasure Island* sounded like we would finally be getting somewhere,

I found no treasure, barely understood the island, and, as previously mentioned, was busy thinking about the girls I'd rather be kissing (many of whom would have been completely creeped out if they had known how often during English class I pictured that happening). Here are reasons reading is dumb in case you didn't already know:

Reason 1: You do it alone. No girls. Not even friends. Just you in your boring, dumb mind.

Reason 2: It doesn't really matter what some character did. That character is not real and never was. Whoop-dee-doo: Holden is depressed. Good for him. The him that is not really him because he is NOT. REAL.

Reason 3: You don't actually have to read anything because teachers lead class discussions. Then, you can just find out what things in books are supposed to mean. Dumb . . . Though, now that I say this, it is actually only partially dumb because it does save more time for the aforementioned thinking-of-kissing-of-girls. So half dumb, half cool.

Reason 4: (and shhhh, don't tell) If you don't read all of those books your class is assigned, guess what? You still can go to college! And guess what else? You still can be successful! Really. I did it. I barely read *Animal Farm* or *A Connecticut Yankee in King Arthur's Court* and I was still accepted. In fact, I graduated, and I'm writing this essay on a plane right now! I get to travel for my job! On planes! How cool is that? Take THAT assigned chapters of *Fahrenheit 451*.

Now, there is one small disclaimer for the dumbness of reading that I must point out: *some* girls. At one point in high school, a girl you are way into is way into something. For her, it was Kurt Vonnegut. And that girl has a real obsession with *Cat's Cradle*. So, as you want to get to the kissing part, you try to read the book and it barely makes sense but you read it anyway and then try to talk to her about it. So fine.

Then, in college, more women like more books. You find yourself pretending to read poetry because your creative writing professor is super attractive and you might, like me, find yourself rereading e. e. cummings and Kim Addonizio over and over. Suddenly that "pretty how town / (with up so floating many bells down)" makes total sense to you, it is your completely totalitarian homogenizing college campus! You have to Break The Mold! So fine, what happens in *some* books matters a little and might affect you *sometimes*.

Then, suddenly, you are an adult and you find friends, *some* of whom are self-professed "readers." At first, trying to fit in, you go to a bookstore and stare blankly at the shelves. How DO you pick a book? How the heck do you go about picking a book? Then you remember someone talking about *The Grapes of Wrath* or *The Solitude of Prime Numbers* or *The Hunger Games* and you think, "Jeez, a lot of books start with the word *The*."

Right after that, you pick one of the many *The* books by yourself, without it being assigned, because you feel closer to the people you care about when you do. You want to read a book. I know it sounds strange, but you actually want to.

And yes, maybe one time, when you're older and married to a beautiful woman, she and you get upset with one another and huff into separate rooms. You have nothing to do all locked up in there, so you pick up the book you were reading and you find yourself on page one-hundred-and-whatever of *The Fault in Our Stars* or three booklets into *Building Stories* and you watch those made-up people doing made-up things that feel just like you. Only "you" on the inside. You feel less alone. You understand yourself more.

You then pick your head up. Close that looking-inside-of-you book. Walk over to the door. Turn the handle. Then go out to your beautiful wife to fix what has come undone. You are actually compelled to be better because some dumb book helped you see yourself more clearly. NOT reading is dumb. There, I said it.

● ● ● ● ●

Christopher Lehman is the author of books for teachers, including *Falling in Love with Close Reading* (with Kate Roberts) and *Energize Research Reading and Writing*. Additionally, he is the founding director of the Educator Collaborative, a think tank and educational consulting organization working to innovate the ways educators learn together. Previously, he was a classroom teacher, literacy coach, and a senior staff developer at the Teachers College Reading and Writing Project at Columbia University. While reading wasn't always his thing in school, he did love school. He holds degrees from the University of Wisconsin-Madison, New York University, and Teachers College, Columbia University. He writes all over the Internet for wide range of publications as well as at his blog, ChristopherLehman.com. You will also find him on Twitter @iChrisLehman where he tweets too much about zombies and teaching. Though not teaching zombies. An earlier version of this essay appeared on the Nerdy Book Club blog and is adapted with permission.

Dawn MacKeen

Baba's Journals: Learning About My Family's History

O ur car was speeding down the hot asphalt road through eastern Syria. On all sides, the desert stretched out flat and unwelcoming. Unsure of my direction, I checked my grandfather's journals, re-reading his words. Yes, we were headed the right way. In this unfamiliar terrain, I'd be lost without

these pages, each one doubling as a map to this region, and to his life. Now, a narrow river appeared, playfully splashing some blue. The Khabur, I realized. The driver slowed as I looked out at the banks where my grandfather, whom we called "Baba," had camped, nearly a century earlier, beside thousands of other Armenians, all starving, sleep-deprived, and terrified of the armed guards nearby. Already, the caravan before his had been massacred. I tried to picture his facial expression, his fear.

Sweating in the backseat, I pored over this translation of his memoir, double-checking the names of villages, like this one, *Suwar*, where he'd been interned. In recent weeks, this had become my daily routine, as I retraced his steps from his home outside modern-day Istanbul, across the country's interior, and into Syria, once all part of the Ottoman Empire, following his deportation path. Through each region, I'd re-read what he'd written about these places, not wanting to miss a single detail of how he had survived the Armenian Genocide, the 20th century's first holocaust, when some one million others did not. This was a completely different reading experience than I'd ever had before. I'd grown obsessive, my life orbiting around his every sentence. In the past, reading had only transported me to different places in my mind; now it had led me to cross an ocean and journey thousands of miles so I could actually stand where he stood. There, miles from the Iraq border, I burrowed in and read some more:

> *I, too, had lost hope of surviving, but I considered myself lucky—as strange as that might sound—because from our family I would be the only victim. My family had been left behind, while, every day, I witnessed thousands perish with their entire families. "I will be sacrificed, but my family will survive," I would say to myself, and thus I was consoled.*

I could almost hear his soft, gentle voice, so matter-of-fact about his fate. This was the man who smiled non-stop when I was child, the man whose knee I remember clearly, because I was about that tall.

Though my mother could recite his trials by heart, she had trouble reading her father's own account. He'd penned it in Armenian, her first language, but she never really learned the written script. But that didn't stop her from trying: for years, she'd carry loose papers, slowly translating his words into English so she could share them with the world. He'd survived, he'd written, for this purpose: "Being an eyewitness to those fiendish savageries, that satanic pogrom, I vowed it as my duty to put to paper what I saw."

I thought about that as we left Suwar behind us, and kept driving. The terrain was desolate and cracked, only periodically marked with boxy, mud-colored homes. This was the most severe stretch of terrain I'd travelled so far during my two-month trip across Turkey and Syria, a few years before the latter country descended into civil war, and again became a river of blood. I read onward:

> We got on the road and walked until evening.
> We stopped at a place. We were amazed that
> there were no massacres. Let them massacre, so
> we would be no more. We were still reconciled
> with death. Ah, so sweet seemed to be dying!

My eyes welled up, though I'd read it countless times before. Since my grandfather died when I very young, he couldn't tell me about his difficult past face-to-face. And my mother's version, simplified for children, somehow always felt like folklore. After a relative translated his two journals into English, I could finally read his story. I'll never forget the day, several years earlier, when I boarded a cross-country flight to attend a friend's wedding, with a copy of the journal in hand.

By now, after spending so much time with him, I could anticipate his reaction to any situation, his words giving me the biggest gift—the gift of getting to know my grandfather decades after his death.

As the cabin lights dimmed, I opened it up, and began to turn the pages feverishly, my mouth agape. With each escape, I couldn't believe the endangered protagonist was my own grandfather. I started to shake, finally understanding what my mother was trying to tell me; how he'd lived through the most trying times imaginable; how he'd personally witnessed so many dead, he thought it numbered a million. Slowly, I realized the chain reaction of his survival—I couldn't believe my mom existed, that I existed, my aunt and uncle, my cousins, my cousins' children, my whole family. With a heavy heart, he had relayed these stories to his daughter, but he had also documented it for future generations to learn what had happened to him and his people.

As I sat in the car in Syria, scrutinizing more passages, I had the sudden sensation that he was sitting beside me, guiding us. I could almost see his finger point to the places he wanted us to stop and look. Ahead loomed a hill, a ghostly hill. On top sat a small Armenian Church, denoting a massacre site. "Mrkada," the sign read. This was where he tried to flee the sentries, but had been spotted. I read some more, and became worried about him all over again, though I knew what he'd do. By now, after spending so much time with him, I could anticipate his reaction to any situation, his words giving me the biggest gift—the gift of getting to know my grandfather decades after his death.

● ● ● ● ●

Dawn MacKeen is a freelance reporter living in Southern California. She is the author of a forthcoming book about her grandfather, which will be published by Houghton Mifflin Harcourt in 2015. Previously, she covered health and social issues as a staff writer for Salon.com, *Newsday*, and *Smart Money Magazine*. Her articles have also appeared in the *New York Times Magazine*, the *Sunday Times Magazine* (London), *Elle*, and the *Los Angeles Times*.

Claudia S. Dybdahl & Paul C. Ongtooguk

From Norwich to Nome: Reading in America

*N*orwich, Connecticut, 1950s . . . I was the best reader in first grade. The school was housed in a white, wooden building at Four Corners and my room was on the ground level with floor-to-ceiling rectangular windows that pushed out to let in the sweet smell of lilacs. During reading, we would take our books from our desks and Miss Dale would stand in the front. She dutifully called on each child to read aloud while the rest of us followed along. The slower readers only got to read one sentence.

Claudia S. Dybdahl

I sat at my desk in the back waiting for my turn. Sometimes, as the anticipation built, my hands would sweat. I listened to Martha stumbling through "jump and play" and lingered in the images of Mother and Father, Dick, Jane, and Sally. I was just like Jane. I was a middle child and had a sled, roller skates, and ribbons in my hair. My mother wore dresses when she cooked dinner. My father played catch with us in the backyard when he came home from work. We took car trips and we played guessing games. Each school day I was swept into Jane's life and daydreamed about how I could live out her adventures after school.

Paul C. Ongtooguk

I peeked ahead to see how far we were from the end of the story. My turn was always the same. Miss Dale would let out a small but distinguishably tired sigh and say, "Claudia, will you finish the story for us?" I was the closer. The days when I could read two or three pages were the best. My voice lifted the words from the page and delivered them to the class with an ease that was tinged by a seriousness of purpose. Miss Dale sometimes smiled.

Claudia went on to earn a Ph.D. in Reading Education.

Nome, Alaska, 1950s . . . I remember Spot. He was so clean. Dogs in Nome were sled dogs that were kept chained outside and their coats reflected conditions on the ground—rain, mud, or snow. Jane wore fancy dresses outdoors, Mother wore high heels, and Dick's shirt was always neatly pressed. The whole family looked scrubbed. I waited for them to wear out their shoes in the dirt, or for the mosquitoes or a cold wind to drive them inside but it never happened. It was like a reversal of circumstances where the inside had been taken outside and things turned out to be in a better order. One time Father and Dick went fishing. Father caught a big fish and Dick caught a little fish and the story ended. I wanted to know what happened to the fish—did they share them, freeze them, cook them, go back for more? But instead Dick hopped on his clean, shiny bicycle. My bike was coated with mud, and the spokes were broken and bent from the rocks and gravel that were thrown up as I pedaled through streets and in between houses. Something that I did not understand was unfolding in these stories and I was on the wrong side of the bubble. Dick and Jane held the world in their hands and ran and played in it at will. There were no uncertain rains. I, on the other hand, had to learn how to scan the horizon for opportunity as my world was unpredictable and the storms could be fierce. I did not learn to read in first grade or in second grade. I came late to reading and comic books were my teachers. My first sight words were *Bam, Bang,* and *Boom* and the reverberations that were set off inside my head swept me through a dusty set of *Encyclopedia Britannica. Zygote*—fertilized beginning— seemed right by the time I got to *Z.*

> I was looking at thousands of books about Alaska Natives and Eskimos. It was like coming around a bend and finding an ocean that went all the way to the horizon that I hadn't even known was there.

My years in junior high and high school were heady times for Alaska Natives. In Washington, D.C., the Alaska Native Claims Settlement Act was being negotiated. We were in the national spotlight. At home, Alaska Natives were taking charge of our health care system and we began to imagine jobs beyond vocational training. Ambition bubbled to the surface. I was pretty sure that what was happening was important enough to be in books and that I would read about these things

Open a World of Possible: Real Stories About the Joy and Power of Reading © 2014 Scholastic

in high school. When nothing showed up, I finally asked a teacher when I was going to learn about myself. "When are we going to show up in the books?" The teacher explained that there were no books about Alaska Natives because everything that Eskimos know is told but not written down. I never questioned his statement of the fact.

After high school I ended up at the University of Washington and Suzzallo Library, a neo-gothic structure of overwhelming beauty and size. I hadn't given up on my certainty that Alaska Natives would eventually be written about, and one day I asked the librarian if she knew of any such books. Surprisingly, she handed me a pencil with no eraser and some little squares of paper and explained the rules for the non-circulating collections of the library. I could look at the books in the stacks and write down the call numbers. I would give the call numbers to another librarian and she would bring the books to me. The books stayed in the library, but I could sit at a table and take notes. By this time, I expected that there might be an arm's length of books and papers. I was eager, curious, and excited.

The next thing that I remember is sitting on the steps and trying to breathe. The section that she led me to was as big as a house. I was stunned. I was looking at thousands of books about Alaska Natives and Eskimos. It was like coming around a bend and finding an ocean that went all the way to the horizon that I hadn't even known was there. Everything was rescaled. The world was different. I was a lifetime behind. Why had this been kept a secret?

• • • • •

Anchorage, Alaska, 2014 . . .

Claudia S. Dybdahl is a professor of elementary education at the University of Alaska, Anchorage, and is currently serving as faculty in the Center for Research and Alaska Native Education. She has dedicated her career to working with students and teachers to improve reading instruction in our schools.

Paul C. Ongtooguk is an assistant professor at the University of Alaska, Anchorage, and is currently serving as the director of the Center for Research and Alaska Native Education. He has dedicated his career to transforming educational opportunities for Alaska Native students.

Marcelle M. Haddix

The Year I Met Carrie White, Miss Celie, and Ponyboy Curtis

When I was in the fifth grade, my dad was laid off from his job, and as my family began to struggle financially, we lost our first home. It was a modest home nestled in a residential area of Milwaukee,

Wisconsin. I have memories of running with the other neighborhood kids, capturing bugs and worms, and playing make believe with my dolls and action figures. In this home, my imagination grew. Suddenly, I had to leave all of that behind. We moved to the second-floor apartment above my grandmother's daycare center. The daycare was located in the inner city on Martin Luther King Drive, sandwiched between a church, a community center, the post office, and a corner store. While it was the heart of the black community, its hustle and bustle city life did not mirror the residential environment to which I had grown attached. Being displaced from my childhood home at the beginning of my adolescent years was a traumatic experience for me. Already a fairly introverted child, this transition forced me further into isolation. I spent long hours alone; I no longer wanted to go outside and explore the neighborhood around me. My life was spent being shuffled from school to church to our upstairs apartment.

At the time, I attended an inner-city Catholic school. In seventh grade, we had a young teacher who made the practice of reading central to her classroom. Not only did she introduce the class to young adult texts that piqued our interest, but she also encouraged us to bring in other books to read during our independent reading time. One of the first books she had us read was *The Outsiders* by S.E. Hinton. Now, why would the lives of a group of white teenage boys in a gang in the 1960s resonate with a classroom of mostly black, Puerto Rican, and Italian kids from the inner city in the 1980s? But they did resonate—I felt like Ponyboy Curtis was one of us. And, like him, I understood what it meant to be displaced from one's home and to cultivate community in unknown places. During a time when I felt like an outsider, the characters I met in the books I read affirmed my existence.

I began reading ferociously, building my community with characters like Alice Walker's Miss Celie and Stephen King's Carrie White. Because of characters such as Ponyboy Curtis, Miss Celie, and Carrie White, I acquired an eclectic taste for reading books. All different yet the same, these characters demonstrated courage and confidence that came from places of fear. That year, I began leaving our upstairs apartment and exploring my new neighborhood. Almost daily, I walked to the local library which was just three blocks away. I got lost in the stacks and engrossed myself in the lives of characters both different from and the same as me. This moment in my life confirmed the power of great stories with unfamiliar yet relatable characters and informs my practice of making sure my students today read literature that represents diverse stories and experiences. Such encounters with diverse texts and characters can open up a world of new possibilities.

> During a time when I felt like an outsider, the characters I met in the books I read affirmed my existence.

• • • • •

Marcelle M. Haddix is the Dean's associate professor and program director of English education at the Syracuse University School of Education. She directs the Writing Our Lives project, a program geared toward supporting the writing practices of urban youth within and beyond school contexts. Haddix's scholarly work is featured in *Research in the Teaching of English, English Education, Linguistics and Education,* and the *Journal of Adolescent and Adult Literacy.* Her awards and recognitions include the American Educational Research Association Division K Early Career Award; the National Council for Teachers of English Promising Researcher Award; and the Syracuse University Meredith Teaching Award.

Anna Sumida

Solving a Mystery

*M*y heart's desire was to have golden blond curls and to look like Jane from the Dick and Jane books. As early as first grade, I knew that I did not want to have small, slanted eyes, straight black hair, and a razor-edged line of bangs running horizontally across my forehead. Even though I looked

Anna at age 12

like the pictures of Japanese children I saw in my afterschool program's Japanese-language *chomen* (readers), I didn't want to look or act Japanese. I wanted to look "American." Born in Hawaii, a Japanese-American, I never saw myself in school or library books.

Contributing to my desired identity were the images I was bombarded with on TV. Every day I watched episodes of *Leave it to Beaver* as my mother cooked dinner. I distinctly remember wishing Mom would dress like Mrs. Cleaver. Beaver's mom seemed

the "perfect" housewife with waisted dresses, flared skirts, and matching belts. My mom wore faded shorts. Beaver's family ate off dinner plates. I ate from a *chawan* (rice bowl). They used forks and knives. I used chopsticks. The books and media I was exposed to consistently made me feel alien.

But then one day in first grade, a book rocked my world. A tall, skinny picture book in the children's section of the library piqued my curiosity because the title was a question. Something like *How Big Is Big?* The book progressively took me on a journey from objects I thought were big, beyond trees, to the sun, and eventually into the universe—unimaginably BIG—then suddenly the book reversed in the opposite direction; objects got smaller and smaller until they were unseeable—electrons and neutrons of an atom! Chills ran up my spine. There were things bigger than I could ever know and smaller than I could ever see? I wanted more. Instinctively, I gravitated towards nonfiction to unlock a way of knowing that invigorated my soul.

One weekend, a door-to-door salesman knocked at our home selling *The World Book Encyclopedia*. My parents hemmed and hawed. It was expensive. But somehow they found a way to purchase it. Too young to read it at the time, I noticed Mom occasionally used the encyclopedia for answers to questions my brother, sister, and I asked. She pointed to black-and-white photos or diagrams and constantly looked up words in a paperback dictionary to explain further.

Books and words satisfied my curiosity but *still*, why did I feel like I didn't have a place in the books read at school? Was I abnormal? I was uncomfortable in my own skin, feeling displaced and inferior.

I didn't realize it as a child, but the predominance of Japanese spoken at home underexposed me to English vocabulary. My grandparents only spoke Japanese—arriving on a ship from Japan circa 1910 as immigrants to work on Hawaii's sugar plantations. Since my family lived with them, my parents frequently conversed in Japanese. Was this why fiction was difficult for me?

Our next-door neighbor was Caucasian. When she spoke, she sounded intelligent. Why couldn't my parents speak like her? Why couldn't I speak like her children? Her five children retold, in vivid detail, every Nancy Drew and Hardy Boys mystery, tracking the numbered series. Their favorite album was *The Sound of Music* and they belted out the songs like they were part of a mini-Broadway show. Books they read at home and from the library were all about Euro-American children and families that looked like them. I felt invisible in books.

Fortunately, my affinity for nonfiction continued and allowed me to peel away invisible layers to uncover my confused sense of identity. As a Japanese-American growing up in the 50s and 60s, I subconsciously negated my identity and marginalized myself to dominant Euro-American culture as seen through school curricula, mainstream literature, and mass media. I began to find myself through nonfiction.

> I gravitated towards nonfiction to unlock a way of knowing that invigorated my soul.

Nonfiction continues to nurture my wonderings and point my internal compass towards a better understanding of my identity. Nonfiction helps to calibrate my sense of agency in a complex world.

• • • • •

Anna Sumida received her doctorate in curriculum and instruction from the University of Hawaii with a focus on critical theory and cultural studies. With a passion for social justice and educating children to be agents of change, she has served Native Hawaiian children and families through the campus and community programs of Kamehameha Schools for 29 years. Given the Excellence in Teaching Award by the Hawaii Council of Teachers of English, she also produced an award-winning educational film for parents on early literacy; published articles in *Language Arts* as well as other educational journals; and co-authored *Elevating Expectations: A New Take on Accountability, Achievement, and Evaluation*. She is currently co-authoring *Arting, Writing, and Culture: Teaching to the 4th Power*.

Barry Lane

A Poem Is Not a Pepsi

*I*f I told you that I communed regularly with people who lived 400 years ago, you would not believe me. If I confided to you that there were imaginary humans who never breathed a single breath but were as alive to me as friends I know and love, you would think me a lunatic. If I pointed to

some marks on white paper and said to you I could stare at them and through this process meditate with the mind of the person who made them, you might think I was a member of some cult religion.

But I can do all these things because I am a reader.

I did not always possess these magical powers. I grew up in the land of shadows deep in the cave, staring for hours at the flickering images on the box. I watched shows and absorbed the light and darkness. In between sales jingles that still rattle around in my head many years later, I sat in silence, drawing in the stories. At the end of the night, I turned off the light.

Looking back, I still remember those empty moments as a child when the box went mute. I was left with very little because I never really participated in the stories I watched—I was a spectator. My television fed me visions, but I never created my own until I became a reader.

It is hard to tell the exact moment I attained these magical powers, but it was long past childhood. I remember reading the philosophical novel *Siddhartha* by Herman Hesse during my freshman year of college and not wanting the book to end, absorbing with awe the "Dialogues of Plato" (how could something so ancient feel so contemporary?), falling into short stories by Guy de Maupassant and O. Henry, and relishing those surprising last moments where a plot twists and you see another side of the

> A poem is not something we consume, but in some mysterious way it consumes us and from this process something new is born.

character you thought you knew. And then one day I stumbled upon Rainer Maria Rilke's "Fourth Duino Elegy" and gasped when I read:

> *Who shows a child who he is, who sets him in his place among the stars and puts the measure of distance in his hand, who makes the child's death out of gray bread and leaves it there in his mouth like the core of a lovely apple. Murderers are not hard to understand, but this, that one can contain the whole of death, even before life has begun, can hold it in one's heart gently, and not be angry, this is indescribable.*

Reading this passage for the first time I remember thinking, "I don't really have a clue what it means, but it is so true, so utterly human." It seemed to reach past my mind to something more elemental and eternal at the core.

My friend Charles Boyer introduces literary analysis to his college students with a tagline I love: "A poem is not a Pepsi." A poem is not something we consume, but in some mysterious way it consumes us and from this process something new is born. Call it comprehension. Call it wisdom. Call it hope. Reading is not a skill; it is a miracle.

●　●　●　●　●

Barry Lane lives in Vermont and has written many professional books including *But How Do You Teach Writing?*, *After The End*, *Revisers Toolbox*, and *51 Wacky We-Search Reports*. His latest project, co-authored with Colleen Mestdagh, teaches kindness to children through original songs and lessons. It is called *Force Field for Good*. You can find more information about Lane's work at www.discoverwriting.com.

Michael W. Smith

The Great-Heartedness of Books

I've lived in Philadelphia for 22 years now and have been in the same book club for 21 of them. I was the host of our last meeting. My book choice: Anthony Marra's *A Constellation of Vital Phenomena*. It's always a bit nerve-wracking to pick a book for my club. For the last 20

years, I've endured teasing about a book I chose that no one liked except me. But this time I had hit a home run. Marra's book is set during the Chechnyan wars. It tells the story of a group of people who struggle to survive under horrifyingly destructive conditions.

I'm a little ashamed to say that I didn't know anything about the Chechnyan wars. I hadn't followed the news. But even if I had, I couldn't have fully comprehended what it means to live in such dire circumstances. After reading Marra's book, I think I have a much better understanding of the horrific challenges even though I know that my reading experience obviously pales in comparison to the experiences of those who lived through the horrors that Marra chronicles.

Nevertheless, reading *A Constellation of Vital Phenomena* opened up my world: I got to see ordinary people, flawed like me, face those horrors with dignity and courage. I was privileged to observe them reach out to others with small gestures of kindness that allowed them to keep their humanity against all odds.

After we had discussed Marra's book and club members were leaving, one of them grabbed my forearm and squeezed. "Thank you for this," she said. "It has changed my life." Mine too, I think. I hope I have learned enough to act with grace and kindness when I face the relatively minor struggles of my life.

This is just a recent example of what's been an ongoing life theme. I think back to my adolescence when my dad, an inveterate reader himself, shared with me the book he had just finished: Claude Brown's *Manchild in the Promised Land*, the story of Brown's coming of age in Harlem. "Read this," he said. "It's something you should know about." So I did. And the walls of our all-white suburb in which I grew up came down, at least a little. Now, as a father and husband myself, my own family is multi-racial. I don't know whether it would have been if my dad's book hadn't sent me down a new path.

I think back to the time when I had just finished Hermann Hesse's *Siddhartha* and ran weeping to my girlfriend's house to try to explain to her what had happened to me as I read of Siddhartha's spiritual journey. I didn't know exactly what had happened to me—still don't, I guess. But something had.

I think back to the time I read Jumpa Lahiri's amazingly wise story *Unaccustomed Earth* and how it made me resolve to bring her great-heartedness to my relationships with my own friends and family. I'm not sure how I'm doing, but I do know she's helping me try.

My friend Jeff Wilhelm and I recently finished a research study of why kids read what they read outside school: *Reading Unbound: Why Kids Need to Read What They Want—and Why We Should Let Them.* Our most important finding is that the kids we studied read books to help them navigate their lives' journeys.

> The great-heartedness of books is an enduring gift. Every time I open a new one I know there's a real chance that it will change my life.

Michelle explains:

You can look to books, I think, and characters for their influences . . . You can look at oh, so I made a mistake like that so that could be why they reacted that way and realized also how the characters reacted in real life, you know? Maybe I shouldn't have done that. And you can reference your own experiences off of books. And you can kind of "Yeah, so I shouldn't do that again because the character also found that very offensive." Kind of like a cautionary buddy.

Helen chimes in:

Sometimes when, like, big stuff happens in my life, I'll think about what my favorite character would have done, the ones I admire most. And then sometimes I follow their example and sometimes I don't . . . They all have different approaches, different ways they approach things, and then I try to apply that to my life, to see which way works for me. Characters are just ways of thinking, really.

Throughout my life, books have provided me with many "cautionary buddies" and new ways of thinking. Books have helped me discover alternative perspectives and once unimagined options. The great-heartedness of books is an enduring gift. Every time I open a new one I know there's a real chance that it will change my life.

● ● ● ● ●

Michael W. Smith is associate dean for Faculty Development and Academic Affairs in Temple University's College of Education and chair of the Department of Teaching and Learning. He joined the ranks of college instructors after 11 years of teaching high school English. He has won awards for his teaching at both the high school and college levels. His research focuses on how experienced readers read and talk about texts as well as what motivates adolescents' reading and writing both in and out of school. He's shared that research and the instructional ideas that derive from it in 14 books and over 60 articles and chapters. When he's not working, Smith is likely to be watching or talking about sports, reading, or playing with his granddaughter.

Communion

*An old tree had sprouted branches that,
growing straight up, resembled a green harp.
There I could hide in communion with my
dearest friends—a tree and a book.*

~Alma Flor Ada

Alma Flor Ada

My Communion With Books

*T*he fascination began with words. The old ballads my mother sang as lullabies excited my imagination:

Las mañanas de San Juan	*On the morning of the Feast of St. John*
se levanta el Conde-Niño	*the Child-Count wakes up*
a dar agua a su caballo	*and gives his horse water*
a la orillita del mar.	*at the sea shore.*

Even though I lived inland I knew the joys of being by the sea. I imagined the fresh breeze filled with the smell of seaweed and the salty taste on my lips, giving water to a horse in the early morning. The fact that I could anticipate the romance between the count and the young princess just made my anticipation at hearing my mother's ballad a greater pleasure each time.

The words were Cuban writer's José Martí's verses sung by my grandmother to her own made-up tune:

Quiero a la sombra de un ala	*Under the shade of a wing*
contarte este cuento en flor	*I'll tell you this story in full bloom*
la niña de Guatemala	*of the girl of Guatemala*
la que se murió de amor.	*the girl who died for love.*

What magical images those verses evoke. In my tropical island, shade was always welcome, but to imagine sitting under the subtle shade of a wing, to listen to a story in bloom, provoked an indescribable joy in me. What kind of illness was love that would cause the death of a girl in Guatemala? How could the poet ever forget this girl who loved him so dearly?

By the age of three, my grandmother had taught me to read. Combining her love for books with her love for the earth, she traced for me in the dirt the names of animals and plants we saw on our outings through our old farm. For each new letter there was a story. The *v* in *vaca* had the shape of the horns of the cow they milked to offer us a glass of fresh milk; the *b* in *burro* resembled the donkey's long ears. I don't remember all the stories, but even today I can feel the warmth of the sun on our faces as she traced the word *rosa*, and showed me how the *r*, in her old-fashioned handwriting, looked like the wall of a garden, and the little lop on top was the rose that had climbed the wall to see the marvels of the world. Looking up to our own garden's walls, and hearing the wonder in my grandmother's voice, I felt this letter held both the fragrances around us and the promises to come. Yes, the name *Rosalma*, chosen many years later for my daughter, in the rose garden of Saint Rose of Lima, was the blooming of that seed of wonder planted when I first learned the letter *r*.

Learning to read was followed by the magic of the first book my mother gave me, her own long saved copy of Johanna Spyri's *Heidi*, a bit of magic to be followed by many more.

I discovered the perfect place for reading: an old tree, felled by a storm, had refused to die and had sprouted branches, that, growing straight up, resembled a green harp. There I could hide in communion with my dearest friends—a tree and a book. From that tree trunk I sailed the straits of Malaysia with Emilio Salgari's *Sandokan*, seeing the brave prince fight the invading British forces; I trembled with fear and hope in Robert Louis Stevenson's *Treasure Island*; and laughed with the mischief and misadventures of Richmal Crompton's *Just William*.

While I enjoyed the new worlds that books opened, the most extraordinary feeling they provoked was that they had been written only for me. How special they made me feel, how well understood. It did not matter that there could not be two more dissimilar landscapes than our Cuban farm and the Swiss Alps. The wind swishing through our bamboo grove by the river was the same wind Heidi heard swishing through the pine trees, and while she visited Pedro's blind grandmother, I had my own blind great-grandmother I rushed to from my outings. Above all, I understood Heidi's love for her surroundings—it was my love for mine.

And the more I read and reread Louisa May Alcott's books, the clearer it became that she could not have been writing for anyone but me. And could Sarah's misfortunes and her resilience, that I read and reread in Frances Hodgson Burnett's *A Little Princess* be anything but a call to my soul? Of course I knew other people had read these books, and continued to do so, but nothing changed the feeling that they had been written uniquely for me.

> Books remind me, each day, to never forfeit my dreams.

What might sound like a preposterous childish idea at first is actually an extraordinary insight. Contrary to what proponents of standardized testing would have us believe, each book has been written exclusively for each individual reader and gets re-written as it is read.

Because—to be meaningful—reading must be a dialogue. It is only when the reader encounters the text with a full range of feelings, emotions, and experiences and compares them with those proposed by the author that true reading begins. And it is only as the reader recognizes the ideas in the text, or is surprised by them, that reading becomes enriching and reaches its potential.

What motivated such conflicting opinions about Heidi by the people around her? What did each one want from her or for her? What could Jo March have done to curb her temper? Why was it important that she continued to harbor her dreams? Silent questions such as these led me to a profound observation of the people around me and to a better understanding of their motivations. I am moved to ask: *What if something would have been different? What other possibilities are there? Who has been left out? Who will reap the benefits? What will be the consequences? Who will be affected by them?*

Books inspired and continue to inspire me to be a kinder, more caring, courageous, and supportive human being. They move me to ask myself how I can contribute to make social realities more equitable, more inclusive, more responsible . . . what can I do to help create a just society, the only road to enduring peace? Books remind me, each day, to never forfeit my dreams.

● ● ● ● ●

Alma Flor Ada, professor emerita at the University of San Francisco, has devoted her life to advocacy for peace by promoting a pedagogy oriented to personal realization and social justice. A former Radcliffe Scholar at Harvard University and a Fulbright Research Scholar, she is an internationally renowned speaker. Dr. Ada's professional books for educators include *A Magical Encounter: Latino Children's Literature in the Classroom* and *Authors in the Classroom: A Transformative Education Process,* co-authored with F. Isabel Campoy, about their work promoting authorship in students, teachers, and parents. Dr. Ada's numerous children's books of poetry, narrative, folklore and nonfiction have received many prestigious awards such as the Christopher Medal (*The Gold Coin*), Pura Belpré Medal (*Under the Royal Palms*), Once Upon a World (*Gathering the Sun*), Parents' Choice Honor (*Dear Peter Rabbit*), NCSS and CBC Notable Books (*My Name is María Isabel*), and the Marta Salotti Gold Medal (*Encaje de piedra*). In 2012, she received the Virginia Hamilton Literary Award in recognition of her body of work for children. Dr. Ada is also the author of a book of memoirs, *Vivir en dos idiomas,* and two novels for adults, *En clave de sol* and *A pesar del amor.* She has been awarded the Distinguished Professor Award at the University of San Francisco, the American Education Research Association (AERA) Hispanic Issues Award for Research in Elementary, Secondary, and Postsecondary Education; the California Association for Bilingual Education (CABE) Lifelong Award; the California Council for Higher Education 2011 Award; the 2012 Literary Award of the American Association of Hispanics in Higher Education; and the 2014 OHTLI Award from the Mexican Government "bestowed on renowned Latino leaders who have distinguished themselves for the contributions to the advancement and empowerment of Mexican communities abroad." Dr. Ada has also established an endowment for the California Association for Bilingual Education (CABE) to provide scholarships for future teachers.

Carmen Agra Deedy

How Reading Changed My Life: Owning the Written Word

M y father was 14 years old when he learned to read. He was born in 1924, during the nascent years of the Cuban Depression. At age six he attended a rural school long enough to conclude that the endless days and stinging yardsticks were not his cup of *café con leche*. After one particularly severe beating, he never returned.

As a newly emancipated six-year-old, he spent his days plundering mango groves, chasing guinea hens, and dozing on the warm rocks that lined the riverbank. When he grew tired of these diversions, he gathered pebbles in his pockets and used them to pelt his erstwhile teacher during the unfortunate man's evening constitutional.

When his mother was presented with evidence of this hooliganism, as well as her son's chronic truancy, she accepted the news with the resignation of a woman long defeated by poverty and fertility. Still, she declared that if he refused to go to school, then he must work like everyone else.

By the time he was 14, one of my father's tasks was the mile walk to the town bakery to pick up bread from Antonio, the ill-tempered proprietor. After this he did various farm chores; the remainder of the day was his to spend at his pleasure.

Then, a serendipitous encounter with *Prince Valiant* changed the trajectory of his young life.

It happened one morning when he entered the bakery to find the irascible Antonio laughing as he read the syndicated comic strip in the local newspaper. My father asked what was so funny, and in an act of uncharacteristic benevolence, Antonio handed him the paper. My father was captivated by the ink drawings but, how to make sense of the story? With only pictures for clues, the characters were enigmas, about whose lives and exploits he could only guess. He handed the paper back, bought his loaf of bread, and left.

But the images of fierce knights and fair ladies remained with him. He had to know their story.

On the following morning, he lingered. When he was certain the last customer had left, he asked the baker if he would read the comic strips aloud to him. The man shot him a questioning look; when it went unanswered, Antonio shrugged, pulled up his stool, and began to read.

This tryst became a weekly affair, and might have simply ended one day—as abruptly and unceremoniously as trysts often do—with one or the other giving in to boredom or discontent.

Instead, my father arrived one morning to find Antonio in a fury; he had scorched the day's bread. When he spied my father, he snapped, "Don't think I'll be making time to read to you today! You're too damn old for it!"

Stung by the reproach, my father backed out of the door and ran to the river, a place he could always find solace. He was too ashamed to go home, too ashamed to tell anyone what had happened, too ashamed to do anything but sit on the riverbank and sob and swear childish oaths. His misery soon turned to resentment. He scrambled to his feet, wiped his nose, and scooped up a handful of pebbles.

From the bakery door he could see Antonio asleep on his stool; arms crossed, chin on his chest. Fresh-baked loaves of Cuban bread lined the shelves. My father's hand tightened around the pebbles.

> I wrestled with words again and again until, slowly, they became mine.

"What do you want?" demanded Antonio, jerking awake. Startled, my father stepped back. "And why can't you read? Didn't your mother send you to school?"

"She tried," said my father, "And leave my mother out of it."

Antonio didn't respond immediately.

"Do you want to learn?" he asked, at last.

"Not if it's going to turn me into an angry jackass like you," said my father.

"Very well then. As I see it, two paths lie before you: you can either sit around and wait for others to read to you at their whim, or you can learn to read and never again be at the mercy of an angry jackass who decides to stand between you and knowledge. Your decision."

My father's reply was to have generational repercussions.

"Teach me," he whispered.

His fingers relaxed and the handful of pebbles clattered to the ground.

They began with *Prince Valiant*. Before long they graduated to the obituaries. Classifieds followed, and then full-length articles. My father became obsessed with words. Once all but invisible to him, he now saw them everywhere: painted on storefronts, splashed across the back of an iodine bottle, printed on the head of a nail . . .

I asked him once how it was possible that he had not noticed words before when they had been all around him. I was a young author then, spending increasingly more time with poor, often marginally literate children. I desperately wanted to understand.

"They were not mine," he said quietly. "Just like new shoes and shiny toys, *I did not believe written words belonged to me.*"

I felt a rush of blood that made my ears ring.

That was it.

That simple explanation would change the way I would talk to children about reading from that day onward. I am a reader for many reasons—and despite many more, including an assessment of dyslexia at age 28—but I am the daughter of a voracious reader and an intellectually curious person. Books and magazines and maps were ever-present in our home. I never doubted that words belonged to me. And because I knew this, I persevered; I wrestled with words again and again until, slowly, they became mine.

My father was 14 years old when he learned to read. It was a hunger that could not be sated, and he passed on that same appetite for words and books and stories to his daughters. We did our utmost to transfer that love to our own daughters and sons. And they, in turn, have book-rich lives that they are bequeathing their children.

And that is how reading changed my life.

● ● ● ● ●

Carmen Agra Deedy's award-winning books include *Martina the Beautiful Cockroach* (Pura Belpré Honor Award, E.B. White Book Award Nominee, ALA Odyssey Audio Honor Award), *The Yellow Star* (Christopher Award, Jane Addams Peace Association Honor Award), *The Cheshire Cheese Cat* (Cybil Award for Middle Grade Readers), and the *New York Times* bestseller, *14 Cows for America*. She hosts the Emmy Award-winning Georgia children's program, *Love That Book!* Deedy has been a guest speaker at the TED Conference, the Library of Congress, and the Smithsonian Institution. An avid supporter of libraries, she is an author advocate for the American Library Association. Her forthcoming picture book is titled *The Brave Little Rooster*.

Roy Blount, Jr.

Still Learning

I'm still learning to read, but here's how I began: by looking at the page as my mother read to me aloud. Especially formative, I believe, were the stories of Uncle Remus—African American folktales recalled by 19th century writer Joel Chandler Harris from his childhood on a plantation.

Harris was a forlorn little kid, a stutterer born out of wedlock. These stories, both scary and avuncular, had absorbed his rapt Irish-American attention. As a still-stuttering and painfully shy adult, Harris found ways to spell the tales he'd heard, to get them down on paper. "By and by" he spelled "bimeby," for instance. Dialect. Hard to read today, and politically embarrassing, but music to me then and now, like the blues. Harris's adventurous, out-of-the-box spelling formed my mind's ear.

My mama she done told me, "Sound out the words." Not just isolated words, but words in the context of a story, in the consistency of a literary voice, in the dialectic of cultural mingling, in the cuddling urgency of my mother's complicated dreams. So words on a page are mother's milk to me (a bottle baby).

But you can't get all of English by written word of mouth. Got to learn to spell correctly. My mother also acquainted me with the dictionary, which sounded out the words officially, in the full heterosymphonic, crazily inconsistent, and expanding glory of American English. A good dictionary is also music to me—sort of classical, but with notes and chording derived from Latin, from Yiddish, from Shoshone . . . I can never remember how many *r*'s in "embarrassing."

> My mother also acquainted me with the dictionary, which sounded out the words officially, in the full heterosymphonic, crazily inconsistent, and expanding glory of American English.

Have to look it up every time. Embargo . . . embark . . . embarrass. One dictionary traces it back to the Portuguese for "halter." (Hmm. Am I the only one who thinks here of "halter top"?) But better check that against another dictionary . . . Nobody ever finishes learning to read.

● ● ● ● ●

Roy Blount, Jr., is the author of 23 books about everything from the first woman President of the United States to what barnyard animals are thinking. His latest is *Alphabetter Juice: The Joy of Text*, now out in paperback from Farrar, Straus, and Giroux. Before that was *Hail, Hail Euphoria: Presenting the Marx Brothers in Duck Soup*, *Alphabet Juice*, *Long Time Leaving: Dispatches From Up South* (which won the 2007 nonfiction award from the New England Independent Booksellers Association), and *Feet on the Street: Rambles Around New Orleans* (which the *New York Times* called "a wild, unpredictable ramble through a wild, unpredictable town"). Blount is a panelist on National Public Radio's *Wait, Wait . . . Don't Tell Me*, ex-president of the Authors Guild, a member of PEN and the Fellowship of Southern Authors, a New York Public Library Literary Lion, a Boston Public Library Literary Light, a usage consultant to the *American Heritage Dictionary*, and an original member of the Rock Bottom Remainders. He comes from Decatur, Georgia, and lives in western Massachusetts. In 2009, he received the Thomas Wolfe Award from the University of North Carolina.

Juan Felipe Herrera

ABC

"**A**hhh, Behhh, Cehhh," I repeated out loud, ambling sideways through the streets of Escondido, California, at the age of five, tuning my voice to my mother's as she read me the first three letters of the alphabet from a late 1800s Spanish primer she had discovered at *La Segunda,* the local second-hand store. It was like singing and almost like storytelling with a harmonica—like the one my father would jiggle in his hands making it flutter like a dove, and then sparkle and sizzle like a tiny orchestra of Texan accordionists as he paused and spoke about catching a train, at 14, to *El Norte,* the USA, in 1896. Letters and words and stories were all honey-coated *música* to me—until I was spanked in first grade for speaking in Spanish.

In third grade, in front of the class, after inviting me to sing (and after I yanked myself up from my desk after three years of silence), Mrs. Sampson said, "You have a beautiful voice." Beautiful?

From that day forward, words and sentences and books, I discovered, when read and recited, could heal a tender heart. Even though we moved from barrio to barrio, reading became my place of rest, my garden. The more I read out loud, the more I played with words and dreamed up stories. Soon, I discovered that if I played softly, carefully, with words, I could write a poem. And if I read the poem to others, for others, I could inspire them—this became my life's mission as a poet.

What is a poet's garden? A poet is an intense reader who loves to read the same sentence many times to catch the kind notes of each letter, like the *A* that opens and flies by you like a flock of geese or the *J* that makes you smile when you pronounce it. Yet, most of all, a poet deeply listens while reading—to delight in the deep-inside stories and meanings. On rare occasions, someone speaks up and reveals his or her innermost story. That is when you write—write fast and slow and then go, writing until the poem is born, blossoms, and glows.

My brother-in-law, Roberto, a Vietnam War veteran, was a moody man. No one asked him why he was always so serious and jumpy. They knew it had to do with what he had experienced in that terrible conflict. But, what was it, really? After years had passed since his return from Vietnam, we sat down together and suddenly, he burst with his story. I scribbled it down after I came home—a poem with his words. He read and read it, over and over. Everyone in the family did. Even the Veterans of Foreign Wars local hall wanted copies. They poured over it, noticing its familiar volleys and voices about life and death. Reading—whether a poem or a personal remembrance or just one phrase, such as, "You have a beautiful voice"—can put a broken human being back together again.

These days, as California's Poet Laureate, I amble through schools, libraries, and community centers throughout California inaugurating parks and new bridges rising tall over emerald-colored bays. At strawberry farms I give away books, trading stories with families until the moon comes up. Hear me call out the letters of the alphabet, like Mama did—*A* is for *All,* *B* is for *Beautiful* and *C* is for the new *Challenge* of this *Century*—to read all voices, in all languages, about all peoples. ABC—it is that easy.

> From that day forward, words and sentences and books, I discovered, when read and recited, could heal a tender heart.

• • • • •

Juan Felipe Herrera is an author of 29 books that include poetry, fiction, nonfiction, children's books, and young adult novels. His most recent is *Portraits of Hispanic American Heroes,* published by Dial. A graduate of the University of California in Los Angeles, Stanford University, and the Iowa Writers' Workshop at the University of Iowa, he travels the country promoting reading, writing, and creativity encouraging everyone he meets to tell their stories. He has garnered many awards, among them the Guggenheim Fellowship in Poetry, the National Book Critic's Circle Award, the PEN USA Award, the Josephine Miles PEN Oakland Award, and the Latino Hall of Fame Award in Poetry. He is professor of creative writing at the University of California in Riverside. Appointed by Governor Brown, Herrera is currently serving as California's Poet Laureate.

Lily Wong Fillmore

On Learning the Language of Literature

I grew up in a small California town at the foot of the Gabilan Mountains—Steinbeck Country—so interests in language, culture, and literacy came naturally to me. It wasn't Steinbeck, however, who influenced me as much as the people and the places Steinbeck wrote about. Many of the students at my elementary school in the 1940s were, like myself, learners of English as a second language. They were the children of Mexican, Croatian, Portuguese, Filipino, Chinese, and Japanese immigrants who worked on the farms and orchards of the coastal valleys. We learned English from one another and from the children of the Dust Bowl migrants who fled the environmental disaster that turned their farms and homes in Oklahoma, Arkansas, and the Texas panhandle into a wasteland. To a Chinese-speaking kid, anything that was not Chinese was English, and I was an equal opportunity learner who picked up as many colorful invectives as my classmates had to offer, from their home languages or from English ("nunnaya beezwaks",[1] "kaiyatay-lavohka"[2] and "bucka-dahdi"[3] were favorites). In the spirit of sharing, I taught them some equally useful expressions in Cantonese.

It is no wonder, then, that I would have taken an interest in language and culture since everyone I knew was looking for common ground on which to bridge our differences. School was where that could happen. The English I learned from my classmates was great for schmoozing and for verbal self-defense as needed, but it did not always satisfy other literacy contexts. Few of us had parents read to us at home, so school was where we would learn the English needed for reading, and the books we learned to read there would provide opportunities for the linguistic upgrades we needed for reading pleasure.

Miss Sally Mayer was the teacher who introduced me to a literary world beyond the one inhabited by Dick and Jane. Miss Mayer read real books to her fifth-grade class—meaty, complicated books that took weeks, even months, to read, at the rate of a half-hour's worth each day, right after lunch. The books she read were ones the students, especially those of us who were not yet fluent

---

1 "None of your beeswax," = "Mind your own business," or "bug out!"

2 "Cállate la boca" = "Shut your mouth," or "shut up" in Spanish

3 "Bakatare" (pronounced bock-a-tah-dee) = colloquial Japanese for "stupid fool"

enough in English or in reading, could not possibly have managed on our own. The most memorable of these books, *Green Mansions* by W. H. Hudson, was about a man who finds himself in a rainforest where he encounters a strange girl who communicates in bird songs. Now, as I look at the text, it was a wonder that our teacher thought we could follow it. Most teachers would have judged it to be far too linguistically demanding even for native English-speakers of our age. It was an enormous act of trust, both in her own ability to make the story come alive for us, and in our ability to comprehend and appreciate it.

Green Mansions is a fantasy tale of adventure and romance. As a protected Chinese child of the female persuasion, romance was a topic about which I had considerable curiosity but zero knowledge and even less experience. Listening to this story of danger, adventure, love, superstition, misunderstanding, and finally, of tragic loss—the cry of anguish as Abel imagines the moment his beloved Rima falls from the treetops and into the fire the Indians have set in the forest, resonated with my 11-year-old soul. "O cruel nature!" I memorized this line, thinking it a handy lament to have in my own linguistic repertoire. I wanted to relive the moments of the story, of the protagonist's awakening senses as he chases down the mysterious bird girl and discovers the beauty of the natural environment. I wanted to find the places in the text that described events I had not fully understood when it was read aloud to us, and read them for myself so I could discover what they meant.

> How does one learn the language of literature that is so different from everyday spoken language except by reading books?

I was first in line to check the book out from the school library after Miss Mayer returned it. That book, in its rough pea-green muslin binding, transported me to the Guyanese jungle where, over the course of however long it was in my possession, I read and reread the passages, savoring the beautiful descriptions, and reimagining the events. What I only partially understood when Miss Mayer read it to us became vivid experiences as I lingered over the text. The language that etched in my mind forever the sounds, smells, and colors of the jungle became a part of my expectations of the kind of vivid experiences one could find in books.

How does one learn the language of literature that is so different from everyday spoken language except by reading books like this? From *Green*

Mansions, I gained an appreciation for beautifully complex language—what is called academic language these days—as I discovered that people in books did not talk the way my friends and I talked to one another. Those who populated stories such as *Green Mansions* were infinitely more formal, eloquent, polite, and often downright verbose, especially when addressing objects of affection.

> *Rima, you are like all beautiful things in the wood—flower, and bird, and butterfly, and green leaf, and frond, and little silky-haired monkey high up in the trees. When I look at you I see them all—all and more, a thousand times, for I see Rima herself.*

The florid use of language in this over-the-top declaration of love was poetry to my ears, and became a standard against which to judge the sincerity of any such commendation I might receive from anyone in the future. My taste in literature has evolved and changed since then, as has my admiration for rhetorical flourishes in speech. What has endured is a fondness for the artful use of language in written texts.

In my own efforts to improve language and literacy instruction for English learners and for other language-minority students, I find it useful to reflect on my own experiences as an English learner long ago, and to wonder what would have happened had it not been for educators like Sally Mayer who trusted her students to get something out of the beautiful literature she read to us, even if we didn't understand every word. I think about that especially when I hear people asking where they can find literacy materials that are suitable for their students' English proficiency level. What I learned from Miss Mayer is that academic English is not a prerequisite for reading difficult materials. It is, instead, an outcome—a result—of reading them.

● ● ● ● ●

Lily Wong Fillmore, professor emerita, University of California at Berkeley, is a linguist (Ph.D. in Linguistics from Stanford University) and an educator (volunteer teacher in farm labor camps, 1954–1964; member of Berkeley's Graduate School of Education faculty, 1974–2004). Much of her research, teaching, and writing have focused on issues related to the education of language-minority students. She has conducted studies of second language learners in school settings on Latino, Asian, American Indian, and Alaskan Native children. Since her retirement from the Berkeley faculty in 2004, she has worked with educators in urban school districts to improve academic language and literacy instruction for English learners and other language-minority students.

Marilyn Jager Adams

Dreams

My father said he would not send a girl to college. It would be a foolish waste of money. But I was determined to go anyway. I knew exactly what I wanted to do. I wanted to teach math in urban schools: good for the heart, and good for the mind.

Between programming computers and decent typing skills, I earned my way through undergraduate school. (Back then, state universities were sufficiently affordable that a kid could really do that—a tragically lost opportunity in today's world.) I programmed management rosters and statistics for the psychology department, I wrote systems programs as a GE intern, and I worked as a Kelly Girl whenever I had a few days here or there.

Since money was so hard to come by, I was determined spend it well. Planning to major in math and minor in education, I enrolled in the Arts & Sciences honors program and signed up for the best courses I could find. As a math major, I was required to take physics, and the university I attended offered many options—physics for dummies, physics for regular people, physics for medical students, physics for engineers, and physics for physics majors. I chose to enroll in honors physics for physics majors. Alas, within the first few weeks, my honors physics teacher pulled me aside. He told me that he had never had a young lady in one of his classrooms and he didn't intend to start with me. Why was I there? He suggested that I major in education and minor in math. He felt that would be more suitable.

I did earnestly try to want to major in education, but there were issues. The biggest one was that the major carried an extremely heavy credit requirement. By now, I was a sophomore. If I shifted to education, I would never be able to finish my degree on time, and I would never be able to take another non-education course of my choice.

I ended up majoring in psychology and minoring in mathematics. Working with preschoolers, I did my honors thesis on the relationship between syntactic development and logical competence. My plan was that, when I finished, I would apply for the Teacher Corps. But, my mentors in the psychology department strongly encouraged me to go to graduate school in psychology. Well. This seemed a totally radical proposition. So I gave it a shot. I decided to apply only to schools that I knew I couldn't get into without help from providence. If my fairy godmother wanted me to go to graduate school, I would. I ended up getting into all of the schools and headed for Providence.

At Brown, my advisor's specialty was attention (a topic that should be required of all curriculum and software developers). Meanwhile, his best buddy's specialty was speech perception, forcing me to become thoroughly versed in the science of phonemes. Then, as fate would have it, a fancy new tachistoscope appeared, so I did my thesis on visual word recognition.

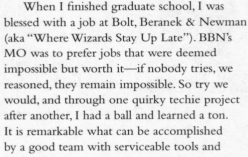

Reading enriches our dreams even as it offers means for realizing them.

When I finished graduate school, I was blessed with a job at Bolt, Beranek & Newman (aka "Where Wizards Stay Up Late"). BBN's MO was to prefer jobs that were deemed impossible but worth it—if nobody tries, we reasoned, they remain impossible. So try we would, and through one quirky techie project after another, I had a ball and learned a ton. It is remarkable what can be accomplished by a good team with serviceable tools and dedication to a mission. Yet, all along, my fairy godmother kept pinging me, kept reminding me of why she'd sent me to school. Among projects she dropped on me were a computer program using animated graphics to provide phonological feedback for deaf children, a diagnostic test of decoding abilities, a "thinking skills" curriculum for barrio students in Venezuela, and, of course, the Center for the Study of Reading.

I had not been at BBN long when the U.S. Department of Education released an RFP for a multidisciplinary Center for the Study of Reading. We teamed with colleagues at the University of Illinois and won the contract. It was through the Center for the Study of Reading that I was appointed to write *Beginning to Read*. At that point, I had been working with the Reading Center for 10 years. Though I already knew a lot about a reading, what I knew turned out to be neatly filed away in separate little mental buckets. Forcing everything to fit in the same big bucket made all the difference, causing the intersections between pieces —their mutual dependencies and synergies—to become visible. What I was beginning to understand was not just the requirements of learning to read but, more importantly, how reading helps us to develop, organize, distinguish, and refine our knowledge and thought.

What I've learned since then is that teaching reading to a classroom full of kids is an incredibly difficult challenge—so difficult that, as evidence attests, our schools may fail except with those kids who get extra help at home. The problem is that, given its scope and intricacies and its dependence on what the child brings to the table, learning to read requires far more individual time and attention than one teacher can offer to every student.

In other words, good classroom reading instruction is not an impossible challenge. We are rich enough and we are smart enough—we can solve this problem. And it's worth it. Our children's lives depend on it. Through reading, we can see through each others' eyes, feel through their hearts, think through their minds, and learn through their lessons. Reading enriches our dreams even as it offers means for realizing them.

● ● ● ● ●

Marilyn Jager Adams is a visiting scholar in the Cognitive, Linguistic, and Psychological Sciences Department at Brown University. She is the author of several books including the landmark *Beginning to Read: Thinking and Learning about Print*. She has also been active in the policy arena serving, for example, on NAEP's Planning, Steering, or Standing Committee for Reading since 1992 and on the Development Team for the *Common Core Standards in English Language Arts*. She is currently a principal scientist for Scholastic's new technology-enhanced programs, *System 44* and *iRead*. Asked how she did with her own life aspirations, Adams responds, "To contribute to education? The opportunities have been beyond my wildest dreams. Whatever I've accomplished, I owe most of all to public education and to libraries. And to my fairy godmother."

Timothy Rasinski

Fluent Reading: The Power of Rhythm and Music

We all have our own unique literacy journeys in life. Mine was upbeat. I was an early reader—I started school already knowing how to read. But I still recall reading with amazement Dolores Durkin's seminal study of children who started school knowing how to read. These children were  not exceptionally intelligent. What they had going for them were parents who read to them every day. As I considered this important finding, I could not recall either of my parents reading aloud to me in the traditional manner.

After reading Durkin's work, I called my mother and asked her why she never read to me (or my brother or sister who were also early readers). She gave me an earful and reminded me that when I started school as a first grader, I was sent to the second-grade classroom for reading instruction because I could already read. She pointed to a couple of significant events in my early years.

My father was a musician who played on weekends in local clubs in Akron and Cleveland. He would rehearse several days a week after coming home from work in the factory. After taking a quick shower, he'd come downstairs, get out his sax or clarinet, and would ask me and my brother and sister to join him. My mother would pass out the lyrics, and as my father played, we all sang along.

Back to my phone conversation, my mother asked: "Were you reading or not?" I had never considered this reading, but as I reflect on it as an adult, I now see that I *was* reading—for a purpose! And since my dad often rehearsed the same songs week after week, we were repeatedly singing the same texts. Looking back, I see that this was an early example of fluent, repeated reading.

My mother loved short rhythmical texts and quite often, after I had said my prayers each evening, she would recite a poem, nursery rhyme, or song for me, drawing from her songbook or anthology of poems. Early in the week, she would read her poem and we would discuss it a bit. Then, as the week wore on, she would ask me to recite the poem with her. By the end of the week I would often read the poem to her on my own. Moreover, since

Open a World of Possible: Real Stories About the Joy and Power of Reading © 2014 Scholastic

she had the actual text with her as we read, I was able to match the words I was reciting with the words on the page. I was reading! We did this little routine quite often and I am convinced that this, along with my father's song rehearsals, was how I learned to read.

It's interesting to note that many of the instructional methods that I advocate for young readers today are based on my own experiences at home as an early reader.

In *To Kill a Mockingbird*, Scout delivers one of my favorite quotes: "Until I feared I would lose it, I never loved to read. One does not love breathing." When I contemplate all the ways in which reading has made my life so meaningful, joyful, and enlightened, I am stunned and awed by its influence. I can't imagine a life without the ability to read and my heart breaks when I think of all the children (and adults) for whom reading is such a painful struggle. Those who work to help children become fluent and joyful readers are, in my opinion, doing the same essential work as medical doctors who help their patients breathe.

> Those who work to help children become fluent and joyful readers are, in my opinion, doing the same essential work as medical doctors who help their patients breathe.

• • • • •

Timothy Rasinski is a professor of literacy education at Kent State University and director of its award-winning reading clinic. He has written over 200 articles and has authored, co-authored, or edited over 50 books or curriculum programs on reading education. He is the author of the bestselling books on reading fluency, *The Fluent Reader*, now in its second edition, and *The Fluent Reader in Action*. His scholarly interests include reading fluency and word study, reading in the elementary and middle grades, and readers who struggle. His research on reading has been cited by the National Reading Panel and has been published in journals such as *Reading Research Quarterly, The Reading Teacher, Reading Psychology,* and the *Journal of Educational Research*. Rasinski is the first author of the fluency chapter for Volume IV of the *Handbook of Reading Research*. He served a three-year term on the board of directors of the International Reading Association. He has also served as co-editor of *The Reading Teacher*, the world's most widely read journal of literacy education, and was co-editor of the *Journal of Literacy Research*. Rasinski is past-president of the College Reading Association and he has won the A. B. Herr and Laureate Awards from the College Reading Association for his scholarly contributions to literacy education. In 2010, Rasinski was elected to the International Reading Hall of Fame. Prior to coming to Kent State, he taught literacy education at the University of Georgia. He taught for several years as an elementary and middle school teacher in Nebraska.

Meenoo Rami

Finding My Home in a New Language

*D*o not bend. Handle with care.

Those are the first words that I began to decipher and understand in the English language. As a 12-year-old Gujarati kid who was moving from India to America, I had to adjust to many things at once. The most important: finding my home in a new language. I come from a literary home. As a young child, I grew up reading at my father's feet. He had a home library filled with thousands of books and I would sneak in there and read for hours. I don't remember the particular books and I can no longer read in Gujarati, but I know that I loved reading and that I learned early on from my father about the power of words to transport and transform us.

But what happens when the very things in which you ground yourself and your reality become foreign? What happens when you have to build your language life over again? What happens when you lose your voice overnight? And what happens when you become silenced but you have so much to say and so many questions? Sometimes, the right teacher or guide comes your way and you're never the same again.

You're lucky if you find a teacher like Mrs. Cerwin, who taught generations of kids like me at River Trails Middle School in Mt. Prospect, Illinois. She, like many other amazing ESOL (English for Speakers of Other Languages) teachers, put the right books in my hand at the right time. From her, I discovered my love of the Boxcar Children series, *Hatchet*, and *Bridge to Terabithia*. In her capable hands, I learned to find my way into a new language home and, no matter how chaotic things were in my life, I was able to return to what I always knew: how to find comfort in books, characters, and faraway places. Through these reading experiences, I was able to make a new home in a foreign place. When I connected with the language, it was as if I had truly arrived. The pace of my word acquisition quickened; after all, I had been a lifelong reader, I just needed help with the new English vocabulary. I was already a believer in the power of words and wanted very much to unlock this new language puzzle. Learning and mastering a new language was like finally arriving at my destination and being able to put my bags down, unpack, and settle in.

What does reading make possible?

Voice: Reading gives us a voice when we feel as though we have none. It empowers us, through the courage of others, to find our own voice. When Atticus Finch stands up for Tom Robinson, we learn what it means to have the courage to stand up for unpopular beliefs in our community. Through our reading, we learn to see the ways in which moral conundrums are worked out and we are able to try out our own moral compass on situations based in other worlds, other realities.

Belonging: The right book can be a home for the reader. As C. S. Lewis wrote, "We read to know that we're not alone." Books can show us that our experiences, even our deepest and most personal ones, can connect to others who have walked a similar path. Books can be both windows and mirrors for us; we can discover new ways of seeing the world. For some of us, books aren't just an escape from reality; they allow us to carve a space for ourselves in a reality that can be less than kind at times.

Agency: Readers are also writers, designers, and creators of our own experiences. When we enter other worlds in books, we are inspired to reimagine, recreate, and reframe our realities. Words of others inspire us to write our own. If we can experience the power of stories to transform us, then we can also imagine the power to tell our own stories. More than anything else, reading has the power to remind us of our own power.

> Through these reading experiences, I was able to make a new home in a foreign place.

My journey from an ESOL kid at River Trails Middle School to a teacher of English at the Science Leadership Academy was only possible because a teacher like Mrs. Cerwin helped me find my language home. For that, I will forever be grateful.

• • • • •

Meenoo Rami teaches her students English at the Science Leadership Academy in Philadelphia. She is the author of *Thrive: Five Ways to (Re)Invigorate Your Teaching.* The founder of #engchat, Rami has become a mentor to teachers across the country and a sought-after speaker. You can reach her on Twitter @meenoorami or at meenoorami.org.

Ruth Culham

Cigarettes, Comic Books, and Reading

I learned to read because my parents smoked. True story. When I was little, it was pretty much a nightly routine that we would join my grandparents for dinner and afterwards, the four adults would smoke up a storm and talk for hours. Even then I hated smoking and couldn't wait to

be excused and make my escape. The timing of my exit was critical—at a precise moment between the first and second cigarettes, I would gather my plate and glass, and ask to be excused. If I asked too soon, the answer would be "No." If I waited too long, I'd have to suffer one more round of smoking.

I always retreated to the bathroom. My grandmother hid a stack of comic books for me under the bathroom sink—hidden because she knew my mother wouldn't approve, making them all the more attractive to me. I remember them well: Huey, Dewey, and Louie, Archie and Veronica, and Atomic Mouse. She knew I'd be bored in no time on my own, and since I was the only child in the house and there was no TV, she provided the contraband. I loved my grandmother for lots of reasons, but this one was high on the list.

This happened when I was only three or four, at the most. I couldn't read. All I could do was look at the pictures and try to figure out what was going on. But something magical happened during those long evenings locked away in my grandmother's bathroom . . . the words started to make sense. By the time I reached first grade, I was reading. Maybe not fluently or deeply, but I was reading. And because my teachers didn't know about differentiation, they stuck me in a corner of the classroom with books and left me alone.

> It was just me and comic books, paper, pencils, and crayons—plenty of resources to learn to read and write for a motivated six-year-old.

The gap between my peers and me widened, and by the end of first grade, I could read almost anything. At the same time, I began writing. I learned my letters from what I saw in books. I began with my name and moved on to copy words, all this done quietly, on my own, in what might be the first reading/writing center in the world: my grandparents' bathroom. It was just me and comic books, paper, pencils, and crayons—plenty of resources to learn to read and write for a motivated six-year-old. This may be the only good thing to come from smoking cigarettes—but I do thank my grandmother for starting me on my way to a lifelong love of language by letting me "read" comic books for as long as I wanted.

From the Introduction to Ruth Culham's *The Writing Thief: Using Mentor Texts to Teach the Craft of Writing* (International Reading Association, 2014).

● ● ● ● ●

Ruth Culham is a recognized expert in teaching writing and the author of over 40 bestselling Scholastic and IRA books and resources on the traits of writing and teaching writing using reading as a springboard to success. Her practical yet motivational ideas for teaching writing make her a favorite among teachers. Culham's steadfast belief that every student is a writer is the hallmark of her work. As the author of *Traits Writing: The Complete Writing Program for Grades K–8* (2012), she has launched a writing revolution. *Traits Writing* is the culmination of 40 years of educational experience, research, practice, and passion.

Lester L. Laminack

Finding the Magic of Reading

I was an onlooker, a lusting voyeur.

I sat perched on the wide arm of that oversized chair looking over the shoulder of my brother. He sat next to my mother, open book spread across his lap. He was in first grade, I was going on five, and I was in awe. I watched in amazement as my brother placed his finger under a word and it spilled forth from his mouth, filling the air with sounds.

I listened to the music of that rhythmic language—

I do not like them, Sam-I-am. I do not like green eggs and ham . . . One fish, two fish, red fish, blue fish . . . The sun did not shine. It was too wet to play. So we sat in the house all that cold, wet day.

It was that music that I carried with me around our upstairs apartment. I walked about chanting, "I do not like them here or there. I do not like them anywhere. I do not like green eggs and ham. I do not like them, Sam-I-am."

I was an onlooker, an eavesdropper longing to join the magical club of readers. I wanted to place my finger under a word just so, and have those words spill forth from my mouth. I wanted to sit in the big chair next to my mother with a book spread across my lap. I wanted to make the music that was somehow trapped on the page waiting for the touch of a magic finger. I wanted that finger to be mine.

I listened and watched every evening. I carried the music everywhere, chanting the memorable language that continued to resonate long after.

I did, of course, hold the books and lick the tip of my index finger before carefully turning each page. I did chant the music as I touched the words and I did believe with the faith of childhood that I had found that magic.

Then I went to first grade. I met Dick and Jane. See Dick. See Jane. I met Spot. Run, Spot. I met Sally. Oh, Sally! I met Puff. Get down, Puff. I sat in small circles as we took turns telling everyone to "Look," or "Get down" or "Run, run, run." We took turns saying those words, touching them with our fingers, but the music was gone. There was no memorable language. Nothing would resonate long after.

I did, of course, learn to read. As I recall, that was neither a remarkable event nor a struggle. Just another occurrence in the journey called childhood.

But somehow, the magic and the music had vanished. It wasn't until third grade when I finally heard the music again, it played on the slow-paced, smooth, southern voice of Mrs. Hand, our school librarian.

It started with Uncle Remus tales and moved to weekly adventures with Henry and Violet and Jesse and Benny as they struggled to survive in that old boxcar with their adopted dog, Watch. I longed to be Henry, the brave leader. I longed to dam up the stream and make a pool that doubled as the refrigerator. I could taste the cold milk and feel the crack in Benny's cherished pink cup as I drank with him.

It was Mrs. Hand who revived the music I longed to hear. And I continued to cherish the sound of it. Although I had the power to take hold of that sound with my ear, I still could not echo it with my voice. That would take a few more years.

In the fifth grade, my family moved to Key West. It was supposed to be a short stay so we rented a furnished place. It had no TV. The weather was warm and pleasant even in the fall evenings and filling the time outdoors with my brother and friends was no challenge. But the night, the dark and quiet night, was another thing altogether. We played cards and board games, but that grew old quickly. At my mother's suggestion, I resorted to reading a book. We bought a copy of *The Wonderful Wizard of Oz*. It took only a few pages before I was hearing the music, the rhythm of the story, the voices of the characters, and finding myself living among Dorothy, the Tin Man, the Cowardly Lion, and the Scarecrow.

> I wanted to make the music that was somehow trapped on the page waiting for the touch of a magic finger.

I had found it. And once you do, it is yours forever.

● ● ● ● ●

Lester L. Laminack, Ph.D., is professor emeritus of Western Carolina University in Cullowhee, North Carolina, where he received two awards for excellence in teaching. Laminack is now a full-time writer and consultant working with schools throughout the United States. His academic publications include *Learning Under the Influence of Language and Literature, Reading Aloud Across the Curriculum, Climb Inside a Poem, Cracking Open the Author's Craft, Unwrapping the Read Aloud,* and *Bullying Hurts: Teaching Kindness Through Read Aloud and Guided Conversations.* His newest professional book is *The Writing Teacher's Troubleshooting Guide.* Laminack is also the author of six children's books: *The Sunsets of Miss Olivia Wiggins, Trevor's Wiggly-Wobbly Tooth, Saturdays and Tea Cakes, Jake's 100th Day of School, Snow Day!,* and *Three Hens and a Peacock* (2012 Children's Choice K–2 Book of the Year Award).

Maxie Moua

Navigating Through Literacy

*I*n eighth grade, I was told that I was in a "guinea pig" class. Mrs. Clark, a hardcore English teacher and grandma who often told us about her motorcycle trips, was given a group of students on which to test her new approach to Advanced Placement (AP) English. It was in Mrs. Clark's class that I became more serious about challenging myself. In high school, I took all the honors and AP English classes I could. Mrs. Clark became a mentor to me, as did Ms. Norton, my eleventh- and twelfth-grade English teacher, who encouraged me to join the Writing Club. In 2012, I was the first Hmong-American female student to enter the *California Writes!* contest and my poetry submissions won the Silver Key Award—which led to other writing. I drew a lot of inspiration from my Hmong background.

My parents and two older sisters fled Lao Communists by crossing the guarded Mekong River to Thailand and moved from refugee camp to refugee camp. In 1985, with sponsorship from an American family in Minnesota, my family was able to leave the Thai camps at last and come to America, eventually settling in Fresno, California.

Although five of my siblings and I were born here, I was immersed in both Hmong and English and learned English as a second language. Watching children's TV shows like *Teletubbies* or *Power Rangers* helped my English, while getting chased by my siblings or scolded by my parents influenced my understanding of the Hmong language. By the end of Kindergarten, I was at a second-grade reading level so I was moved up, but I soon discovered that I wasn't prepared for a lot of the second-grade coursework. However, I excelled in reading. I remember having so many shiny stars under my name for reading that at the end of the school year, I got to attend a carnival my elementary school held to reward the students who read the most books.

I used to translate for my parents when they came to Open House or school meetings. I was happy that I could help my parents—it made me feel smart and responsible, but it was also challenging. Sometimes I would see my dad hold a magnifying glass up to a piece of mail, trying to sound out a word.

He would ask me what it meant, and I would try to break it down in Hmong as best as I could, but he still looked confused. Or my mom would come into my room and ask me to read a letter she had received, and I would respond in broken Hmong.

It's a common problem that the younger Hmong generations face in America. My siblings and I struggle to transition from English to Hmong because many English words are not easy to translate. Reading and speaking English year after year has definitely built up my English literacy skills, but how can I balance my Hmong literacy as well? One summer in high school, I took a Hmong native speaking class taught by Mr. Yang. Given my trials communicating in Hmong to my parents, I enjoyed learning how to read and write Hmong and committed to Hmong literacy just as I have with English literacy.

> My parents made me stay in school where I met teachers who have impacted both my English and Hmong literacy journeys.

I once wished that my parents could read to me and tuck me into bed at night. I once wished they could understand the poetry that I've written about our culture and our family. But it wasn't my parents' fault that they were refugees, and it wasn't their fault that their homelands suffered through war. My mother and father pushed me in school and gave me the chance to learn how to communicate in English instead of marrying me off at a young age as is the tradition. My parents made me stay in school where I met teachers who have impacted both my English and Hmong literacy journeys.

I am Hmong-American, and literacy is my privilege.

• • • • •

Maxie Moua was born and raised in Fresno, California. She is a Horatio Alger California Scholar and now attends the University of California, Berkeley. Moua finds happiness when she doodles and creates handicrafts; she lives to learn. She aspires to learn more about the Hmong language and to teach it. Moua loves her mom, dad, two sisters, and five brothers very much and wants to thank them for their unconditional love.

J. Richard Gentry

A Dyslexic Lover of Books Learns to Read

*T*he first word I learned to read in school was "Dick," a version of my own name. That single word in large black type on the first page of my first book appeared with Dick's picture. He looked just like me: about my size with sandy hair and blue eyes. Dick was decked out in a red sweater and

khaki shorts just like I loved to wear. On the next two pages, I mastered, "Look, look," followed by "Oh, oh, oh," and I really felt proud. A lot of people have chided my first book but I cherished it. After all, it was my first! I read about Dick and Jane, Baby, Spot, and Puff, and I loved the characters—especially Puff. To this day, an orange cat is my favorite pet.

How ironic that my mother, who taught me to read in first grade, was also my first-grade teacher. Ironic because more than 50 years later, I would be writing books for parents of babies and toddlers and working to produce educational apps showing parents how to be *their* child's first reading teacher; and ironic because I caution them not to wait until first grade. Natural reading begins in preschool. First grade is much too late to learn to read in English if you are dyslexic like me.

The first signal that dyslexia would both sidetrack and enhance my life with books occurred the same year I read Dick and Jane. A dyslexia warning sign surfaced during my first-grade mid-year reading test. Already conscious of my slow reading rate, I sped ahead, marking many sections of the test before I was supposed to be doing them. I raced to get ahead so that I would have more time for the longer reading sections that slowed me down. I remember finishing the matching sections—sounds with words and words with pictures—I aced them all even without hearing the instructions. I matched pictures of three-car segments of trains—variations of a flat car, a box car, and a caboose—that were somehow supposed to be analogous to matching letter sequences in three-letter words. Train-car matching was a riveting "reading" skill! The county elementary school supervisor administering the high-stakes test scolded me for moving ahead through the test booklet.

On that test day in first grade, the county supervisor hinted at the unnamed dyslexia nemesis that would follow me for the rest of my life:

Open a World of Possible: Real Stories About the Joy and Power of Reading © 2014 Scholastic

"He will always be a good student," she told my mom, "but he'll have to work hard at it." Her prophesy would perfectly describe my life with books.

A dyslexic's reading history can be as quirky as the required reorganization of circuitry in the dyslexic reader's brain. Here are some snippets of what books mean to me:

- In first grade, the refrain "I think I can, I think I can" from *The Little Engine that Could* coached me in optimism and hard work.

- In the middle grades, my independent reading ranged from Bible stories to the Boy Scout manual. By eighth grade, I was one of the youngest Eagle Scouts in America. Even though I later abandoned my quest to become a preacher, I kept many of those values. These days some have accused me of being a preacher of literacy.

- I own a collection of antique spelling books including an 1829 edition of Noah Webster's blue back speller, my great grandfather's speller from his one-room schoolhouse (the same one my grandmother used), the full set of the horrible spellers I had in elementary school that didn't help me learn to spell at all, and the spelling books I authored for America's schoolchildren up to the present day.

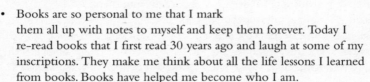

Books are so personal to me that I mark them all up with notes to myself and keep them forever.

- Books are so personal to me that I mark them all up with notes to myself and keep them forever. Today I re-read books that I first read 30 years ago and laugh at some of my inscriptions. They make me think about all the life lessons I learned from books. Books have helped me become who I am.

Dyslexia be gone. I can't imagine life without books.

●　●　●　●　●

J. Richard Gentry, Ph.D., is a teacher, researcher, and author of influential journal articles, books, and policy papers on reading, spelling, writing, dyslexia, and best practices in literacy education. He is breaking new ground in baby/toddler reading. His recent books include *Raising Confident Readers: How to Teach Your Child to Read and Write—From Baby to Age 7* and *Fostering Writing in Today's Classroom,* coauthored with educators Jan McNeel and Vickie Wallace-Nesler. Dr. Gentry is the author of *Spelling Connections,* a spelling series for Grades K–8 from Zane-Bloser. He blogs for *Psychology Today.*

Adria F. Klein

On the Road: Talking My Way into Reading

I remember reading inside my head at a very early age, but the words would not come out of my mouth—at least not in a way I was willing to share. I had difficulty pronouncing words so that others could understand me. My first-grade teacher usually "forgot" to call on me. Even when the familiar text simply said,

"Look. Look, look. Look, look, look," I faltered. The words came slowly from my mouth and were painful to my ears. My very crooked teeth made it tough for my tongue to move to make the sounds that were so fluent inside my head. I covered my mouth with my hand whenever I talked so people wouldn't see as the words came out.

I had plenty to say, I just never said it. When I was small and my dad was still alive, we would go on Sunday drives from St. Louis to nearby places in Illinois. I remember how he tried to get me to talk, but my sister filled in for me and I was happy to have her do so. He came up with a plan—in truth, a bribe. He paid me a quarter to talk on the trip and my sister a quarter to be quiet or, at least, to give me a chance to find my voice. We talked about everything we did, everything we heard, and most of all, we shared stories, songs, and poems. My reading helped me to find my voice, to talk, and to share in the back seat of that old Buick as we crisscrossed the Mississippi River on those Sunday afternoons.

Later, as a mother, I did everything I could to get my own children to talk, as oral language is one of the most important roads to reading and writing. When my son was about three, I was teaching in New Mexico, and directing plays after school to earn extra money. We couldn't afford a babysitter, so when his dad had to work late, I took my son with me. One evening, he was running up and down the bleachers in the school auditorium that also served as basketball court, cafeteria, and theater. My son's footsteps echoed on the bleachers and I asked him to come over and talk to me. I said, "David, there are three reasons you need to stop climbing on the bleachers. One, you might fall and hurt yourself. Two, the noise is making it hard for us to hear each other as we work on the play. And, three, I think you would enjoy watching the play." David responded positively to my sharing the reasons why, and sat down to watch the rehearsal.

One of my students said, "Wow!" He told me that he had never heard that many words from his parents at one time. He explained that he mostly got told what to do: "Do your homework. Eat your dinner. Brush your teeth." He didn't hear the reasons, didn't know the whys, and the talk was at the command level, mostly one-way communication. He didn't have the language modeling in early conversations with others that builds a path to literacy. Parents and teachers need to model language through stories, songs, and poems, and share their thinking through conversation.

I recalled my own reluctance to talk. The Sunday rides in the Buick: the talk, songs, and poems filling our car with language—and, yes, the feeling of a quarter growing warm in my little hands.

Talk builds interest in the world. It motivates children to find their voice. Oral language development and thinking about the whys of the world led to the reading and writing that changed my life.

As an educator, I have focused on studying the ways in which children think and learn and develop language. My research focuses on this intersection, what I define as Integrative Language Processing. I believe that a love of reading comes from an enthusiasm for learning, a true curiosity about people and the world. And this learning starts with the joy of talking to, with, and by children.

> Hug your children by surrounding them with love and language. Talk is the road that leads to reading and changes lives.

My newest grandchild, my daughter's wonderful little girl, Wren, is just over a year old. Our talk is enhanced by video chats as often as possible. She doesn't live nearby, there aren't many car rides yet, but there is the joy of seeing her face, of knowing that she understands that Grandma is on the phone. Wren can already wave and say "hi" and "bye." Just this week, she hugged the phone to send love to Grandma. Hug your children by surrounding them with love and language. Talk is the road that leads to reading and changes lives.

• • • • •

Adria F. Klein, Ph.D., is a professor emerita of reading education at CSU San Bernardino where she was the chair of the Department of Elementary and Bilingual Education. Currently, she is a visiting professor and program director for early intervention at Saint Mary's College of California. A former president of the California Reading Association, she also served on the International Reading Association board of directors. Dr. Klein is the co-author of many professional books and articles including *Interactive Writing, Guided Reading,* and *Shared Reading* as well as a number of children's books. As a senior consultant for the nonprofit New Teacher Center, she has been the principal investigator for a Hewlett Foundation funded grant on oral language development for PreK–Grade 3 and contributed to the development of the open source website (oral-language.newteachercenter.org), as well as the oral language assessment application, OLAT. She works with large urban school districts around the United States as well as in a number of countries including Hungary and Australia.

Enrique A. Puig

Transcending Language:
From Hola *to* Les Misérables

I grew up in Miami at a time when a name like *Enrique* was strange and very few people spoke Spanish. Thanks to my parents and grandparents (not to mention my friends in the neighborhood), I grew up fully bilingual in a household that was rich with *Hola* and *Paris Match* magazines in addition to *El Diario de las Americas* newspaper. Every morning, Radio Reloj opened the world to us and increased my vocabulary exponentially.

My paternal grandfather worked for Pan American Airlines in the 1940s and '50s and the toss-away magazines from the planes provided us ample reading material. One person's trash is another person's treasure! Did I read French? No. But with my English and Spanish and the many pictures, I was able to determine roughly what the text said in the glossy *Paris Match* magazines. When I couldn't figure something out, I'd ask; although the adults around me didn't speak French either, they had other sources of information mysteriously at their fingertips to help me "decode" what I was attempting to understand.

Somewhere along the way, I figured out that reading was a tool or a key to learn many other things. Although radio was a major source of new vocabulary, it was the printed words and pictures in those magazines that opened the world of literacy to me. Those stories and pictures were my passport to places I only dreamed of seeing—the Eiffel Tower, St. Peter's Basilica, the Louvre, Gaudi's Basílica i Temple Expiatori de la Sagrada Família, the Danube River—the list goes on. They fed my imagination and prompted me to become more than a little Cuban kid growing up in Miami.

Over time, I realized that language, like all of the arts, was a powerful instrument for transcending. Dick and Jane made me see that

The ability to read is humanity's legacy.

there were similarities and differences among families and gave me options for my future. Archie, Reggie, and Jughead introduced me to the awkwardness and fun of adolescence. In *Cheaper By the Dozen* (the book, not the movie, and my literate turning point) by Frank Bunker Gilbreth, Jr. and Ernestine Gilbreth Carey, I realized that we all have a story to tell. Then Jules Verne, Alexandre Dumas, and Victor Hugo taught me about the human condition. The Gilbreths' story about the antics of the father and siblings made me laugh; while Jean Valjean wrenched my heart to tears over a loaf of bread. Interesting that while I started with *Paris Match,* to date my favorite book is Hugo's *Les Misérables*—and although I'm biliterate, I still don't speak French! Yet Verne, Dumas, and Hugo were instrumental in developing my love affair with reading. The late Marie Clay was right—we do take different paths to common outcomes. Now my goal is to ensure that my granddaughter Alessandra lives in sea of language, print, and stories. The ability to read is humanity's legacy.

● ● ● ● ●

Enrique A. Puig, Ed.D., is the director of the Morgridge International Reading Center at the University of Central Florida and former director of the Florida Literacy and Reading Excellence project; a multi-million dollar grant charged with providing professional learning opportunities in Florida. He currently teaches graduate and undergraduate K–12 content area reading at UCF. Puig taught for 25 years in Orange County Public Schools, Florida, and has worked with numerous school districts from the U.S. Virgin Islands to Washington. He is author of *Guided Reading and Spanish Speaking Students* and co-author of *The Literacy Coach: Guiding in the Right Direction, 2nd Edition,* and *The Literacy Leadership Team: Sustaining and Expanding Success.*

Grace Mah

Worlds Possible Beyond English

Nelson Mandela said, "If you talk to a man in a language he understands, that goes to his head. If you talk to him in his language, that goes to his heart."

My story of reading, writing, and speaking English started in preschool. As a second generation Chinese-American, my first language was Mandarin Chinese. Both of my parents are from China, and it was natural for them to speak Mandarin to me when I was born. When I went to preschool in the 1960s, my teacher was not particularly knowledgeable about ESL (English as a Second Language) students and she told my parents, "Grace may be 'mentally retarded' because she can't communicate." Remember, this was the sixties, and enlightened attitudes about multilingualism and special needs were not part of the times. The teacher's pronouncement so freaked out my parents that they stopped speaking Mandarin to me and my siblings and talked only English to us from then on. So, my Mandarin language skills are on par with the abilities of a four-year-old.

During the time I was in school, I loved reading, writing, and speaking in English. I was able to join the library's summer reading program every year, and take honors and AP English classes in high school.

It wasn't until I had my first son that I developed a passion for bilingualism and biliteracy. When I enrolled him in a Mandarin/English bilingual preschool, I was amazed at how quickly and naturally he learned both languages. The preschool used a 50/50 immersion model where Mandarin and English were used equally to teach the content material. There were no "Mandarin lessons" for vocabulary and grammar. Rather, Mandarin and English were the medium to teach about colors, animals, rocks, and flowers—typical preschool fare.

I was pleasantly surprised to find that after two years in this preschool, my son was able to recognize over 220 Chinese characters and was quite fluent in Mandarin. He had surpassed my own reading vocabulary in that language.

So, when I was investigating Kindergarten for my son, I was quite taken by the Spanish immersion elementary school program that our school district offered. In the classroom, I observed the children learning Spanish, seemingly without effort. All of the Kindergarten standards were being taught in Spanish such as family, home life, and jobs in the community. They were not learning Spanish vocabulary and conjugations, as in an enrichment language class. They were learning standard school content with Spanish as the medium.

It was magical—the dynamics of the teachers interacting with the students and the ease with which the students were reading, writing, and communicating in Spanish. I wondered, "Why can't we do this in Mandarin?" And thus began my long road to initiate and establish a Mandarin immersion elementary school program in my local public school district.

The benefits of bilingualism and biliteracy to children are multifold: increased cognitive brain functions, greater understanding of multiple cultures, and advances in professional opportunities. With the increasingly shrinking global economy, our future American citizens must be able to comfortably maneuver, build rapport, and conduct business with the nations of the world.

As our U.S. Secretary of Education said, "Today, a world-class education means learning to speak, read, and write languages in addition to English . . . This isn't a matter of getting ahead—it's a matter of catching up."

Not only is reading crucial to American education, but the world of possible is even bigger when you learn another language.

> Not only is reading crucial to American education, but the world of possible is even bigger when you learn another language.

• • • • •

Grace Mah is a member of the Santa Clara County Board of Education in California. She initiated a Mandarin Immersion Program in the Palo Alto Unified School District in 1998. A recovering engineer, Mah spent 18 years in the high-tech industry before having children and finding her passion for education and bilingualism.

Jane Hansen

Reading Opens Up a World of Writing

*T*he *Bean Trees* by Barbara Kingsolver led me to my own writing. Kingsolver wrote about armhole aprons hanging on hooks on the porch. Armhole aprons! That's what my grandma wore! I'm writing a poem about her—I *need* that line! I read differently from then on, and found borrowable ideas of all kinds, from punctuation to format to genre. As a researcher, I always encourage people to read as writers.

Sometimes the books I read influence me in a less direct way. They strike a chord my writer self loves to hear. I recently read *The Latehomecomer: A Hmong Family Memoir* by Kao Kalia Yang and noted these special words on page 200:

> *I stayed up all night typing the essay on our gray typewriter at the dining table, slowly . . . The sound of slow keys being clicked . . . Flexing careful fingers every few minutes. Trying to find a rhythm and a beat in the clicking of the keys, the mechanical whirl at the end of each line . . . It took me a long time to think it through . . . but the writing calmed something inside of me.*

Sometimes my calm, as with Kao Kalia Yang, starts with a bit of tension. When I heard poet Seamus Heaney read many years ago, he said, "Your geography is more important than your history." In my notebook, I wrote about the openness of the Minnesota land around my family farm, part of which became:

> *In Southern Minnesota/children race, arms o u t s t r e t c h e d through fields of summer, waves/of blue and green that never stop until forever . . .*

With thanks to Patricia MacLachlan, the author of *Sarah Plain and Tall*, for the idea of the waves of blue and green. I think of the authors who give me ideas for writing—and for the craving to write that reading brings.

● ● ● ● ●

Jane Hansen started her teaching career in Liberia, as a Peace Corps volunteer, and then taught in New Jersey, Minneapolis, Hawaii, and Iowa. After earning her doctorate at the University of Minnesota and a professorship at the University of New Hampshire, she moved to the University of Virginia for her second professorship. Throughout her decades as a professor, she served as a researcher who visited classrooms twice a week to study children as writers, and wrote about them *When Writers Read* and *The PreK-2 Writing Classroom: Growing Confident Writers.* She has been active in NCTE, IRA, served as president of LRA, and is currently president of the Reading Hall of Fame. Upon retirement as professor emerita, she continues as co-director of the Central Virginia Writing Project.

Imagination

I was creating my own excitement, exploring yet another universe with my new literary friends that I met in the pages of a book.

~José M. Cruz

Walter Dean Myers

I Am What I Read

I could have been an alien, dropped from some strange planet into the Harlem of the 1940s. I didn't know who my real parents were, or why I wasn't with them. My name, I was told, was Walter Myers and the name of the people I was living with was Dean. There were

odd things I couldn't do—like sing a song on key when I started Sunday school. I remember Mrs. Bellinger, a large busty woman asking me if I could hear the songs she was trying to teach us. It really didn't bother me that much because I liked the songs and holding hands with other kids as we gathered on Sunday mornings to go to Abyssinian Baptist Church.

Later, when I started public school, I discovered that the other children and my teachers couldn't understand my speech. I began my nearly eight years of speech therapy to try to clear up my enunciation. It didn't work very well and I found myself somewhat isolated socially. Alone with my books. I liked basketball and the fact that I was always big for my age. I wasn't the kid that bullies confronted. Still, I sensed a difference between myself and other kids my age.

My stepmom had read to me from the time I arrived in New York. She often worked cleaning apartments or, if she were lucky, in some factory setting. When she wasn't working, she would do the chores around the house and then would read from the magazines she enjoyed. Most of the magazines were love stories and I would sit on her lap and watch her finger move across the page, word by word, as she read aloud. I didn't understand much about the stories, I just enjoyed sitting on her lap, but soon I discovered the connection between the words she was pointing to and what she was saying. She was reading. It didn't take me long to figure out the more familiar words and then the patterns. By the time I was four or five, I could sit in my favorite chair, a sturdy wooden chair with a cushioned seat and back, and read to Mama.

It was no big deal. Magazines had words in them and I had learned to read those words. As Mama had, as I thought that everybody had.

I don't know where the books came from that I discovered. *The Little*

Engine that Could comes to mind as an early book. I liked *The Three Little Bears* and *Little Red Riding Hood*, too. By eight, I was leading a dual life. I played in the streets all day, and at night I would come home and spend a lot of time with stories. It was my very special world. As time went on, the stories stayed in my mind. They were with me like secret friends and would pop up in the oddest places. In the middle of a stickball game, for example, or on a tree-climbing expedition.

As I grew older, I was surprised to find that the things I couldn't do were somewhat odd to other people. I was tone deaf, had almost no ability to distinguish colors, and still couldn't speak well. What I could do, and what was slowly taking over my life, was appreciating and dealing with words and language.

As time went on, the stories stayed in my mind. They were with me like secret friends.

Once I began to read, I began to exist. I am what I read—all the books, all the papers, all the stories. I think that's what I've always been. Writing is just an extension of my reading life.

And I love it!

• • • • •

Walter Dean Myers won the Council on Interracial Books for Children Contest in 1969, which resulted in the publication of his first book, *Where Does the Day Go?* Since then, he has won more awards than any author for young adults, and is one of the most prolific writers, with more than 110 books to his credit. He is the recipient of the Margaret A. Edwards Award for lifetime achievement in writing for young adults. He has won the Coretta Scott King Award five times and received two Newbery Honors. His book, *Monster*, was the first winner of the Michael L. Printz Award, a National Book Award Finalist, and a *New York Times* bestseller. He delivered the 2009 May Hill Arbuthnot Honor Lecture, a distinction reserved for an individual who has made significant contributions to the field of children's literature. Most recently, he served as the National Ambassador for Young People's Literature, a post appointed by the Library of Congress.

Walter Dean Myers (1937–2014) changed the face of children's literature by representing the diversity of the children of our nation in his award-winning books. He was a deeply authentic writer who urged other authors, editors, and publishers not only to make sure every child could find him- or herself in a book, but also to tell compelling and challenging stories that would inspire children to reach their full potential. My favorite quote from Walter is a clarion call to embrace the power of books to inform and transform our lives: He said, "Once I began to read, I began to exist." He will be missed by all. —*Richard Robinson*

Jon Scieszka

The Seed

*H*ere's the story that made everything possible for me.

A kid plants a carrot seed.

His mom tells him she's afraid it won't come up.

His dad tells him he's afraid it won't come up.

His older brother just flat out tells him it won't come up.

But every day, the kid weeds and waters his one-seed carrot patch.

Nothing comes up. And nothing comes up.

Everyone keeps telling the kid it won't come up.

But the kid keeps weeding and watering.

"And then, one day, a carrot came up . . .

. . . just as the little boy had known it would."

And the last page, the last image, is the kid wheeling away a single carrot so huge that it completely fills his wheelbarrow.

This story, *The Carrot Seed*, written by Ruth Krauss and illustrated by Crockett Johnson, exploded my three-year-old mind and reshaped it in the most perfect Zen way . . . that needs not a bit more explanation.

● ● ● ● ●

Jon Scieszka was appointed the first National Ambassador for Young People's Literature in January 2008. Born in Flint, Michigan, Scieszka earned a bachelor's degree in writing from Albion College and a master of fine arts degree from Columbia University. He held a number of teaching positions in the first through eighth grades before taking a year off to develop ideas for children's books. He is the author of many bestselling children's titles, including *The Stinky Cheese Man*, which won a Caldecott Honor medal, *The True Story of the Three Little Pigs*, and the Time Warp Trio series. Scieszka is the founder of Guys Read, a nonprofit literacy organization. For more about Jon Scieszka's work, see www.jsworldwide.com/proclamation.html.

Ralph Fletcher

A Chance to Live Many Parallel Lives

*R*ecently, during an author visit to a school, a fifth-grade boy asked me: "When you were a kid, what did you want to be when you grew up?"

"I wanted to play centerfield for the Boston Red Sox," I replied without a moment's hesitation.

"Well, you could still do it!" he told me.

I smiled. "I don't think so. I'm too old now. Plus, I was always a very average athlete. I wasn't good enough."

"But you could write a book where the main character plays centerfield for the Red Sox," he persisted.

True! Being a writer means being able to create an existence you couldn't live in your real life. The same thing is true for reading. When I'm reading, I can be a teenaged kid with cancer or an inmate in a mental ward. I can live on a remote lighthouse off the coast of Australia in 1920. One day, a boat washes ashore with a baby on board—alive!

Humans are fiercely curious. One life simply isn't enough to live. Reading books has allowed me to explore a myriad of other existences.

John Updike once said: "We contain chords someone else must strike." I think that Updike was talking about love, but his comment resonates with books and reading. The books I've read have struck chords within my soul, chords I never knew I had.

> The books I've read have struck chords within my soul, chords I never knew I had.

• • • • •

Ralph Fletcher travels around the U.S. and abroad, helping teachers find wiser ways of teaching writing. He is the author of many books for young readers including *Fig Pudding, Flying Solo, Twilight Comes Twice, Also Known as Rowan Pohi,* and *Marshfield Dreams: When I Was a Kid.* His professional books for teachers include *Boy Writers: Reclaiming Their Voices, Pyrotechnics on the Page,* and *What A Writer Needs, 2nd Edition.*

Margarita Engle

Reading and Writing Across the Hyphen

*M*y mother is Cuban and my father is American, so I think of myself as Cuban-American, with a hyphen built into my memory. I was born and raised in Los Angeles, but the most thrilling experience of my childhood was spending adventurous summers on the island, where I met my grandmother, great-grandmother, and the entire extended family. I was immersed in the Spanish language and Cuban culture, and I also fell in love with tropical nature, leading me to become a scientist as well as a poet.

The 1962 Missile Crisis transformed my childhood into a devastating "before" and "after." Travel to Cuba became impossible. My life was sliced in half.

During the early, pre-Crisis years, I loved poetry, and I read every poetry book I could find. Emily Dickinson and Robert Frost were available in the library. José Martí and Federico García Lorca were on my mother's bookshelves. When it came to prose, stories about horses were my favorites. I was a city girl who treasured rural summers in my mother's hometown of Trinidad, on the south-central coast of Cuba, and on a nearby family farm at the foot of wild green mountains. Over there, my cousins galloped fearlessly. They were expert *guajiros*—farmers, and *vaqueros*—cowboys. Their days were spent rounding up free-roaming cattle and performing rope tricks. At home in Los Angeles, my days were spent reading *The Black Stallion,* and the legend of Pegasus, told and re-told in various mythology books that seemed more real to me than my daily life. Those larger-than-life horses were my escape from smog, noise, traffic, and the impersonal crowds of anonymous city streets.

In my mind, poetry and stories were not separated. Reading and writing were natural outgrowths of each other, like grafted fruit trees or transplanted flowers. I experimented with haiku, ballads, sonnets, fables, and short stories. I longed to understand the wide world that lay beyond U.S. borders, but there were no authentic multicultural children's books. None. Not one. Instinctively, I switched to grownup books, searching for stories that would help me reclaim the experience of belonging to more than one country. The first book I bought with my own money was

Things Fall Apart by Chinua Achebe. I was ten years old.

One year later, when I was in junior high, the Missile Crisis maimed my world. It was not a war. No shots were fired, but for Cuban-Americans, the hyphen was no longer a bridge. It became a chasm, dividing the halves of families as thoroughly as if we were separated by galaxies. During my teen years, it seemed easier for American citizens to walk on the moon than to visit relatives in Cuba. Gradually, I created my own island within my imagination. It is an island that is still with me now, a place where my voice is free to fly back and forth across the boundaries of history. It is a place made of words, in a written world where neighboring countries can learn about each other, with the hope of someday re-establishing diplomatic relations and free travel. In that written world, the hyphen is once again a bridge.

> I created my own island within my imagination. It is an island that is still with me now, a place where my voice is free to fly back and forth across the boundaries of history.

• • • • •

Margarita Engle is the Cuban-American author of *The Surrender Tree*, which received the first Newbery Honor ever awarded to a Latino/a. Her young adult verse novels have also received multiple Pura Belpré Awards and Honors, as well as three Américas Awards, and the Jane Addams Peace Award, among others. Margarita's newest verse novel is *Silver People, Voices From the Panama Canal*. Books for younger children include *Mountain Dog, Summer Birds, When You Wander*, and *Tiny Rabbit's Big Wish*. Margarita lives in central California where she enjoys hiding in the forest to help train her husband's wilderness search and rescue dogs. For more about her work, see www.margaritaengle.com.

Richard L. Allington

Imagining Life in Another Time

*A*s a child I was fascinated by history and historical fiction. I spent hours at my desk in the one-room country school I attended through sixth grade reading books with an historical emphasis. In college, I was an American history major because I thought I was going to become a high school history teacher and football coach. In the end, I became a fourth-grade teacher and then a reading specialist. In both of those roles, and as a father as well, I became a purveyor of historical texts. I read and recommended such texts to my students and my children.

One book, *The Matchlock Gun* by Walter Edmonds, began my journey into historical texts. It was my "home run" book! I think I was in third grade when it first captured my imagination. *The Matchlock Gun* is a heroic story set during the French and Indian War near Albany, New York, where I ultimately worked for much of my professional life.

I have recommended that book to many elementary school students as well as to my own children. When I talk about the book, I try to set the historical stage and ask children to imagine living in the wilderness with not a neighbor in sight. I even point out the Eurocentric perspective the author takes and ask readers to consider how the story might be told differently by a member of the Iroquois nation.

I must also note *Turn Homeward, Hannalee* by Patricia Beatty, another historical text that I found compelling as a child and continue to recommend as an adult. This book is set during the Civil War and features a Southern working class girl as the heroine. As is the case with *The Matchlock Gun*, this book invites readers to

> I love how such books bring history to life and help students consider just how different children's lives were compared to today.

imagine life as a child during an historical era that is very different from today. I love how such books bring history to life and help students consider just how different children's lives were compared to today.

History and historical fiction allow me, as a reader, to imagine life in another time and in different social environments. My love of history informs and enriches my life. I'm addicted!

● ● ● ● ●

Richard L. Allington is a professor of education at the University of Tennessee. He was an elementary school classroom teacher and a Title I director in poor rural schools prior to beginning his career as a teacher educator and instructional researcher. His research interests include reading/learning disabilities and effective instruction, especially in classroom settings. His publications include over 100 articles, chapters, monographs, and books. He served or serves on the editorial advisory boards of *Reading Research Quarterly, Review of Educational Research, Journal of Educational Psychology, Reading Teacher, Elementary School Journal, Journal of Literacy Research,* and *Remedial and Special Education.* Dr. Allington has served as president of the National Reading Conference and the International Reading Association. He received the William S. Gray Citation of Merit from IRA for his contributions to the organization and the profession. He was co-recipient (with Dr. Anne McGill-Franzen) of the Albert J. Harris Award for contributions to improving professional understanding of reading/learning disabilities and was elected to the Reading Hall of Fame. Dr. Allington is author or co-author of several books including *Classrooms That Work: They Can All Read And Write, Schools That Work: All Children Can Read And Write,* and *What Really Matters for Struggling Readers: Designing Research-based Programs.*

Marilyn Burns

Reading Your Way Into Math

I remember my father reading to me after I was tucked in to go to sleep. Grimm's Fairy Tales were a constant favorite and I was enthralled by the stories. I was amazed that those black marks on the pages somehow turned into such engrossing tales. And I was impressed that my father seemed to hear the voices as he read dialogue from villains or princesses or knights. I was hooked by the desire to read, to have access to those stories, and to hear those voices for myself.

By first grade, I was reading stories on my own. But I knew I wasn't really reading yet. I still wasn't hearing the voices that my father did. In retrospect, I was probably reading Dick and Jane and it would have been hard even for my father to give those stories a dramatic reading. But I thought that when you could truly read, you would hear the voices.

It took a while for me give up that misconception and realize that characters' voices, as well as visual images of how they looked, all existed in my mind. I finally realized that I could conjure them up for myself. At last, I was a reader. It was up to me to bring meaning to those black marks, and I could do it. I still marvel today that those black marks are not only capable of creating stories with voices and pictures, but can also give life to powerful emotions. What an achievement of humankind!

With my love of reading, majoring in mathematics seemed an odd choice. It was only after teaching for 10 years or so that I made an important instructional connection between the two. I remember thinking in my early days of teaching that I could help my students become successful because math didn't rely on reading. We didn't read in math class, we did math, and I presented that view to my students.

This was another misconception. And just as I can't remember the moment that I gave up the notion that hearing voices was part of reading, I can't recall exactly when I gave up the notion that reading wasn't part of learning math. Eventually, I embraced the idea that both had the same goal—bringing meaning to black marks on pages. Both reading and doing math involve creating visual images. Both can engender emotions and, yes, even when doing math, I've experienced pleasure, delight, and amusement, along with consternation, confusion, and frustration. The shift I made in my teaching was to help my students experience the full breadth of doing math. And to make that shift, I started including children's literature in my math teaching.

My goal was to find worthy literature that also could be useful for math lessons. *How Big Is a Foot?* by Rolf Myller, first published in 1962, was one of my early finds and is ideal for helping students understand the reason and benefit for standard units of measure. Eric Carle's *Rooster's Off to See the World*, published in 1972, poses a perfect problem for Kindergarten children to figure out how many animals went off to see the world. *17 Kings and 42 Elephants,* written by Margaret Mahy in 1987, is a rollicking poem of a jungle journey. Laura Geringer's *A Three Hat Day* is a sweet love story that introduces even young children to the idea of permutations. And part of Laura Ingalls Wilder's 1932 classic, *Little House in the Big Woods*, is perfect for a fractions lesson when, in Chapter 10, Laura and Mary grapple with figuring out how to share their two cookies so Baby Carrie gets a fair share.

Books are a way to tempt students who are generally reticent about math. They're a way to entice math-oriented students into the wonder of reading. I'm hooked. My collection was initially small, but I now have hundreds of children's books on my shelves, including many recently written books and also nonfiction titles that I regularly use for teaching math.

> Both reading and math have the same goal—bringing meaning to black marks on pages.

• • • • •

Marilyn Burns, the founder of *Math Solutions,* is one of today's most highly respected mathematics educators and authors. Over the course of more than 50 years, Marilyn has taught children, led in-service sessions, presented at conferences, contributed to professional journals, written more than a dozen books for children, and created more than 20 professional development resources for teachers and administrators. In 1996, Marilyn received the Glenn Gilbert National Leadership Award from the National Council of Supervisors of Mathematics for her influence on mathematics education. In 1997, she received the Louise Hay Award for Contributions to Mathematics Education from the Association for Women in Mathematics. In 2010, Marilyn was inducted into the Educational Publishing Hall of Fame by the Association of Educational Publishers. You can find titles and authors of the children's books that Marilyn recommends for teaching math at www.mathsolutions.com/documents/lessons_chart-2.pdf and teacher.scholastic.com/products/math-concepts-skills/math-reads/math-books-topics.htm.

Kwame Alexander

How to Read a Book

First, find a tree—a
Black Tupelo or White Crabapple
will do—and
plant yourself.

(It's okay if you prefer a stoop, like
Langston Hughes)

Once you're comfy,
Peel its gentle skin,
like you would a Clementine
the color of sunrise.
The scent of morning air
and sweet butterfly kisses.

Next, dig your thumb at the bottom of
each juicy section and POP the
words out
piece by piece
  part by part
    page by ruffling page

Then, watch a novel world unfold
down the rabbit hole.

Oh, the places you can go.
A summer balloon ride.
A polar express.

Bring your favorite
purple crayon
and oodles of cotton candy
for all the rainy, snowy days.

Lastly, when the sun is so quiet,
get cozy between the covers and
let your fingers wander (where
  the sidewalk ends, and the wild
  things are)

Squeeze every morsel
of each plump line
until the last drop
of magic

    d
   r
     i
       p
      s

from the giving tree
and bursts of orange
explode
beneath the good night moon.

Don't rush though:

    Your eyes need time to taste.

    Your soul needs time to wonder.

    Now, sleep

    Dream

    Hope

    (you never reach)

    The End.

● ● ● ● ●

Kwame Alexander is a two-time NAACP Image Award Nominee and author of 17 books, including *The Crossover* (a middle-grade novel), *Acoustic Rooster and His Barnyard Band* (a picture book about a rooster that starts a jazz band with Duck Ellington), and the YA novel *He Said/She Said*, a Junior Library Guild Selection. He's also a poet, publisher, literary editor, playwright, producer, speaker, performer, teacher, and book festival founder. He believes that poetry and literature can change the world, and he uses it to inspire and empower young people. Alexander is the Poet Laureate of LitWorld, and, through his Book-in-a-Day literacy program, he has created more than 3,000 student authors of 64 anthologies of poetry and fiction. A frequent speaker and workshop presenter at conferences in the U.S., he also travels the world planting seeds of literary love (Brazil, Italy, France, Turkey, Canada, and Ghana are recent stops). Recently, Alexander led a delegation of 20 writers and activists to Ghana where they delivered books, built a library, and provided literacy professional development to 300 teachers as part of LEAP for Ghana, a literacy program he co-founded. From 2005–2011, Kwame was the founding producer of the Capital BookFest, an annual touring book festival that reached more than 10,000 book-lovers in Charleston, South Carolina, Washington, D.C., and Richmond, Virginia. A version of this poem will be published in 2016 in a children's book entitled *The Book Party*.

Pam Muñoz Ryan

Stories of My Imagination

Before books, there were the stories of my imagination. I didn't come from a print-rich environment, but I came from a story-rich tradition. First, both of my grandmothers were storytellers of sorts—of family incidents, neighborhood shenanigans, and their personal trials and journeys, all recounted over and over again while walking with them around their yards, or next to them on a porch swing after a big dinner.

In addition, I was blessed with an un-choreographed childhood. I was the oldest of the three sisters in my family and the oldest of the 23 cousins on my mother's side. I directed my minions—sisters and cousins—and they often obliged. I was the benevolent queen, the mom in the pretend family, the conductor of the picnic table train, the doctor who saved lives, and the heroine who saved the day. Over time, that power dwindled, only to be rekindled when I became a writer.

My earliest memory of reading from a book was at my Mexican grandmother's house. She lived only a few blocks away from us and I spent much of my afterschool and free time there. In her living room, on the bottom shelf of a bookcase, was an entire set of encyclopedias. I'm not sure how they came to be there. She was a fan of buying things from door-to-door salesmen—an enormous juicer, a vacuum, cleaning supplies, cosmetics—so I suspect someone talked her into a set she could buy over time.

I became intrigued with the encyclopedias because in the middle of each volume was a section printed in color. I studied the illustrated anatomy pages with the plastic overlays, the botanical plates, the illustrated fairy tales, but once I reached the *G* encyclopedia, I never went any further. I had found a section devoted to illustrated Greek myths. Prometheus's liver was eaten by an eagle. Echo was destined never to speak for himself but only to repeat the words of others. Pan became the cause of sudden unexplained anxiety. And glorious Pandora unleashed the world's misery. Horrible. Frightening. How I loved them!

In fifth grade, I discovered the library. We had moved across town and I was new to the neighborhood. It was summertime and I didn't yet know anyone. I started riding my bike to the small branch library nearby, filling my bike basket with books. That memory is so vivid that even today I can relive the exact route I took down the alley, through the Knights of Columbus property, over a bumpy dirt field and into the parking lot of Green Frog Market, to wait for the stop light on the corner, ride down Bernard Street to Baker Street, and park my bike in front of the library.

Like the route to the library that is etched into my memory, so those books of my young adolescence are carved into my soul: *Treasure Island, Swiss Family Robinson, Anne of Green Gables, Little Women,* and the Sue Barton, Nurse series. If I loved a book, I read it many times.

The act of reading and escaping into books allowed me to live many more lives than my real one. Books allowed me to travel beyond Bakersfield, California. They helped put my world in perspective, especially when I did not fit in. I was comforted by the characters' lives, living them vicariously, as I muddled through my own.

Later, all of those dots on the path— hearing family stories, the luxury of dramatic play, reading and loving books—eventually led me to my writing life and the most wonderful gift in return, readers.

I cherish what one of my young readers wrote to me. He said, "I love books because if anything ever happens to me in life, like what's in a story, I can think how to *be.*"

That is the power of reading.

> Hearing family stories, the luxury of dramatic play, reading and loving books—eventually led me to my writing life and the most wonderful gift in return, readers.

• • • • •

Pam Muñoz Ryan has written over 30 books for young people, including the young adult novels *Esperanza Rising, Becoming Naomi León, Riding Freedom, Paint the Wind, The Dreamer,* and the upcoming *Echo.* Among other honors, she is the recipient of the NEA's Civil and Human Rights Award, the Virginia Hamilton Literary Award for Multicultural Literature, and is twice the recipient of the Willa Cather Award, the Pura Belpré Medal, and the PEN USA Award. She was born and raised in Bakersfield, California, holds a bachelor's and master's degree from San Diego State University, and lives near San Diego with her family. For more information, visit www.PamMunozRyan.com.

Sharon M. Draper

My Journey from Reader to Writer

By the time I could walk, my mother had already introduced me to books. She and I would visit our neighborhood library once a week, where the chairs were just the right size and the books were placed low to the floor, just at the right level for little people like me. I reveled in the magnificent array of

reading materials from which I could choose, especially brand new books, still crisp and unsoiled by little hands. The pages, stiff like brand new soldiers, turned slowly, almost squeaking on the binding as they opened to page after page of unimagined pleasures. I loved the crackle of the protective plastic coverings, the smell of the ink on the page, the feel of the thick, golden pages on my fingers, and the magical words that waited for me. I loved Dr. Seuss and how he played with words and characters. Gentle Horton, who heard a Who, and hatched an egg. Bartholomew and his five hundred hats. The magic of McElligot's Pool.

I still love the smell of a library, and whenever I enter one, I breathe deeply of that almost intoxicating library smell. It's sort of like dust and ink and magic all mixed together. The library of my childhood had wooden floors, which gleamed first thing in the morning with fresh wax and creaked when you tiptoed across them to find a book on the shelf. The shelves, also made of wood, held row upon row of possibilities, all brightly jacketed and waiting to be opened and discovered.

I remember the ducks crossing a busy street in *Make Way for Ducklings*. I'd never been to Boston, and for that matter, had never seen a real duck, but that didn't make the story any less compelling. That book led me to Robert McCloskey's *Blueberries for Sal*. I'd certainly never encountered a bear, and I know I'd never picked blueberries, but the books became my passageway into a world so much larger and more exciting than the small house in which we lived.

I delighted in the antics of Tigger and Winnie the Pooh, not the animated, television version that children now associate with those characters, but the words and pictures which came alive as I read A.A. Milne's wonderful stories. I knew I'd recognize the Hundred Acre Woods should I ever pass by, and Christopher Robin would be a delightful playmate, I was sure, even if he did wear those short pants all the time. (I remember thinking that Christopher Robin's mother had very little fashion sense!)

I marched in a line with Madeline, enjoyed the adventures of Curious George, and was lulled to sleep by the soothing words of *Goodnight Moon*.

By the time I started school, I was a fluent reader. I don't remember ever learning to read—it just happened gradually as I progressed from listening to the stories my mother read, to reading them with her, to finally reading them by myself. I breezed through Kindergarten, even though the teacher frowned on children being "too advanced" and knowing "too much" before getting to her classroom. She felt that parents just didn't have the knowledge to teach a child to read, and surely I had learned something incorrectly. But since she had her hands full teaching the rest of the class how to read the "right" way, I had plenty of time to look at books and read on my own.

By first and second grade, we were deeply immersed in the Dick and Jane books. These were the required readers that our school, and most schools in the country, used at this time. The stories surrounded a white, privileged family that consisted of Mom, Dad, Dick, Jane, Baby Sally, and Jip the dog. They lived in a lovely house, drove a nice blue car, and nothing bad ever happened to them. "See Jane run. Run, Jane, run. Jane can hop." These were the kind of sentences found in the early books. It never occurred to me that this family did not represent my own, or those of most of the children in my class. I thrilled in their adventures, and each year, the text would become more difficult, and the adventures of Dick and Jane would get more complicated, but still, nothing worse than a rainstorm ever happened to them. I read the stories at school and at the library, absorbed them, and even identified with the characters and adventures presented to me. But there were no children of color in any of the books.

As I got older and was able to go to the library by myself, I discovered Beverly Cleary. Beezus and Ramona, Henry Huggins, and Ribsy were all characters I could accept, laugh with, and understand. Even though their world was still woefully lacking in cultural diversity, everything wasn't perfect. They didn't have much money, and they had real, albeit humorous difficulties. I'll never forget Henry Huggins trying to get that dog home in a box on the city bus!

I read all of the Little House books by Laura Ingalls Wilder, and then all of the books by Louisa May Alcott. Spiced up with fanciful tales of Danny Dunn and his homework machine, a brilliant invention as far as I was concerned, I proceeded to steal from the rich and feed the poor with Robin Hood, run away from home and get lost with Pinocchio and Tom Sawyer, and long for home with Heidi. I read all of Kipling, all the Baum stories about the Wizard of Oz, and delighted in Peter Pan's Neverland, where children refused to grow up and could fly!

As I look back, I realize that almost none of the books I loved included characters who looked like me. I'm sure that influenced my writing later on.

By the time I got to the sixth grade, I had read most of the books in our small school library and most of those on the children's side of the public library. The librarians knew me by name and often let me take home 10 or 12 books at a time. I read them voraciously and took them back to be exchanged for more. One librarian in particular, Mrs. Pratt, a bespeckled woman of great girth, guided my reading, encouraged me to read wider and deeper, and even offered me new books to take home to review for the rest of the children who visited the library.

I was frustrated, however, because I had nowhere to grow. Back then you had to be 14 to get an adult card and I was only 11 and a half. Mrs. Pratt recognized my dilemma, and one day when I walked in she announced with great anticipation in her voice, "I have a surprise for you!"

"A new book has come in?" I asked.

"Better than that!"

"The sequel to *Caddie Woodlawn*?"

"No." She grinned like a schoolgirl, then handed me a green library card.

Now, library cards for children were yellow. Adult cards were white. I had never seen a green one. I looked at her quizzically. "What's this?" I asked.

"It's a special-permission card," she told me. "With this card, you may check out books from the adult side of the library. The green card means someone will make sure you don't check out books that are too grown-up for you, but as of today, the rest of the library belongs to you!"

I think I saw tears in her eyes. I jumped with excitement, gave her a hug, and ran with joyful anticipation to the great adventure of reading the rest of the books in the library. I am still there.

The books became my passageway into a world so much larger and more exciting than the small house in which we lived.

• • • • •

Sharon M. Draper is a professional educator as well as an accomplished writer, the author of over 30 books. She has been honored as the National Teacher of the Year, is a five-time winner of the CSK Literary Award, and is a *New York Times* bestselling author—her book *Out of My Mind* was on the *New York Times* bestseller list for over a year. She has been honored at the White House six times, and was chosen as one of four authors in the country to speak at the National Book Festival in Washington, D.C. In 2012, she received the Lifetime Achievement Award for contributions to the field of adolescent literature by the Assembly on Literature for Adolescents of the National Council of Teachers of English, as well as the 33rd Annual Jeremiah Luddington Award by the Educational Book and Media Association, also for lifetime achievement. She was selected by the U.S. State Department to be a literary ambassador to the children of Africa and China.

David Lee Finkle

A Reading Tale Told in Comics

I learned to read so I could read the comics pages in the newspaper by myself. I loved reading the funnies so much that by second grade, I wanted to be a cartoonist. I learned to love reading in general so much that by sixth grade, I also wanted to be a writer.

My love of reading and writing led me into teaching, but being a teacher—a middle school teacher—requires me to keep my sense of humor, so I finally became a cartoonist, too.

When I thought of writing about my reading life, it seemed natural to relate that story through comics. So what follows is the story of my reading, told through my alter-ego, Mr. Fitz, who is trying to explain to his student, Spike, how reading changed his life.

David Lee Finkle is a middle school language arts teacher and the creator of the *Daytona Beach News-Journal* comic strip, *Mr. Fitz*. He is the author of *Writing Extraordinary Essays: Every Middle Schooler Can!* and *Teaching Students to Make Writing Visual and Vivid*, as well as the novels *Making My Escape*, and (with his son Christopher) *Portents* and *Portals*. He is probably reading about seven books at once right now.

José M. Cruz

My Mother's Letters, the Sears Catalog, and the Books That Showed Me the Way

I was six years old when my mother left Santo Domingo and the Dominican Republic for New York City. She often wrote long letters describing her life in New York. My Aunt Cecilia read the letters out loud to me, my grandparents, and to my five cousins.

After she read them, I would ask her if I could read each letter myself. The letters were difficult for me to comprehend because I was still learning to read and because I had to decipher my mother's handwriting. I mostly enjoyed reading the postcards she sent of various New York landmarks such as the Empire State Building and Central Park. Sometimes I carried the postcards in my pocket to share with friends or to prove that my mother actually lived in America. After reading and spending hours looking at the postcards, I began to think that one day, I was going to live in the Empire State Building and go swimming in the lakes in Central Park.

In Santo Domingo, we had a neighbor who was a tailor. He kept a couple of old Sears catalogs in his shop. He used to allow the neighborhood kids to sit inside and keep him company while he worked. While there, we liked to play a game called "*Eso es mio,*" meaning, "that's mine." In this game, we turned the pages of the catalog and whoever touched the page first got to claim all of the items on that page. Even though the catalog was in an unfamiliar language, I longed to be able to read English so that I could read the descriptions of the pictured items. I couldn't wait to come to America to buy everything in the Sears catalog.

When I finally did arrive in New York, five years after my mother's departure, I was disappointed that we did not live in the Empire State Building. I also discovered that I could not go swimming in the lakes in Central Park. But, at long last, being reunited with my mother and living together in New York more than compensated for this disappointment.

I arrived in New York in the middle of September. A week after my arrival at P.S. 165 in Manhattan, Ms. Guild, my teacher, gave my class a homework assignment I would never forget. She said, "Your homework today is to become a member of the Public Library. By Monday I expect every one of you to have a library card." She specifically said, "Go to the Bloomingdale Branch located on West 100th Street." We went to the library and took our passports for identification. That day, my mother and I became members of the NYC Public Library and we had our membership cards to prove it. I did not believe it when the librarian told me I could borrow any book I wanted. When I saw all the books, I was beyond excited. It was my first time in a library and my heart was pounding.

Reading was difficult for me because I was still learning English, but my struggles with the language did not deter me from taking out as many books as I could carry. When I read I was transported to another universe. It was as though the author had written me a letter which I did not understand at first, but if I didn't give up and kept at it, eventually I could. What kept me reading was that I felt as though each author were writing to me; it was like reading my mother's letters. Ernest Hemingway, Guy de Maupassant, and John Steinbeck became my good friends. I am grateful to my teachers, Mr. Newman and Mr. Erlich, who introduced me to all these great writers, and I am also grateful to Sister Grace Anne Troisi, a Sister of Charity, and her friend Connie Anestis, who insisted that I read the "great" novels.

> I was creating my own excitement, exploring yet another universe with my new literary friends that I met in the pages of a book.

Reading not only introduced me to a universe I never would have known, it also kept me out of trouble. The inner city was filled with opportunities to go in the wrong direction; there were gangs, drugs, and plenty of other self-destructive distractions. Often, in school, I would hear people say, "Did you hear about this person who was shot, or stabbed, or died of an overdose?" Although I was not an angel, when it came to these common tragedies in the community, I was out of the loop. "Man, José, where have you been? You never know what's happening. You miss all the excitement!" my friends would say.

In fact, I was creating my own excitement, exploring yet another universe with my new literary friends that I met in the pages of a book.

● ● ● ● ●

José M. Cruz was born in the Dominican Republic and arrived in New York at the age of ten. He is a product of the New York City public school system and graduated from Manhattanville College in 1975 with a B.A. in Economics. He has a J.D. from the CUNY Law School and was admitted to the New York State Bar. Cruz also has an M.S. from the Bank Street College of Education. For the past five years, he has been the principal of Mathematics, Science Research & Technology Magnet High School in Queens, New York. Cruz loves his work and he believes that what teachers do in the classroom today determines what our world will look like tomorrow.

Kathy G. Short

Reading to Imagine and Transform

Growing up in Archbold, in a rural northwest corner of Ohio with few neighbors, books opened up new worlds, transporting me beyond the confines of my little community. Taking advantage of any available moment to read, I kept books with me at all times. One day, my second-grade

teacher even caught me sliding a library book out of my desk, sneaking a look between spelling words on the weekly test.

A large stack of books was always beside my bed and I often read late into the night, carefully hiding my flashlight beneath the covers so my parents wouldn't discover that I was still awake. I also regularly snuck through the cornfields behind our house to a tree that became an oasis for me. There I could sit and read for hours without being bothered by my four younger brothers. The books came from our town library because our school was too small to have its own library. Over time, I checked out every book in the library's Childhood Biography series, fascinated by the diverse people in those books—all representing lives of possibility so different from my own.

In many ways, my fascination with books defied deficit conceptions of families like mine. By eighth grade, both of my parents had dropped out of school to work on the family farm and had married quite young. My father sold auto parts and my mother cleaned houses. They did not buy books, read themselves, or read aloud to me. No one in my extended family had ever graduated from college. According to the statistics, I was "at risk." The books in the town library literally transformed my life, transporting me to other places and times to experience the many different ways in which people lived and thought around the world.

My reading focused on the real lives of people, both contemporary and historical. When I was in sixth grade, however, I discovered books of another sort. I was babysitting, bored by TV, and looking for something to read when I came across Hans Christian Andersen's fairy tales. I was swept away into a world of imagination. For the first time, I experienced a world of possibility, a "what if" that was no longer bounded by "what is."

These worlds of possibility became the foundation that later supported my interest in issues of social justice. I was no longer willing to accept the world "as it is"—instead, I was determined to imagine a world that could be better and more just. That ability to imagine an alternative world is essential to being able to take action and to work for change. Imagination had always seemed outside of my reach, an extra "frill" that practical, hardworking people like my family members didn't need. Books allowed me to see that imagination is essential to considering perspectives beyond my own and really listening to others in order to work for transformation and change. Without imagination, we are stuck in the present moment, frozen in time and place. Books extend the present moment, allowing us to reflect on the past and imagine the future.

> Books allowed me to see that imagination is essential to considering perspectives beyond my own and really listening to others in order to work for transformation and change.

• • • • •

Kathy G. Short is a professor in Language, Reading, and Culture at the University of Arizona with a focus on inquiry, dialogue, and global children's literature. She has worked extensively with teachers all over the world to develop inquiry-based curriculum and has authored multiple books and articles, including *Creating Classrooms for Authors and Inquirers, Literature as a Way of Knowing, Talking about Books,* and *Stories Matter: The Complexity of Cultural Authenticity in Children's Literature.* She is director of Worlds of Words (www.wowlit.org), an initiative to build intercultural understanding through global literature and was president of USBBY, the U.S. national section of IBBY, the International Board of Books for Young People. Short was named the 2011 Outstanding Educator of the Language Arts by the National Council of Teachers of English and served on the 2014 Caldecott Medal Award Committee. She is currently president-elect of the National Council of Teachers of English.

Regie Routman

Becoming a Reader

*M*y earliest memory of reading was seeing my mother quietly reading, day after day, in the pale light of late afternoon. I envied her that zone of peacefulness and privacy and knew not to disturb that sacred time. She tried to invite me into that world by insisting I read old-fashioned

classics such as *When Knighthood Was In Flower*, first published in 1898. She handpicked similar masterworks at our local public library, and I rebuked and resisted every one of them. I have no childhood memories of learning to read in school, of being read to at home, or of enjoying reading. Other than romantic comic books, which I savored well into my teens, reading was an unpleasant chore, something that had to be done whether one liked it or not.

I was 15 before I formed my first unforgettable reading memory. It stems from an overnight with my grandmother. She read aloud *Gone With the Wind* by Margaret Mitchell with such emotion that I was spellbound. I finally got it! So this was what reading and hearing great literature could do for the mind and spirit—transport me to another era, enable me to enter the fascinating and complicated lives of different characters, prompt me to rethink my own hopes and desires and become so thoroughly lost in a riveting story that time stopped and nothing else mattered. I was drawn in to savor the sounds and rhythms of well-crafted language—and I was hooked for life.

I became an avid and discriminating reader. Reading became as necessary to me as breathing. Today, I read for many reasons including relaxation, curiosity, and to learn about the world around me—I want to be a knowledgeable citizen. How do I find the books I most enjoy? I rely on the Sunday *New York Times Book Review*, friends' and colleagues' raves, bookstore recommendations, book sale browsing, and books written by authors I love. Of all the possessions in my home, I am most proud of my walls of books, the books I buy because I have to have them—not just to read but to touch, rearrange, revisit, cherish, and lend. Those books define me—fiction, nonfiction, professional books—and say much about who I am, what I value, and what kind of reader I am.

Reading continues to keep me grounded, relaxed, invigorated, and joyful. My mother would be proud. I spend many a late afternoon and evening lost in the pages of a book. I bring my reading interests and passions into the schools where I teach. I always introduce myself to students through great books. I choose the books for students as carefully as I choose for myself and base my choices on their interests and curiosity. "I'm so excited, kids. Have I got a book for you!"

I open the book and begin to read aloud. Soon the room goes silent and I can see that students are engaged. A great book has once again worked its charm and captured listeners' hearts and minds. And afterwards, as always, I hear a chorus, "Will you read it again? Can I read it?" The reading magic has begun, and it is contagious.

> A great book has once again worked its charm and captured listeners' hearts and minds.

• • • • •

Regie Routman is a longtime teacher and author of many books and articles for teachers and leaders. She has been a teacher of all the elementary grades, a Reading Recovery teacher, a reading specialist, a teacher of students with learning disabilities, a mentor teacher, literacy coach, and national leader for improving schoolwide literacy achievement. Currently, she conducts weeklong residencies in diverse schools in the United States and Canada where she does demonstration teaching and coaching in classrooms, most of which have large numbers of English language learners and struggling readers. Her latest book is *Read, Write, Read: Breakthrough Strategies for Schoolwide Literacy Success* from ASCD. See Regie's website (www.regieroutman.org) for her "What I'm Reading" blog, her books and resources, and her professional development offerings including the video- and web-based virtual residency series on reading and writing: *Regie Routman in Residence: Transforming Our Teaching.* Regie lives with her husband Frank in Seattle, close to her son, daughter-in-law, and darling granddaughters.

Teresa Mlawer

My True Sanctuary: A Bookstore With Soul

Growing up in Cuba, I did not have access to many books at home or at school, but there was no lack of stories flowing at home. Both my parents were born storytellers. My mother told my sister and me many stories about Cuba—the struggle for independence from Spain and

her own struggle, after losing both her parents at a young age, to raise her two younger sisters and keep their small family together. She was a woman of strength and courage, and she passed those values on to us.

My father, on the other hand, regaled us with stories about Spain, his native country. When he was only 13 years old, he journeyed by sea to Cuba and, with pluck and courage, survived his younger years there and ultimately succeeded in his new country. From his vivid imagination, he created brave, strong characters—often young girls and women—who triumphed in one adventure after another. I treasured my father's stories the most because they transformed my small world, and invited me to discover different lands, distant places, and invisible friends without having to leave the comfort and safety of my own room.

Sunday mornings were special. Even though we already knew how to read, my father delighted in entertaining my sister and me with the comics section of the Sunday newspaper. He also encouraged us to share our own stories with him and my mother. These sweet memories have remained with me for more than 65 years.

School was also a sanctuary. Even though I did not have access to many books at school, I had wise and dedicated teachers

> My father's stories transformed my small world, and invited me to discover different lands, distant places, and invisible friends without having to leave the comfort and safety of my own room.

who instilled in me a love of learning. I never wanted to miss a day of school, not even when I was sick—so I often pretended that I was not! School was a magical place, second only to my home.

It was not until I was 17, when I arrived in the United States, that I discovered books. Driven by a desire to learn English, I began to devour them. Lucky for me, I landed my first job in publishing more than 50 years ago, and it was love at first sight. I fell in love with the written and spoken word. I became a passionate reader of adult, children's, and young adult literature. I have read thousands of children's and YA books and continue to do so today.

My real transformation came when I joined Lectorum in 1976. It was at this Spanish bookstore, located on 14th Street in Manhattan, that I discovered my true sanctuary: a bookstore with a soul.

The books that rested on old-fashioned wooden shelves represented the dreams and aspirations of so many talented writers. I felt a great sense of responsibility to both the writers and the readers, thinking of myself as the ambassador of these wonderful books. Without a doubt, my years at the Lectorum Bookstore were not only the happiest of my life, but also the ones that made me the person I am today.

● ● ● ● ●

Teresa Mlawer began her career in publishing in 1963. She was at the helm of operations at Lectorum Publications from 1976 until her retirement in 2012. Among her many functions at Lectorum, Mlawer served as editorial director, where she oversaw the acquisition, selection, and editorial development of Spanish-language books for children and young adults. A pioneer in Spanish-language publishing in the United States, Mlawer has translated over 300 children's books from English to Spanish. She has dedicated her life to the cause of literacy, especially among Hispanic children in the U.S. and Latin America. As a well-known specialist in children's literature in Spanish, she works with publishers, educators, and librarians to bring the best authentic literature to children. She is a strong and vocal advocate for Latino authors and illustrators in the United States. In 2012, she was selected by the Federation of Spanish Publishers from Argentina as one of the 50 most influential people in the Spanish publishing world. For the last three years, she has been a member of the Board of Directors of ConTextos, an international nonprofit organization that works with under-resourced schools in El Salvador.

Charles R. Smith, Jr.

About Me

Growing up where I grew
my young eyes knew
that blood red bandanas
represented Pirus
while Crips sported blue
and when the two met
sometimes bullets flew
piercing bystanders
with innocent eyes
poking holes of pain
inside family's lives.
But while some squeezed triggers
and others got high
I turned to books
to let my mind fly,
I turned to books
for joy and inspiration
to be something in life
and avoid incarceration.
Books provided hope
along with education
allowed me to dream
and provided motivation
to express myself
through words on a page,
allowed me to laugh

cry
and vent rage,
allowed me to love
hate
and engage
myself in the world
and all that I see
each book provided
to me
entry
to a wide opened world
of adventure and mystery,
science fiction
biography
sports and history.
Great men
great women
great stories
great lives
made great impressions
on my young hungry eyes
inspiring me to dream
of lands across the sea
like Hawaii
Japan
France
and Italy,
been there
been there
been there
done that,
Aloha
Koniichi wa
and Bonjour in a beret hat.

I've scuba-dived with sharks
sea turtles and fish
got a tattoo of dolphins
flipping around my wrist
I've soaked in jacuzzis
under moonlight
in the crisp autumn breeze
of an Arizona night.
I've touched stars from ships
that sailed Caribbean waters
I've kissed the hand
of Ambassador's daughters
I've shaken hands with presidents
and perhaps the best
b-ball player, Michael Jordan
and I must confess
that I've also met
Larry Bird
Magic Johnson
Dr. J and Wilt
Chamberlain
Shaq
and Kevin Garnett.
I've taken bullet trains
ridden European rails
hopped metros in Paris
surfed waves under sails
blowing in the breeze
billowing blue sky
on tropical seas.
I've changed time zones
six times in one day,
smacked volleyballs on beaches
in sunny L.A.,
sank jump shots
and splashed
nets on Maui
on a ship
against
a crew
from Bali.

So many sights and sounds
that I can write down
of the life that I've lived
from the books that I found
filled with words
that planted the seed
of dreams for me
when I chose to read.

• • • • •

Charles R. Smith, Jr., is an award-winning author, photographer, and poet with over 30 books to his credit. He won a Coretta Scott King Award for his photographs accompanying the Langston Hughes poem, "My People," and a Coretta Scott King Honor Author Award for his biography on Muhammad Ali, *Twelve Rounds to Glory*. Many of his books have also garnered reluctant reader awards, proving that kids who don't like to read, do like to read his books. Charles R. Smith, Jr., was born and raised in Los Angeles, California. He currently lives in Poughkeepsie, New York, with his wife Gillian, and their three kids, Sabine, Adrian, and Sebastian. You can find him on the web at www.charlesrsmithjr.com.

Joanne Yatvin

Dancing in the Library

*M*iss Lehlbach, our grade school librarian, invited our class into a world of fantasy when she introduced us to delightful characters we would not have met on our own: Mary Poppins, the Wizard of Oz, Dr. Doolittle, and the Hobbit, to name a few.

For me, the best part of knowing Miss Lehlbach was being one of her Library Helpers who checked out books after school and loaded the returned books onto carts. When it was time to close the library for the day, she would shut the door and pull down the shades. Then the fun began. She taught us songs, recitations, and the Elephant Dance, in which we climbed on chairs, danced over tables, and called on others to join us. I still remember the words and the dance.

Because I trusted Miss Lehlbach, I asked her to recommend books for me. At first, she found my favorites—books about girls who were growing up to be strong and independent women. But after a while she led me to a variety of books I would never have chosen on my own, and they never disappointed me.

Over the years, my personal bookcase has grown very crowded. At times, I've had to move some books to others shelves or give them away. But I still keep a special place close by for my favorites, which I return to again and again—my tribute to Miss Lehlbach.

> Our librarian introduced us to imaginary stories and wonderful characters that we would not have met on our own.

• • • • •

A past president of the National Council of Teachers of English, Joanne Yatvin, Ph.D., has more than 40 years experience as a classroom teacher and school administrator. Yatvin is a supervisor of student teachers and former adjunct professor at the Portland State University Graduate School of Education. She is also the author of *English-Only Teachers in Mixed-Language Classrooms: A Survival Guide, A Room with a Differentiated View: How to Serve All Children as Individual Learners,* and *Teaching Writing in Mixed-Language Classrooms: Powerful Writing Strategies for All Students.*

Inspiration

Nothing can equal the power of an adult who puts the right book in a child's hands at the right time.

~Nancie Atwell

Dorothy S. Strickland

The Gift of Reading: Pass it On

"*D*orothy, I'm so glad to see you. I saved a book especially for you." It was the voice of Mrs. Luex, the librarian at the neighborhood branch library that I visited regularly in Union, New Jersey, where I grew up. She reached down under her desk and pulled out that special book and handed it to me with a smile that seemed to say that she had been waiting all week just for me. The library in our part of town was located in a storefront nestled among several small businesses, including a delicatessen, dry cleaners, and drug store. At age 11, I was old enough to walk to the library all by myself and Mrs. Luex had become one of my favorite people in the whole wide world. She was perfectly round—round body, round face, and hair that was pulled back neatly into a perfectly round bun. She was always welcoming and pleasant. To think that she would select a book just for me made me feel very special. Whatever she selected would be read along with the books I selected on my own.

Born into an African American working class family with parents who migrated from the South with limited educational opportunities, I don't recall ever seeing either of them reading a book. My father, however, read the daily tabloid newspaper with enthusiasm, and often quoted portions of it to the rest of us. Fortunately, my parents indulged my love of reading and seemed to know how important it was to me. Little did any of us know that I would one day become president of the International Reading Association and the State of New Jersey Professor of Reading at Rutgers University.

My love of reading and my passion to share that love with others have been at the center of my professional life. My career began as a fourth-grade teacher. I loved reading aloud to my students each day after lunch. I purposely selected chapter books. The end of each chapter always left them wanting more. At no other time during the day did I have everyone's complete attention. According to our annual standardized tests and my own accounts as well, most of my students prospered in reading. Yet, there were two, I felt, who were not progressing as well as they could.

This prompted me to return to school for a master's degree in reading disabilities and later led to my appointment as a Learning Disabilities

Specialist. All of this made me more determined to foster a love of reading as I worked toward improving my students' ability to read. Later, I became involved in teacher education and wrote extensively on reading education with an emphasis on sharing books with children at home and at school. My research and writing on the importance of family storybook reading became an important part of my presentations to parents and as well as educators.

My love of reading is, no doubt, grounded in my love of story. To this day, I find few things as engrossing as a good novel. The feeling of fear and suspense when the protagonist is in trouble and the relief that comes when all is well are as powerful as real-life experiences.

Though much of my reading today consists of reading to learn and to keep informed, reading for pleasure holds a very special place in my life. It is, indeed, a refuge—a place where I can have a great time inside my own head. Reading has broadened my world, made me more reflective in my beliefs, and expanded my personal universe.

> To think that she would select a book just for me made me feel very special.

Many years after my childhood experiences at the library, I became a professor of children's literature in a teacher education program. One evening, I told my students about my early experiences with Mrs. Luex, my childhood librarian, and my students shared similar stories of their own. At this point in my life, I was both an experienced teacher and a parent of three. Yet it suddenly occurred to me that Mrs. Luex had, no doubt, made many other children feel just as exceptional. What a gift it is to make someone feel special and encouraged. There is no better way for me to repay that gift than to pass it on.

●　●　●　●　●

Dorothy S. Strickland, Ph.D., is the Samuel DeWitt Proctor Professor of Education Emerita at Rutgers University. A former classroom teacher and reading specialist, she is a past president of the International Reading Association and the IRA Reading Hall of Fame. She received IRA's Outstanding Teacher Educator of Reading Award and the National Council of Teachers of English Outstanding Educator in the Language Arts. Strickland was a member of the panel that produced *Becoming a Nation of Readers, Preventing Reading Difficulties in Young Children*, the National Early Literacy Panel, and the Validation Committee for the Common Core State Standards. Her many publications include *Learning About Print in Preschool Settings; Bridging the Literacy Achievement Gap, Grades 4-12;* and *The Administration and Supervision of Reading Programs.* Strickland is a member of the New Jersey State Board of Education.

P. David Pearson

Pay It Forward

I went to a one-room schoolhouse in the wide open spaces of the Sacramento Valley in post-World War II California. In 1947, when I started first grade, all 42 of us—from first graders through eighth graders—were taught by Mrs. Millsap, a matronly lady in her early sixties,

 who was driven daily to and from the school by a retired Mr. Millsap in their sporty 1936 Model A coupe. The rest of us arrived by foot, horseback, and even tractor.

That year, I was one of six students in first grade, along with four girls and one other boy— Denny. Denny was my comrade in games and adventures in the rice paddies that stretched out along the prairie between our houses.

When Mrs. Millsap got around to the first graders (the second day of school), she handed each of us a copy of the first pre-primer (*Skip Along*, I think, was the name). It featured Alice and Jerry—a duo not unlike Dick and Jane. I listened in awe as Mrs. Millsap and two of my fellow first graders took turns reading from the book. I was dumbfounded! I hadn't, until that moment, realized that I couldn't read. As the baby of a family of six children, I had been read to frequently (my mom, Lora, and my older sisters, Patty and Joyce, took turns), but I had never realized that other children my age could read. The cruelest blow of all was that Denny was one of those two readers. Think of it—we had raced one another through rice paddies, and, all the while, he had been able to read!

I arrived home that day in tears. My first question to my mother was, "How come Denny can read, and I can't?" "David," she replied, "Don't you worry. All of your brothers and sisters learned to read, and you will, too. Trust me, David. You just have to give it a little more time."

I trusted my mother completely, so I gave it a little time. I did learn to read the little stories featuring Alice, Jerry, Jip (their dog), and their friends and family. By November, I had started to outpace Denny. By the end of that school year, I was reading a library book or two (and even sneaking books into my bed at night), while Denny was still struggling to decipher the tales of Alice and Jerry.

It wasn't until some 20 years later, when I was a classroom teacher myself, that I finally figured out why Denny was ahead of me at the start. It was Denny's second year in first grade! He had memorized the pre-primer stories—word-by-word, sentence-by-sentence, story-by-story (he didn't even have to look at the print!). But after the three pre-primers, when words looked more alike and memory couldn't carry the day, Denny got stuck, and he never did get through the primer or the first reader, even in that second year in first grade.

The skills I got that year as a first grader laid the foundation for a life of research and writing.

I have had an intellectually rich life as a result of the gift I got from Alice, Jerry, and Mrs. Millsap in first grade. I've been able to study how teachers can scaffold students in learning how to read, understand, and think about text. I wasn't able to help Denny (although you shouldn't feel too sorry for him—I heard he did rather well as a vegetable farmer), but the skills I got that year as a first grader laid the foundation for a life of research and writing that has aimed to extend (pay forward) that gift of reading to all students.

• • • • •

P. David Pearson, Ph.D., is a professor in language and literacy at the Graduate School of Education at the University of California, Berkeley, where he served as Dean from 2001–2010. He has spent the last half-century conducting research to improve the ways students comprehend and think about the texts they read. Among his most popular ideas is the Gradual Release of Responsibility, which he claims to have learned initially in the process of raising his two children and refined trying to teach reading comprehension strategies to young students. In 2012, the Literacy Research Association established the P. David Pearson Scholarly Influence Award to be given annually to honor research that exerts a longterm influence on literacy practices and/or policies. He is the founding editor of the *Handbook of Reading Research*, now in its fourth volume; he edited *Reading Research Quarterly* and the *Review of Research in Education;* and he has served on the Editorial Review Board for some 20 educational journals.

Donalyn Miller

Reading Sent Me to the Principal's Office

*T*he only time I had to go to the principal's office was because of reading. My mother claims this isn't precisely true, but it's my story, so I get to tell it how I want.

A precocious reader, I don't remember a time when I couldn't read.

Knowing how to read by first grade didn't seem like a problem to my mother and me, but my teachers thought differently. Initially enthusiastic about school, I was bored with the phonics worksheets and bland textbook stories that made up our school's reading program. In third grade, my teacher, Mrs. Shugart, introduced us to a new reading activity—SRA cards. Stored inside a large box, each color-coded card included a reading selection on one side and comprehension questions on the back. Mrs. Shugart tested each of us, determining where we should start in the SRA program, and for an hour every day, my classmates and I read the SRA cards and answered questions.

I didn't mind reading SRA cards. I knew I was a good reader and also a little bit of a show-off. I don't remember where I started in Mrs. Shugart's box, but I burned through those cards. Every day, when I turned in my questions, Mrs. Shugart clucked her tongue and scrutinized my work, "Three cards today? Are you sure you're really reading them?" I stood at her desk while she checked my answers against the key. If I missed even one question, she would send me back to my desk to repeat a card—insisting that I read too quickly.

Eventually, I finished the last card in the box. Mrs. Shugart didn't know what to do with me during SRA time, so she made me sit with other kids and help them read their cards. I hated it. One day, Mrs. Shugart returned from the office to find me standing at the chalkboard, chalk in hand, writing the answers to SRA cards on the board. With a gasp, she snatched me by the arm and marched me down to the principal's office. The secretary called my mother.

No-nonsense about behavior and grades, my mother was unhappy about getting a call from school. Waiting for Mrs. Shugart, Mom asked me what happened, "You were cheating? What were you thinking, Donalyn?"

While she talked with Mrs. Shugart and our principal, I sat outside the office in agony—imagining increasingly horrific punishments.

After an eternity, my mother emerged from the principal's office and escorted me to the car. I kept my head down and my mouth shut. As we pulled out of the school parking lot, my mother sighed. "Did you know that Mrs. Shugart was standing there for three minutes before you noticed her? She says that you gave out at least ten answers and she has to skip those assignments with the other kids now."

"Mom, I don't think the other kids will mind skipping those cards," I said, "What's going to happen to me?"

"Well, I asked if you could move to the fourth-grade reading class, but everyone nixed that suggestion. We came up with a different plan. Every day during reading time, you will go down to the library and help Mrs. Potter."

And that's what I did. Every day during SRA time, for the rest of third grade and into fourth grade, I worked as Mrs. Potter's library aide. Looking back, I recognize that spending an hour a day with Mrs. Potter permanently influenced my reading life.

I don't remember what Mrs. Potter looked like, but I can still hear her voice in my head, "Horses? You like horses? Have you met Marguerite Henry? Let's start with *King of the Wind*." After *King of the Wind*, I read every Marguerite Henry book in the library—*Misty of Chincoteague, Brighty of Grand Canyon*, and *White Stallion of Lipizza*. I read Anna Sewell's *Black Beauty*, too.

When I ran out of horse books, Mrs. Potter steered me toward other animal books like *Old Yeller* by Frank Gipson, *Rascal* by Sterling North, and Marjorie Kinnan Rawlings' *The Yearling*. Every book Mrs. Potter gave me launched another adventure.

> I can learn about anything, travel anywhere, ask my own questions, and seek my own answers because I read.

Each time I returned a book, Mrs. Potter spent a few minutes chatting with me about the story, asking what I learned from the book and what parts I liked. Under her guidance, I read a staggering pile of books—Laura Ingalls Wilder's Little House books, *The Borrowers* by Mary Norton, most of the Newbery winners, and selections from the Childhood of Famous Americans series. To me, Mrs. Potter was a magician—able to find a book that matched any random interest of mine.

I took reading for granted before my two years with Mrs. Potter. I enjoyed reading, but I didn't grasp its power until she showed me. From then on, my education belonged to me because I loved to read. I can learn about anything, travel anywhere, ask my own questions, and seek my own answers because I read. Thanks to Mrs. Potter's wisdom and guidance, my life has been one long reading adventure—rich and exciting and *mine*.

● ● ● ● ●

Donalyn Miller has worked with a wide variety of upper elementary and middle school students and currently teaches fifth grade at O.A. Peterson Elementary in Fort Worth, Texas. Donalyn's books, *The Book Whisperer* and *Reading in the Wild*, reflect on her journey to become a reading teacher and describe how she inspires and motivates her middle school students to read 40 or more books a year and develop good lifelong reading habits. Donalyn currently facilitates the community blog The Nerdy Book Club and co-writes a monthly column for Scholastic's Principal-to-Principal Newsletter. Her articles about teaching and reading have appeared in publications such as *Education Week Teacher, The Reading Teacher, Educational Leadership,* and the *Washington Post.*

Patricia A. Edwards

Miss Pat's Saturday School

I was known in my neighborhood as the child who talked just like a
book. I enjoyed reading and practicing what I read on everyone who
would listen—and that included my father, mother, grandmother, sisters,
neighborhood children, and guests who visited my home. I even read to my

dolls and dog when everyone else said they were
tired of listening to me read. Of course, my dolls
and dog were always a very attentive audience.

I looked forward to attending Sunday school
every week because I was the best reader in
my class. I always volunteered to read. If a child
mispronounced a word, I quickly corrected him.
He would say, "Thank you, smarty pants." I would
smile broadly and say, "I'm simply trying to help. I
want to become a teacher one day and show people how to read. Reading
is very important, you know. If you learn how to read when you are young,
you will become an excellent reader when you are older. That's what my
Mama and Grandmamma told me. Didn't your Mama and Grandmamma
tell you that, too?"

One day in Sunday school, I learned a different lesson: Being a smarty
pants wasn't always a wise thing to do. Mrs. Medlock, my Sunday school
teacher, mispronounced a word from the Bible during a Sunday school
lesson and I quickly corrected her. Mrs. Medlock got really mad and told my
mother and grandmother that I was a "naughty little girl" and that I had "bad
manners." I explained to my mother and grandmother, "I am very upset and
confused because I thought that I was helping Mrs. Medlock by correcting
her and saying the word was not *Joshaway*, but *Joshua*. I feel like Mrs.
Medlock shouldn't have told you I was a naughty little girl, when I was really
trying to help her." My mother and grandmother said, "Pat, there's a time
and a place for everything." They told me to keep in mind, even though I
was very young, that many of the adults in my community and church didn't
read that well, but they were highly respected. Correcting Mrs. Medlock in
front of the entire Sunday school class was not the right time and place. I
quickly recognized that if I was going to become a teacher, I should probably
focus on children rather than adults.

At seven years old, I had an excellent plan for how I was going to become a teacher. My Daddy owned a barber shop that was in our backyard, which gave me opportunity to practice my teaching skills on the boys when they came to get a haircut. The song "Where the Boys Are" truly characterized my house. Every Saturday, Daddy cut hair from 7:00 am to 9:30 pm. I sold my parents on the idea that I could have a Saturday School from 8:00 am to 5:00 pm. What really got me excited was that I had a very captive audience. As boys came through the gate that led into my backyard, I would greet them. "Hi, boys! Welcome to the Edwards Barber Shop and to Pat's Saturday School." The boys would often reply, "I didn't come to your house to go to any Saturday School, I came to get a haircut." With a twinkle in my eye, I would say, "Yes, you came to get a haircut *and* to go to Pat's Saturday School."

For those boys who were unwilling to attend my Saturday school, I would say, "Daddy, this little boy told me that he wasn't going to come to my school." My Daddy would say, "Son, can you read?" "No, Sir." "Well I think that it would be a great idea for you to attend Pat's school." With my bright smile, I would say, "I told you so; you have to come to my school. And, if you don't, not only will I tell my Daddy, I'm going to tell your Mama! I know your Mama would want you to learn what I'm teaching because she wants you to do well in school, right? Your Mama has signed the slip for you to attend my Saturday school." I showed all of the boys very quickly the same permission slip.

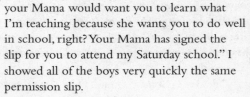

I enjoyed reading and practicing what I read on everyone who would listen . . . I even read to my dolls and dog.

Mrs. Flossie Brown said that Winthrop has permission to come to Pat's Saturday school. Thank you.

If they still resisted, I had another back-up plan. "If you don't come to my school, my Daddy is going to cut all of your hair off. You are going to be a baldy."

Well, I was an excellent recruiter and got my captive audience every Saturday. I read books, I taught the alphabet and how to count, and I had a full curriculum. Oftentimes, I would repeat what I had taught the previous week. If the boys whined, I'd say, "I am reinforcing what I taught. My teacher said that reinforcing what you teach is a good thing." I even kept progress reports on each of the boys who attended my school.

Dear Mrs. Brown,

Winthrop is making great progress in my school.

Patricia Edwards,
Saturday School Teacher

Years later, many of the boys told me how helpful those Saturday lessons were. Even though I was the youngest uncertified teacher in Dougherty County, I'm proud to say that at the tender age of seven, I experienced the real power of teaching.

● ● ● ● ●

Patricia A. Edwards, Ph.D., a member of the Reading Hall Fame is a Distinguished Professor of Language and Literacy in the Department of Teacher Education, and a Senior University Outreach Fellow at Michigan State University. She is an internationally recognized expert in parent involvement, home, school, community partnerships, multicultural literacy, early literacy, and family/intergenerational literacy, especially among poor and minority children. She has served as a member of the IRA board of directors, as the first African American president of the Literacy Research Association, and as president of the International Reading Association. Dr. Edwards is the co-author and author of numerous books including *A Path to Follow: Learning to Listen to Parents, Bridging Literacy and Equity: The Essential Guide to Social Equity Teaching,* and *Change Is Gonna Come: Transforming Literacy for African American Students,* which won the prestigious Edward B. Fry Book Award. She is also the author of the forthcoming *Achieve! Aha Moments, Straight Talk, and Practical Solutions for Helping Students of Color Succeed* and *Different Times, Different Parents, Different Strategies for Engaging Our Essential Partners.* Additionally, Dr. Edwards has been honored with the Albert J. Kingston Service Award and the Jerry Johns Outstanding Teacher Educator in Reading Award.

Gay Su Pinnell & Irene C. Fountas

The Nourishing Power of Literacy: The Right of Every Child

As children, we enjoyed the right of literacy—and, in many ways, may have taken it for granted as we knew it in those early years. It was only later that we became writers and began to develop our professional commitment around one goal—to help all children live literate lives so they could enjoy the exquisite literacy treasures we were afforded as children.

Gay Su Pinnell

Irene C. Fountas

Gay: I am the only child of two teachers. My parents came from farming families. My grandfather could not read or write. The books in our home were mostly for adults because there was no bookstore in our small rural town in New Mexico. The hardware store sold a few children's books, and books for children occupied two shelves of our one-room public library. Nevertheless, I had *Nancy Drew, Black Beauty*, and Andrew Lang's Fairy Books from the library along with the adult books.

Books were woven into family life. Before every road trip, I was in charge of selecting books—50% nonfiction related to the place we were going and 50% fiction of my choice. My father and I would read and discuss the books during the journey.

Teaching was my natural career choice and teaching reading became an inevitable direction. Now, in both my professional and personal life, books are an essential resource. I read electronically but still treasure actual books in print. I reread old favorites and rejoice when I discover a new favorite, especially if the writer has other books I can explore. I never board a plane or go to bed without at least one book in my hand—usually more. I find joy and sustenance in the act of reading and I know always will.

Irene's mother, Catherine Fountas, remains my inspiration. At an advanced age, she is an avid reader, voraciously consuming more books weekly than her family can find for her. What a difference reading can make at every phase of life!

Irene: Though I don't remember having books in my home, I do remember how Mom and Dad tried to plant the seeds of literacy for their six demanding children with the hope that they would pursue education to the fullest. Dad ordered a few bright orange Childcraft books from the Sunday magazine section of the newspaper. His next instinct was that we should all read the encyclopedia to become knowledgeable, so he signed up with the door-to-door salesman to buy one volume one at a time. We eventually had many of the letters, but we never did acquire the complete set. One evening, Dad visited each of us at bedtime and presented us with a small, thick, child-sized black book and told us it was filled with good stories and that we should read the whole thing to learn a lot—it was the Holy Bible.

When I was old enough to qualify for a public library card, I went there frequently, excited about the world of books that had opened to me. I fell in love with fantasy and mystery books—especially Nancy Drew—though I must admit that in school I found even the characters Dick, Jane, Sally, and Spot delightful because I had something to read and think about.

Today I gather books—a collection of treasures—to enjoy every spare moment I have. And, as Gay recounts, she and I ponder how to keep my mom supplied with continuous stacks of books as she consumes more books than both of us and offers us a running critique of our choices. Somehow, I think she is making up for the reading opportunities she missed while she was tending to the demands of her six children.

> Marie Clay . . . opened the doors of literacy to millions of children around the world through Reading Recovery.

Gay and Irene: Our childhoods were very different—but, in one way, they were alike. We both developed a love and an appreciation for literacy that later transformed into a mission that would guide us the rest of our lives—bringing children and literacy together in a joyful and satisfying journey of fulfillment.

A watershed in our thinking occurred when we encountered Marie Clay's theory of the child as a constructive literacy learner. In a little book titled *Reading: The Patterning of Complex Behavior*, Clay wrote eloquently of the remarkable learning that takes place as children become aware of literacy events while adults seize the opportunity to interact with that awareness. We learned about the power of conversation as a model for teaching interactions through which the new and unknown becomes familiar in an ever-spiraling process. Ever more clearly, we could see children as problem-solvers and doers, always working toward more complex ways of responding. These intellectual ideas engaged us and called to us to investigate.

Marie Clay, who created a powerful early literacy intervention, incorporated everything she had learned from an in-depth examination of research and generated a new conversation about the construction of literacy and, ultimately, about teaching the hardest-to-teach children. Her new conversation opened the doors of literacy to millions of children around the world through Reading Recovery—and inform the three foundational points of our life work: 1) a focus on readers/writers and their behaviors; 2) attention to selecting high quality texts for different purposes; and 3) a commitment to elevating teacher expertise. We are ever grateful to those who immersed us in literacy in our early lives, and those who have so richly informed our professional work over the years, and especially to our colleagues—the teachers who make this vision come alive in their work every day with children.

• • • • •

Gay Su Pinnell is professor emerita in the School of Teaching and Learning at Ohio State University. She has worked extensively in clinical tutoring and early intervention for young struggling readers. She received the International Reading Association's Albert J. Harris Award for research in reading difficulties, the Ohio Governor's Award for contributions to literacy education, and the Charles A. Dana Foundation Award, given for pioneering contributions in the fields of health and education. She is a member of the Reading Hall of Fame.

Irene C. Fountas is currently professor and director of the Center for Reading Recovery and Literacy Collaborative at Lesley University where she focuses on the professional development of school leaders and coaches implementing comprehensive approaches to literacy education. She is also engaged in conducting research and implementing development projects related to improving teacher expertise, teacher leadership, and systemic change.

Together, Gay Su Pinnell and Irene C. Fountas have coauthored numerous publications related to classroom literacy, literacy intervention, leadership, and professional development, including *Guided Reading: Good First Teaching for All Children, Guiding Readers & Writers, Grades 3-6, Teaching for Comprehending and Fluency, Grades K–8: Thinking, Talking, and Writing about Reading* and, more recently, *When Readers Struggle: Teaching That Works* and *Genre Study: Teaching with Fiction and Nonfiction Books*.

Kevin K. Green

Lighting the Way for Others

My third-grade teacher, Mrs. Sheneman died recently at the venerable age of 92. As described in her obituary, "For more than 25 years she taught second, third, or fourth grade. She had high expectations for each of her students and loved them dearly."

I was the only African American student in my elementary school until I was in fourth grade. I was most fortunate to have an elementary school teacher like Mrs. Sheneman who reached out to me and helped me hone both my reading skills and my passion for reading. Mrs. Sheneman, along with my mom, Mrs. Lettie C. Green, read to me constantly and introduced me to the world of literacy.

Mrs. Sheneman always expected the most of all of her students and we left her classroom inspired and fully confident in our own ability to read, write, and learn.

The news of her death saddened me but it also brought back happy memories of my eight-year-old self and the joy of her nurturing classroom. Mrs. Sheneman helped make me an avid reader. I started reading all the time on my own—especially comic books such as *Superman, The Flash*, and *Richie Rich*. Later, I read science fiction authored by Isaac Asimov, Ray Bradbury, and Frank Herbert, Jr.

Mrs. Sheneman

These critical literacy and learning experiences ultimately led me to pursue a career in engineering and technology research, inspired, in part, by my early enchantment with science fiction and fantasy books. I know that I owe my current career success to both my nurturing family and my superb and loving teacher, Mrs. Sheneman. A good teacher is like a candle—it consumes itself to light the way for others. Thank you, Mrs. Sheneman, for lighting the way for me.

● ● ● ● ●

Kevin K. Green holds a Ph.D. in electrical engineering and has worked as a computer vision scientist, an educational technology entrepreneur, and a high school math teacher. Among his publications are "Best Practices on How Teachers Can Instill Confidence and Competence in Math Students," a chapter in *Expectations in Education: Readings on High Expectations, Effective Teaching, and Student Achievement*, edited by his father Robert L. Green, and as co-author with his dad of *Expect the Most—Provide the Best*, which explores how high expectations, innovation, and digital technology can reduce the achievement gap.

Jan Richardson

How Reading Changed One Boy's Life—and Mine

*R*eading didn't really change my life until I saw it change the life of a child.

Marcus was a quiet boy who lived with his mother in a shelter for abused women. Because he was the weakest reader in his first-grade class, he became one of my Reading Recovery students. When I explained to his mother that I was going to work with him one-on-one every day, tears filled her eyes. She clutched my arm, and with a quivering voice, softly repeated, "Thank you, thank you, thank you."

Marcus knew his letters but couldn't read at all. Nevertheless, as we worked together, he caught on quickly and grew in competence and confidence. I sent books home with him every night so he could read them with his mother.

One day, Marcus didn't bring his books back. Visibly upset to the point of tears, he explained that he had tucked the books under his cot for safekeeping, but someone at the shelter had taken his book bag during the night. I put my arm around his shoulder and assured him that I would give him more books to take home. "Maybe the person who took your books," I said, "will become a good reader just like you."

A few weeks later, I learned that Marcus and his mother were being moved to a different shelter across town for their safety. I began to worry what his future would be if he couldn't finish the program we had started, develop a solid foundation of reading skills, and continue to grow as a confident reader. Marcus' mother was worried, too; so worried that she put him on public transportation every day and sent him all the way across Washington, D.C. so he could continue to meet with me.

> What a blessing it is to see lives changed forever by the simple yet profound joy of reading.

Marcus eventually graduated from the program as a strong, motivated reader. We had a small celebration and I gave him a book to keep. I'll never forget his ear-to-ear smile. That was the last time I saw Marcus. While I may never see him again, I'm certain that learning to read changed his life forever. The experience certainly changed mine.

Since then, I've taught hundreds (perhaps thousands) of struggling readers, from ages 5 to 75. Each student has fueled my passion for teaching reading. Each one reminds me what an honor it is to be a teacher, what a privilege it is to work with struggling readers, and what a blessing it is to see lives changed forever by the simple yet profound joy of reading.

● ● ● ● ●

Jan Richardson, Ph.D., is a literacy consultant who travels throughout the United States training teachers and providing classroom demonstrations on guided reading. A former classroom teacher (she has taught in every grade, K–12), reading specialist, Reading Recovery teacher leader, and staff developer, Richardson is well known for her practical, engaging presentations. Her book, *The Next Step in Guided Reading,* and DVDs, *Next Step Guided Reading in Action,* provide teachers with practical suggestions and lesson plans for increasing the power and impact of guided reading. She and co-author Maria Walther recently published a new assessment kit, *The Next Step Guided Reading Assessment* for Grades K–2 and 3–6. Richardson is passionate about motivating and accelerating all readers, especially those who struggle.

Penny Kittle

Zookeeper, Spy, Teacher

I became a reader three times. First, I ran a zoo with Dr. Seuss. I had a spot in our living room next to the fireplace where I would tuck myself away from my family. Knees against my chest, I curled into a ball with *If I Ran the Zoo,* studying the letters and illustrations. I could hear

Mom's voice in my ear—each letter a sound I remembered—until suddenly there was meaning. What a moment: I was reading.

I was unstoppable.

I searched the library to find books I could crawl inside. I lived in stories and that was enough—until I met *Harriet the Spy.* She taught me to perch in my closet on boxes of toys behind racks of clothes listening to kitchen conversations through the closet wall. I recorded them in a notebook, just like her, unraveling mysteries, watching my world. I even faked my way through an eye exam so I could have glasses like hers. Harriet taught me to read like a writer.

When I arrived at Oregon State University to become an elementary teacher, I carried a rich reading life inside me. My mother and father assured me that college was woven with rewards. I found one sooner than I expected that first semester in a small room on Monday, Wednesday, and Friday afternoons: Political Science. My professor showed me philosophies that had been rattling around for centuries. He tied impossibly difficult texts together, creating connections across time. I read the seven theories of mankind, as he called them, with wonder.

When I wrote my mid-term exam, the ideas suddenly braided together—I left the exam smarter than when I entered it. I felt a rush of power, of limitless possibility. That weekend I studied for all of my courses differently. I sat with *The Portrait of a Lady* by Henry James, a Norton edition that included nearly 300 pages of textual appendices and literary criticism. I read it all. I scribbled in the margins and layered my ideas onto footnotes. The joy of thinking beside books ate up my evenings.

My professor returned my exam the following week and asked to see me after class. He walked me out into a bright and warm afternoon, the spent leaves swirling at our feet as we surveyed campus. I had a mind for politics, he told me. I glowed. He looked at me closely and said he couldn't believe I was going to waste it teaching the ABCs. I froze there on the steps. How had he missed what was rumbling to life inside me? I had to teach.

Every year I meet kids like Colton, a senior in my English class this fall, who greeted me in September with a high-five and a challenge, "We'll get along fine, but I don't read." Living on a friend's couch, abandoned by both parents, he was in school to play football. I know some good football stories, I countered. He took *The Blind Side* with a smirk, but he devoured it. His backpack slowly filled with borrowed books. When our team missed the playoffs, he spent his Saturdays reading—all day sometimes—because books tell truths and heal loneliness. Reading unwinds the soul. Currently he's studying war memoirs, preparing to leave for boot camp after graduation. He's read 60 books. Imagine the lives he's lived in just one year.

My students need all that is layered in the books I know as well as the ones I have yet to find. I seek what Aristotle called, "True to life and yet more beautiful." I read. I write. I teach. I spend my days between the pages of good books and within the walls of a classroom because it is where I live what I love most completely.

> I spend my days between the pages of good books and within the walls of a classroom because it is where I live what I love most completely.

• • • • •

Penny Kittle teaches high school English and is a K–12 literacy coach in North Conway, New Hampshire. She is the author of six books, including *Book Love* and *Write Beside Them*. Kittle speaks throughout the United States and internationally on empowering students to love reading and writing and to embrace independent thinking through workshop teaching. She is the president of the Book Love Foundation, dedicated to helping teachers build classroom libraries.

Karen L. Mapp

Born to Read

Our three-story home at 420 Orchard Street in New Haven, Connecticut, was where I became a reader. It is where I learned to read, imagine, love, and dream. We shared our home with my great-grandmother, Maude Mapp, as well as my paternal grandparents and two uncles. My brother and I were wrapped in the love and support of three generations of family, not to mention all of the cousins and godparents who lived only a few blocks away.

My childhood neighborhood of the late 1950s and early 60s was incredibly diverse for the times, something I didn't fully appreciate until I was much older. Many neighbors were recent immigrants while others had lived in New Haven for generations. It was within this context that I was exposed to the sights and aromas of lands and people far beyond the boundaries of New Haven.

Jeanne, one of my best friends, lived above her parents' store, China Trading. I loved visiting Jeanne's home. We would wriggle in between the tight aisles in the family store, filled with different Chinese spices and ingredients, various cooking utensils and pots and pans, and rows of books written in Chinese. Jeanne and I would snuggle into a corner with one of the books, looking at pictures of China and the unfamiliar letters and characters. Jeanne would translate, bringing the pictures to life. We both loved to read, and we often shared top honors in elementary school for our reading and writing abilities.

When I asked my Mom how I learned to read, she explained, "I taught you to read when you were around two or three."

> I was then, and remain so to this day, a night owl, and can imagine my poor Mom, as excited as she was by my love of books and reading, also hoping that I would finally tire and go to sleep.

I remember how much I loved Dr. Seuss in those early years. I would squeal with delight when a new Dr. Seuss book was added to my library, and I relished seeing them lined up in my bookcase—the blue cover of *The Cat in the Hat*, the yellow of *One Fish, Two Fish, Red Fish, Blue Fish*, the green and white of *Hop on Pop*, and, of course, the bright orange cover of *Green Eggs and Ham*. Apparently, I would wear out Mom every evening before bedtime, asking her to read the Seuss books, especially *Green Eggs and Ham*, over and over! I was then, and remain so to this day, a night owl, and can imagine my poor Mom, as excited as she was by my love of books and reading, also hoping that I would finally tire and go to sleep.

All of this home-based nurturing support helped me become a strong and voracious reader at an early age. My mom has a picture of me at around age four, setting up a classroom with my dolls and reading to my attentive students. The picture forecasts my current vocation and love— research and teaching.

● ● ● ● ●

Karen L. Mapp, Ed.D., is a senior lecturer on education at the Harvard Graduate School of Education (HGSE) and the faculty director of the Education Policy and Management Master's Program. She has served as the co-coordinator of the Community Organizing and School Reform Research Project and as a core faculty member in the Doctorate in Educational Leadership (EDLD) program at HGSE. She is a founding member of the District Leaders Network on Family and Community Engagement, is a trustee of the Hyams Foundation in Boston, and is on the board of the Institute for Educational Leadership (IEL) in Washington, D.C. Mapp served as a consultant on family engagement to the United States Department of Education in the Office of Innovation and Improvement. She is the author and co-author of several articles and books about the role of families and community members in the work of student achievement and school improvement including *Beyond the Bake Sale: The Essential Guide to Family-School Partnerships* and *A Match on Dry Grass: Community Organizing as a Catalyst for School Reform*.

Nancie Atwell

Secret Gardens

My father was a postal carrier. My mother waitressed. Except for the *World Book Encyclopedia*, which my parents purchased one volume at a time, ours was a house without books. The turning point in my life as a reader came in fifth grade, when my sore throat and achy joints were diagnosed as rheumatic fever. I spent most of the school year off my feet and secluded in my bedroom. Books, the library, and my mother saved me.

She began to scour the shelves of the local library in search of anything she could imagine I might like. At first, I read out of boredom. No child in 1961 had a television, let alone a computer or telephone in her bedroom. But then I began to fall in love—with Ellen Tibbetts, Henry Huggins, Beezus and Ramona, the March sisters, and the heroes and heroines in the Landmark biography series. I escaped my room in the company of Lotta Crabtree, Jenny Lind, Clara Barton, Sam Adams, and Francis Marion the Swamp Fox, and vicariously experienced their perseverance and courage.

When my mother brought home *The Secret Garden* by Frances Hodgson Burnett, I wrinkled my nose at its musty cover and put it at the bottom of the pile. When I ran out of books and was desperate, I finally gave in and cracked it open. I read it straight through. It was my story but not my story. I was Mary; I was Colin. I remember calling downstairs to my mother and thanking her over and over again for the best book I ever read. "Can you get me some more like this one?" I begged. My poor mother tried, but there is only one *Secret Garden*. She renewed it four times for me that winter and spring.

> All that quiet time reading stories chosen for me by an adult who loved me changed me forever—and granted me a passion for stories and the ability to read fast and with feeling.

All that quiet time reading stories chosen for me by an adult who loved me changed me forever—and granted me a passion for stories and the ability to read fast and with feeling. The novelist Graham Greene wrote, "There is always one moment in childhood when a door opens and lets the future in." This was my moment. I became an English major and an English teacher because I was—I am—crazy about books and reading.

Today at my school, the Center for Teaching and Learning, the faculty does for every child what my mother did for me. We show students we love them by looking after them as readers. We give them time every day to curl up with intriguing stories. We scour the shelves of bookstores and pore over reviews in search of titles that will delight them. And we acknowledge the essential *should* in teaching reading: every student should read for the pleasure of it.

While instructional fads will come and go, nothing can equal the power of an adult who puts the right book in a child's hands at the right time. Teachers who cultivate diverse secret gardens—quiet spaces in the school day when every student can venture into a story he or she loves— understand that engaged reading now makes engaged readers for a lifetime.

● ● ● ● ●

A teacher since 1973, Nancie Atwell is the author of the classic *In the Middle* as well as *Lessons That Change Writers*, a year's worth of practical minilessons; *Naming the World: A Year of Poems and Lessons*, a teaching anthology that invites students to unpack and appreciate poetry; and *The Reading Zone: How to Help Kids Become Skilled, Passionate, Habitual, Critical Readers*. In 1990, Atwell founded the Center for Teaching and Learning, a K-8 demonstration school in Edgecomb, Maine, where, until her retirement in 2014, she taught seventh- and eighth-grade writing, reading, and history. Her new book and DVD, *Systems to Transform Your Classroom and School*, describes the culture of engagement and excellence Atwell and her colleagues created by combining smart practice, innovative solutions to common problems of teaching, humane school policies, and traditions that build community. Atwell is the first classroom teacher to receive the major research awards in English language arts, the MLA Mina P. Shaughnessy Prize, and the NCTE David H. Russell Award. In 2011, she was awarded an honorary doctorate by the University of New Hampshire and was named the River of Words Poetry Teacher of the Year.

Douglas Fisher

When I Became a Flashlight Reader

I don't remember much of my early reading life. I don't have memories of Dr. Seuss or bedtime stories or teacher read-alouds. My mom tells me that I was a reasonably good reader, although not typically a motivated one. She says that I read what my teachers asked me to read and not much more.

I've learned that's fairly typical for a boy.

All that changed in fourth grade. While other students might have experienced the so-called fourth-grade slump, my teacher, Mr. Alaimo, jolted me awake as a reader—invigorating my reading life at this critical point in my development.

I vividly remember the day Mr. Alaimo asked us to climb under our desks after he closed the curtains and turned out the lights in our classroom. He read with a flashlight from a book called *The Children's Story* by James Clavell, a rather simple story of a classroom that is taken over by a new teacher following a war. It was the height of the Cold War and I lived in San Diego. We all knew that our city was a main target for the Russians because of the military resources. Mr. Alaimo only read a few pages a day and then discussed the ideas in the text with us as we huddled under our desks. I remember when the students in the story decide to cut up the American flag so that each one could have a piece. I was shocked. I'd never read a book like this. There had to be more.

That's when I became a flashlight reader. I was hooked on books. Late in the evening, often with my covers over my head, I would read (mostly scary) books with a flashlight. I remember reading Stephen King's *The Shining* by flashlight and scaring myself so much I couldn't sleep. But I kept reading so that I could talk with Mike Stroehlein, my best friend, about the book.

> I trace my love of reading directly back to a teacher— a teacher who knew just the right book at just the right time and changed a life.

Reading can also be very personal. I've certainly read a number of emotionally charged books for my own growth that I don't necessarily want to talk about publicly. But more often than not, readers want to talk with others about what they've read. I know I do. All of my friends know how important Auggie, the main character in R. J. Palacio's *Wonder*, has become to me.

I've grown a lot as a reader, moving way beyond scary stories. Today my flashlight is attached to a Kindle, and my colleague Nancy Frey is the one who has to hear most of my thinking about texts. But I trace my love of reading directly back to a teacher—a teacher who knew just the right book at just the right time and changed a life.

● ● ● ● ●

Douglas Fisher, Ph.D., is a professor of educational leadership at San Diego State University and a teacher leader at Health Sciences High & Middle College. He began his education career as an early intervention teacher and elementary school educator. He is the recipient of an Exemplary Leader Award from the NCTE Conference on English Leadership as well as the Virginia Hamilton Essay Honor Award for 2014. He has published numerous articles on reading and literacy, differentiated instruction, and curriculum design as well as books such as *Better Learning Through Structured Teaching*, *Rigorous Reading*, and *Text Complexity: Raising Rigor in Reading*.

Jennifer Serravallo

A Tale of Two Readers

I grew up attending a Catholic elementary school. My teachers put us in ability-based reading groups where we busily read passages in a basal reader and answered questions. I learned that reading in school meant completing tasks such as drawing character webs, making a timeline of a story,

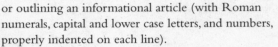

or outlining an informational article (with Roman numerals, capital and lower case letters, and numbers, properly indented on each line).

On the other hand, my childhood summer evenings were spent sitting side-by-side with my siblings, listening to my father read aloud *The Hobbit,* our minds wandering into the Middle Earth while we applied ice packs to our sunburned skin.

During middle school, my classmates and I were asked to highlight new vocabulary in our whole-class novels and then use those words in sentences.

But after school, my friends and I would walk to the local public library and sneak to the stacks that held the 610s: books about "The Human Body." We read every informational text we could find that discussed all the things we were wondering about puberty and sexuality. Reading meant that we were empowered to learn the things that mattered most to us. It meant that we could ask our own questions—and find the answers we needed.

In high school, my English teachers assigned the classics. Shakespeare, Hawthorne, Thoreau, Fitzgerald. Notice I said "teachers assigned" not "I read"—I frequented the bookstore's *CliffsNotes* section and learned how to make A's by parroting other people's interpretations.

After high school, I had a summer job waitressing at a quaint Bed & Breakfast with Ed. Ed was the B&B's chain-smoking, middle-aged gay bartender, and he was perhaps my most important reading teacher. "What are you reading?" he asked the first time we met, and was horrified to hear that I wasn't really in the habit of reading anything. He made it his personal mission to turn me into a true reader, the kind who wouldn't dare board a plane or go on a beach vacation or climb into bed without a book.

Ed spent countless hours talking with me about books. After he got to know me better, he'd often say: "You've gotta read ____," or "You're going to love

_____." He helped me to create my own personal reading canon. For Ed, it was about learning who I was first and foremost because matching books to readers is a very personal thing. He'd never suggest a text that was too hard or irrelevant.

In large part because of Ed's influence, when I dated in my 20s, I dated people's bookshelves as much as I dated the person. The first time I was invited to someone's apartment was my time to scope out their reading life and history. My perusal of their books revealed way more about who these people were than what they told me over lattes at the local coffee shop.

Becoming a reader for me, unfortunately, meant living a different life inside and outside of school. Indeed, this separation between school reading and personal reading is what I've devoted my professional life to trying to remedy.

I want elementary teachers to be like Ed (except for the chain-smoking part). I want them to lean in, get to know their kids, and help them develop rich reading lives. I want classrooms to be filled with great books and stirring questions, and for kids to have the freedom and choice to find the books that keep them interested and wanting more. I want kids to be read to, to read to each other, and to read to themselves and feel free to fall into imaginary worlds. I want this generation of children to grow up and write an essay for a collection like this one in which they thank their teachers and schools for helping them grow into the passionate and thoughtful readers they are today.

> Reading meant that we were empowered to learn the things that mattered most to us.

● ● ● ● ●

Jennifer Serravallo is the author of several books and resources to help teachers get to know their readers, match them to good books, and support them as they develop an independent reading life. Her *Independent Reading Assessment in Fiction and Nonfiction* gives students a choice of books to read independently and allows their teachers to learn about their comprehension, reading habits, and interests from their responses. Serravallo is also the co-author of *Conferring with Readers* and the author of *Teaching Reading in Small Groups* and two versions of *The Literacy Teacher's Playbook*, one for Grades K–2 and one for 3–6. Formerly a senior staff developer at the Teachers College Reading and Writing Project at Columbia University, Serravallo is now a frequent presenter at state and national reading conferences and consults with schools hoping to strengthen their reading workshops.

Linda B. Gambrell

Great Mentors, Great Readers

My maternal grandmother was an avid and enthusiastic reader who read everything from trash to treasure—from "spicy-dicey" detective stories to Tolstoy and Dickens. As she often said, "There is nothing better than a good read!" Because of my grandmother, I grew up loving books.

She was my first and perhaps most significant "reading teacher."

She liked to read poetry—sometimes silly verses and sometimes verses that seemed very sad. I could tell they were sad because of the way she read them aloud—and I would snuggle up to her because I thought she was sad and needed snuggling.

She read Beatrix Potter's *Peter Rabbit* to me over and over again until I had memorized the entire story. I remember "reading" it to my grandmother, carefully turning the pages at just the right time. My most vivid memories, interestingly, are of my grandmother reading aloud to me from the *Compton's Pictured Encyclopedia* about topics as diverse as snakes, George Washington, and how to build a bridge. We sat together, side-by-side on her large, green sofa with overstuffed pillows, as we read and discussed American Indian tribes of the Southeast (Grandmother always insisted that she had Cherokee ancestors).

While I have only vague memories of the fictional stories she read aloud to me, I have vivid memories of my grandmother reading informational text—the encyclopedia, newspapers, and magazines. Today, my favorite "read" is a book that will take me on a real-life adventure where I learn something about other countries and cultures (such as in Khaled Hosseini's *The Kite Runner*), about exciting treks through nature (Jon Krakauer's *Into Thin Air*), about fascinating past eras through historical fiction (Simon

> The central and most important goal of reading instruction is to foster a love of reading.

Winchester's *The Professor and the Madman*), and riveting memoirs (Jeanette Walls' *The Glass Castle*).

Early on in my teaching career I realized that the central and most important goal of reading instruction is to foster a love of reading. We can teach our students all the skills needed for proficient reading, but if they do not choose to read, if they are not motivated to read, they will never reach their full potential as engaged readers. Fortunately, I had a grandmother who was a wonderful reading mentor. In a similar way, we need to mentor our students, children, and grandchildren, so that they develop a deep love of and appreciation for the sheer pleasure of reading.

● ● ● ● ●

Linda B. Gambrell, Ph.D., is Distinguished Professor of Education in the Eugene T. Moore School of Education at Clemson University. She has served as president of the International Reading Association, Literacy Research Conference, and Association of Literacy Educators and Researchers. Her research centers on literacy motivation, reading comprehension, and the role of discussion in teaching and learning and has been published in *Reading Research Quarterly, Educational Psychologist, Elementary School Journal,* and *Journal of Educational Research* as well as in many books she has co-authored and edited. Linda is a member of the Reading Hall of Fame and has received the Literacy Research Association Oscar Causey Award, International Reading Association William S. Gray Award, College Reading Association Laureate Award, National Reading Conference Albert J. Kingston Award, International Reading Association Outstanding Teacher Educator in Reading Award, and the College Reading Association A.B. Herr Award for Outstanding Contributions to the Field of Reading. She currently serves as co-editor of *Reading Research Quarterly.*

Laura Robb

My Reading Champions

My brother Gene was four years older than me. By the time I turned four, I was intensely jealous that he could read and I couldn't. I burned with desire to hold a book and move so deeply into it that, like my brother, I wouldn't even hear my mother when she called us to the table for dinner.

I begged: "Teach me to read, Mom! Please, *please?!*" Finally, no doubt to end the constant nagging, Mom set aside time after lunch for reading lessons, and soon after my fifth birthday, I was reading.

I longed for my father, who was a great storyteller, to read me the books that I couldn't yet read on my own. But my father worked three jobs to pay the rent and feed his family. He didn't have the time or energy in the evening to read to me. Still, every Sunday morning, my brother and I snuggled next to him in bed, waiting for him to tell stories about his childhood. I can still hear my father's voice describing the brutally cold winters on the family farm in Poland. They didn't have enough money to burn wood in the fireplace all night. He told us that he always volunteered to cut onions, turnips, carrots, and potatoes into chunks for the beef stew. I can smell the aroma of that stew and picture my father stirring the mixture, and when no one was looking, popping a chunk of beef into his mouth. "I was always hungry," he explained. Hearing my father's stories drew me closer to books and the stories they held.

My mother took my brother and me on a trolley to the "big" library once a month. In a week, I finished my stack of books and reread each one again and again until we returned them. I'm sure that my father felt my yearning for more books to read. One Saturday afternoon when I was seven, we walked two blocks to the small library in our neighborhood, and my dad filled out forms for a library card. That

Hearing my father's stories drew me closer to books and the stories they held.

Saturday changed my life: I met Mrs. Schwartz, the librarian, and my dad said, "You're old enough to walk to the library yourself." And so I did— almost every afternoon.

In my mind, Mrs. Schwartz was "the keeper of books and the guardian of stories." Some days she read aloud to a small group of us regulars. The best days, though, were slow. On those days, Mrs. Schwartz let me surround myself with books I pulled from the shelves and browse through them to see which ones I'd check out. Sometimes she'd recommend a book and tell me a snippet of the story. But she always let me choose. Books became my friends and were my solace when I felt lonely and not welcomed into the girls' social circle at school.

Yes, reading changed my life. It gave me the drive to work hard in school so I could attend college, become a teacher, and share my love of reading with my students. I can't imagine a life without books and reading. And I can still conjure the voices of my mother, father, and Mrs. Schwartz inside my head. They're with me every time I open the first page of a new book.

● ● ● ● ●

Author, teacher, coach, and speaker, Laura Robb has 43 years of teaching experience in Grades 4–8. She continues to teach each year from December through February to maintain her close learning connection to students. Robb has published multiple bestselling books including *Unlocking Complex Texts, Teaching Reading in Middle School, Differentiating Reading Instruction,* and *Teaching Middle School Writers.* She's developed classroom libraries for Grades 3–9 and co-authored a nonfiction curriculum for middle school, *XBooks and Smart Writing: Practical Units for Teaching Middle School Writers.* Robb speaks at conferences in the United States and Canada and coaches teachers in Virginia. With her son Evan, a middle school principal, she has created the Educator 2 Educator Foundation (e2efoundation.org) that raises money for grants to high-poverty schools to purchase books for their central and classroom libraries. You can contact Robb at www.LRobb.com.

Heidi Mills & Timothy O'Keefe

Believe Kids into Being

*I*t was 18 years ago when we envisioned what might be possible if we created an elementary school grounded in literacy and inquiry. While our vision was solid, we underestimated its power and potential. You see, our students' literacy histories, and their capacity to articulate what reading is and who they are as readers, mirror the insights of the most accomplished authors found within the pages of this book.

At the Center for Inquiry (CFI) in Columbia, South Carolina, we strive to make reading, writing, and learning in school reflect authentic literacy and learning in the world. From the first day of Kindergarten until they graduate as fifth graders, students learn to read and write by reading and writing real books, magazines, and newspaper articles. We "believe" our students into being thoughtful, passionate, and engaged readers and writers by immersing them in a culture steeped in genuine literacy experiences and by talking with them reader-to-reader and writer-to-writer. To do so, we carefully scaffold them by offering instruction at the point of need, guidance, and materials that they can successfully read and write, all the while trusting they will grow into literate beings in much the same way they learned to walk and talk. To offer a glimpse of literacy learning within our school culture, we'll eavesdrop on one of Tim's latest book club conversations.

A Book Club Conversation: Tim and His Third Graders

When I met with a small group of six third graders to discuss the final chapter of *Grandfather's Dance* by Patricia MacLaughlin, four were crying. I was misting over as well. All for good reason. "You know what I said about how it would be a brave move if Patricia MacLaughlin decided to let Grandfather die?" eight-year-old Logan asked, sniffling. "Now I am not so sure I should have said that."

Later that afternoon, when Devyn's mom stopped by my classroom. I related how emotional our conversation about the last chapter had been.

Open a World of Possible: Real Stories About the Joy and Power of Reading © 2014 Scholastic

"I'm not sure how you do it," Devyn's mother replied, glancing at her daughter whose eyes were still red-rimmed from her tears. "Devyn has gone from being afraid of reading to becoming a voracious reader. She *always* has a book in her hands."

After getting to the fifth book of MacLaughlin's Sarah, Plain and Tall series, the children could barely wait for this, the final book. Third-grader Logan and the others had recognized the foreshadowing, the heart pills, the fact that Grandfather had said that he might not be able to attend young Cassie's wedding, and the heartfelt good-bye between Grandfather and an acquaintance. I think we all knew it was coming. But when it happened, and the family found our beloved Grandfather dead in the barn, we couldn't help but cry at his passing. "Think of it," said our student Carl Lewis during our debriefing with the whole class, "These characters are all make believe. She (Patricia MacLaughlin) did this to us with ink spots on a page."

> We "believe" our students into being thoughtful, passionate, and engaged readers and writers by immersing them in a culture steeped in genuine literacy experiences and by talking with them reader-to-reader and writer-to-writer.

Inquiry into Literacy

It's not a coincidence that Carl Lewis talked so eloquently about how authors move readers. Our students regularly talk about books and they also inquire into the reading process itself. Heidi teaches her preservice courses onsite at CFI to immerse her graduate students in the beliefs and practices that make a difference for teachers and learners. She recently asked Tim and his kids to share their inquiry into the reading process with her preservice teachers. We think that the children's responses to the question, "What is reading?" are as compelling as any found in this volume.

Devyn: Reading, to me, is understanding.

Kayla: Reading is learning. Because even if the book doesn't have facts, you still learn as you read. You learn new words and new information all the time.

Tim: Yeah, I think you can learn about human nature, by reading stories. Even in fiction. After reading *Charlotte's Web*, even though most of the characters are animals, I learned about kindness and craftiness, I learned more about human nature. Sarah Beth, what is reading to you?

Sarah Beth: Well, let's say you are reading a book about horses, it's about understanding and feeling like you are in the book. If you are reading a book about horses, you're the rider. You are the one riding the horse and not falling off the horse and your hair is blowing in the wind.

Carl Lewis: Mine goes with Sarah Beth. You have to be in the book if you are enjoying the book.

Ty: Reading to me is like I'm Fireheart in *Warriors* and it's like I'm in the woods and I'm talking to Cloud.

When teachers create cultures of inquiry through literacy, kids live readerly and writerly lives just as adults do outside of school. Kids also get in touch with the reading process and themselves as readers by engaging in inquiry around literacy. While it may not be typical to talk about texts and the reading process so naturally, we know it's possible and it's worth striving for—for all children everywhere.

● ● ● ● ●

Heidi Mills and Timothy O'Keefe have been married for 35 years and have two beautiful boys. Together, they worked with brilliant colleagues to found the Center for Inquiry (CFI), a small school partnership between the University of South Carolina and Richland School District Two in Columbia, South Carolina. The school is nationally known as a demonstration site for inquiry-based instruction, collaborative research, and ongoing professional development. O'Keefe is currently a second- and third-grade teacher at CFI. His classroom has been featured in numerous books, articles, and educational videos. Mills is the John C. Hungerpiller Professor of Instruction and Teacher Education at USC. She has published seven books by leading publishers in education and written numerous journal articles on literacy and inquiry. Mills and O'Keefe are the recipients of the 2014 Outstanding Educator in the English Language Arts Award by the National Council of Teachers of English. They consult with schools across the country on content literacy and inquiry.

Advocacy

I believe if you can turn a kid on to reading, you're saving a life.

~James Patterson

James Patterson

The Lifesaving Power of Reading

As a kid, I was a good student but I wasn't much of a reader. I read what I was assigned but little else. I began to enjoy reading in college, when I could finally read what I wanted to. After high school, I got a job at a mental hospital to pay the bills. It was there that I found myself reading each night

until sunrise in an attempt to get through my shift. Suddenly, I was plowing through serious literature like *Ulysses* and *One Hundred Years of Solitude*. Then I started reading bestsellers—*The Exorcist* and *The Day of the Jackal*—and, I thought, hey, I might be able to do something like that. I might.

But I didn't truly realize the importance of getting kids reading and helping kids to love books until I had a child of my own. When my son Jack was about eight, he was good at a lot of things but he didn't love reading. My wife, Sue, and I sat him down one summer and we told him that he didn't have to mow the lawn, but he had to read every day. Then we took him to a bookstore and helped him pick out books that he would really enjoy. By the end of that summer, Jack had read a dozen books that he loved, and his reading skills had improved dramatically. Jack is now 16 and he loves reading. He's at the top of his class.

It's a simple fact. If kids don't read, they're going to have a hard time getting through high school. Kids who don't read a lot are falling behind in school, which means they are likely to fall behind in life. I believe if you can turn a kid on to reading, you're saving a life. And that's what I'm trying to do, in partnership with parents, teachers, librarians, publishers, other authors, and booksellers—*I want to save lives.*

I created a website, ReadKiddoRead.com, to help parents and teachers find books that kids will love—books that will turn them into lifelong readers. But parents need to get involved, too, and that work starts at home. Parents have to make sure that their kids are reading. They need to understand this: there's no such thing as a kid who hates reading. There are just kids who love reading, and kids who are reading the wrong books. We need to help them find the right books. There are millions of kids in this country who've never read a book they love and that needs to change.

As a part of all this, I began writing kids' books myself and, well, they're really becoming my favorite thing to write. I love that I get to be funny when I write kids' books in a way that I haven't been able to when I'm writing a thriller. I like to tell stories that will work with kids, stories about kids taking responsibility for themselves and their actions. And I think that these types of stories are the ones that resonate with kids. One of the most rewarding things for me has been parents telling me, sometimes with tears in their eyes, that one of my books finally turned their kids on to reading. My ultimate goal is to have kids read a book, and say, "Give me another!"

• • • • •

There's no such thing as a kid who hates reading. There are just kids who love reading, and kids who are reading the wrong books. We need to help them find the right books.

James Patterson holds the Guinness world record for the most #1 *New York Times* bestsellers of any author. In 2010, *New York Times Magazine* featured Patterson on its cover and hailed him as having "transformed book publishing." His awards for adult and children's literature include the Edgar Award, the International Thriller of the Year Award, and the Children's Choice Award for Author of the Year. He's been called the busiest man in publishing, and that's not just because of his own books. For the past decade, Patterson has been devoting more and more of his time to championing books and reading. His website, ReadKiddoRead. com, is designed to help parents, teachers, and librarians ignite the next generation's excitement about reading. ReadKiddoRead was the winner of the National Book Foundation's Innovations in Reading prize. Patterson's Book Bucks programs, which include College Book Bucks, Summer Book Bucks, and Winter Book Bucks, provide book gift certificates to be spent at local independent bookstores. Patterson is currently distributing one million dollars in grants to independent bookstores and is donating over 100,000 books to the military overseas. He has established scholarships in education at 20 schools, including Vanderbilt University, the University of Wisconsin, and Manhattan College. Patterson received a bachelor's degree from Manhattan College and a master's degree from Vanderbilt University. He lives in Palm Beach, Florida, with his wife, Sue, and his son, Jack.

Frank Bruni

Read, Kids, Read

*A*s an uncle, I'm inconsistent about too many things.
Birthdays, for example. My nephew Mark had one on Sunday, and I
didn't remember—and send a text—until 10 pm, by which point he was asleep.
School productions, too. I saw my niece Bella in "Seussical: The Musical"
but missed "The Wiz." She played Toto, a feat of trans-
species transmogrification that not even Meryl, with
all of her accents, has pulled off.

But about books, I'm steady. Relentless. I'm
incessantly asking my nephews and nieces what they're
reading and why they're not reading more. I'm reliably
hurling novels at them, and also at friends' kids. I may
well be responsible for 10 percent of all sales of *The Fault
in Our Stars*, a teenage love story now released as a movie.
Never have I spent money with fewer regrets, because I believe in reading—not
just in its power to transport but in its power to transform.

So I was crestfallen when a new report by Common Sense Media came
out. It showed that 30 years ago, only 8 percent of 13-year-olds and 9 percent
of 17-year-olds said that they "hardly ever" or never read for pleasure. Today, 22
percent of 13-year-olds and 27 percent of 17-year-olds say that. Fewer than 20
percent of 17-year-olds now read for pleasure "almost every day." Back in 1984,
31 percent did. What a marked and depressing change.

I know, I know: This sounds like a fogey's crotchety lament. Or, worse, like
self-interest. Professional writers arguing for vigorous reading are dinosaurs
begging for a last breath. We're panhandlers with a better vocabulary.

But I'm coming at this differently, as someone persuaded that reading does
things—to the brain, heart, and spirit—that movies, television, video games, and
the rest of it cannot.

There's research on this, and it's cited in a recent article in *The Guardian* by
Dan Hurley, who wrote that after three years interviewing psychologists and
neuroscientists around the world, he'd concluded that "reading and intelligence
have a relationship so close as to be symbiotic."

In terms of smarts and success, is reading causative or merely correlated?
Which comes first, *The Hardy Boys* or the hardy mind? That's difficult to
unravel, but several studies have suggested that people who read fiction,
reveling in its analysis of character and motivation, are more adept at reading

people, too: at sizing up the social whirl around them. They're more empathetic. God knows we need that.

Late last year, neuroscientists at Emory University reported enhanced neural activity in people who'd been given a regular course of daily reading, which seemed to jog the brain: to raise its game, if you will.

Some experts have doubts about that experiment's methodology, but I'm struck by how its findings track something that my friends and I often discuss. If we spend our last hours or minutes of the night reading rather than watching television, we wake the next morning with thoughts less jumbled, moods less jangled. Reading has bequeathed what meditation promises. It has smoothed and focused us.

Maybe that's about the quiet of reading, the pace of it. At Success Academy Charter Schools in New York City, whose students significantly outperform most peers statewide, the youngest kids all learn and play chess, in part because it hones "the ability to focus and concentrate," said Sean O'Hanlon, who supervises the program. Doesn't reading do the same?

Daniel Willingham, a psychology professor at the University of Virginia, framed it as a potentially crucial corrective to the rapid metabolism and sensory overload of digital technology. He told me that it can demonstrate to kids that there's payoff in "doing something taxing, in delayed gratification." A new book of his, *Raising Kids Who Read*, will be published later this year.

Before talking with him, I arranged a conference call with David Levithan and Amanda Maciel. Both have written fiction in the young adult genre, whose current robustness is cause to rejoice, and they rightly noted that the intensity of the connection that a person feels to a favorite novel, with which he or she spends eight or 10 or 20 hours, is unlike any response to a movie.

That observation brought to mind a moment in *The Fault in Our Stars* when one of the protagonists says that sometimes, "You read a book and it fills you with this weird evangelical zeal, and you become convinced that the shattered world will never be put back together unless and until all living humans read the book."

Books are personal, passionate. They stir emotions and spark thoughts in a manner all their own, and I'm convinced that the shattered world has less hope for repair if reading becomes an ever smaller part of it.

● ● ● ● ●

Frank Bruni is an American journalist. He was the chief restaurant critic of the *New York Times*, a position he held from 2004 to 2009. In May 2011, he became the paper's first openly gay op-ed columnist.

Lucy Calkins

A Place to Start

Not long ago, when rooting around in the attic looking for a serving dish I wanted for a dinner I was giving, I found an old paperback—its blue cover torn, with a tea stain on the binding. It was titled, in large block letters, *Exodus*. The picture on the cover was of a big tanker ship, a rough looking man with a machine gun, and beautiful woman in a nurse's uniform.

I saw that title, and all of a sudden I was back on the deck of that ship, with Kitty, the American nurse, and Ari, the Israeli soldier, and all around us, a group of orphans, refugees from the Holocaust. The children on the boat had been hidden in attics and basements; they had walked hundreds of miles across icy fields and through dangerous towns. And now, finally, they had almost made it to the Promised Land—but they couldn't land. They had been told to go back, but they wouldn't, and so they'd gone on a hunger strike.

Just seeing the front cover of that book whisked me back in time to the burning hot deck of that ship. I was Kitty again, terrified for these orphans, and amazed by this rough soldier who was willing to sacrifice them rather than have them continue to live without a homeland. Until then, I never knew that a book could take you to places where so much was risked, where characters could be so brave, where sacrifice could be so intense, where people could endure such unbearable danger and loss.

As you might imagine, I never got the serving dish. I stayed in the attic, reading, reading, reading. It was as if, by reading, I could be Kitty. I could ensure that those orphans would survive.

> How do we teach the heart-breaking, soul-searching kind of reading that makes you feel as if you are breathing some new kind of air?

How do we teach *this* kind of reading—the heart-breaking, soul-searching kind of reading that makes you feel as if you are breathing some new kind of air? How do we teach the kind of reading that makes you walk through the world differently because a light bulb is no longer just a light bulb—it is filaments and electricity and the industrial revolution and all that tumbled forth from that? How do we teach the power of reading—reading that allows us to see under words, between words, beyond words? How do we teach the intimacy of reading—of belonging to a community that has a shared vocabulary, shared stories, and shared petitions and projects?

Perhaps the place to start is by thinking about our own lives as readers.

● ● ● ● ●

Lucy Calkins, founding director of the Teachers College Reading and Writing Project, is the author or co-author of more than 40 books including the *Units of Study in Opinion, Information, and Narrative Writing, Grades K–8* written with the TCRWP community and *Pathways to the Common Core*. Her foundational texts include *The Art of Teaching Reading, The Art of Teaching Writing*, and *Units of Study for Teaching Reading, Grades 3–5*. Calkins is the Robinson Professor of Children's Literature at Teachers College, Columbia University, where she co-directs the Literacy Specialist Program.

Robert Needlman, M.D.

How a Doctor Discovered Reading

*T*hroughout grade school, I regarded myself as a "smart boy," and believed that all of my teachers shared in this opinion. So imagine my surprise when my first high school English paper came back with a well-deserved C! Somehow, despite this feedback, or maybe because of it, I stuck with English

and eventually chose it as my college major. It was a struggle. How could I say anything new about a poem that had been famous for centuries? Never one to keep names straight, I had an awful time with big novels. After four years of hair-pulling all-nighters, medical school came as a blessed relief. I had a human anatomy coloring book and a stack of flash cards, and nary an essay to write.

Four years later, I started my pediatric training at Boston City Hospital. Joel Alpert, the visionary chairman of Pediatrics, declared that while the Children's Hospital across town specialized in curing cancer, at Boston City, "Poverty is our cancer." Energized by this challenge, I dove into my work as an intern, which consisted of looking up the latest vital signs and blood test results and repeating them on demand. By the end of three years, having mastered the mechanics of hospital pediatrics, I was all set to start curing poverty, without a clue as to how to do it.

Taking advantage of my bewilderment, the then chief of Developmental and Behavioral Pediatrics, Barry Zuckerman, talked me into yet three more years of training, as a fellow in DBPeds. It was, he pitched, a chance to read and think, catch up on sleep, start a family, and learn, finally, to understand children. The fellowship was, in fact, all of those things.

Barry shared the leadership of his division with Margot Kaplan-Sanoff, a professor of early childhood education, and the trainees included both doctors and masters-level early childhood students. We saw patients together and learned from each other. Implicit in this plan was the idea that pediatricians needed to broaden their view to encompass education, developmental psychology, and public health. This was the incubator for Reach Out and Read.

Down the street from my apartment was a little bookstore where one day I found a copy of Jim Trelease's *Read-Aloud Handbook*. Soon after that, for a noon-time talk, I picked a couple of my favorite picture books and read them out loud to my fellow docs. It was, some said, the best lecture of the year. Working with an early childhood educator, with Barry's encouragement, I wrote a small grant to buy books for the waiting room. First one child would come over for a story, then another and another; parents started reading to their babies.

We brought the books back to the exam rooms and noted what happened when the doctor held out a bright new board book to a young baby; we listened to parents who talked, for the first time, about their aspirations for their young children's education. One mother told me, "By my reading to her, I believe she'll be a reader; and if she's a reader, she could be a writer; she could be a doctor; she could be anything."

> A joyful relationship to books is part of what it means to be healthy.

The intensity of that mother's desire convinced me that I was on to something big. Through her, and others like her, I discovered my true love of reading, not as an academic exercise or personal pleasure, but as a way to make the everyday business of caring for young children more meaningful. From the start, Reach Out and Read was grounded in a simple idea: that a joyful relationship to books is part of what it means to be healthy. This would have remained simply a good idea, but for the work of colleagues like Perri Klass, Pam High, and Alan Mendelsohn, and of like-minded co-workers, volunteers, and community leaders too numerous to name. Their energy, creativity, and perseverance built the program and power it to this day. We haven't cured poverty yet, but we are working on it, one page at a time.

● ● ● ● ●

Robert Needlman, M.D., co-founded Reach Out and Read in 1989. Today, some 12,000 doctors in nearly 5,000 clinics and offices in all 50 states participate, with affiliates in Italy, Germany, Haiti, and elsewhere. In 2007, Reach Out and Read was awarded a UNESCO Confucius Prize. In 2013, the organization received the first David M. Rubenstein Prize, awarded by the U.S. Library of Congress for a groundbreaking or sustained record of advancement of literacy. Needlman is a professor of pediatrics at Case Western Reserve University. He sees patients at MetroHealth Medical Center, Cleveland's county hospital.

Robert L. Green

Dreaming New Realities: Literacy and Learning

*I*t was my older sister Lethia who first led me to the portals that enabled me to begin to understand the world—its realities and its dreams. I was three years old and the portals were books.

During my pre-school years and my primary school education, all six of

my older brothers and sister showered me with books. My parents encouraged them to promote reading in our Detroit home. My parents, who had married in their native Georgia and moved to the Motor City, dreamed of success for their sons and daughters and knew that a good education was the key to that kind of life.

My father never made it past the fourth grade; my mother was in school until the ninth grade. However, they valued education and made it clear to us that educated blacks would have far more opportunities in life. They made sure that we completed our homework and were provided with supplies and books— and not just the textbooks required by schools. In addition, they made it clear that they had high expectations and that we all needed to adopt high standards for ourselves.

I embraced those standards. Reading further enhanced my sense of self-worth. My fourth-grade teacher was so impressed with my reading skills that he once had me read a lengthy book passage before all my classmates. Early on, I shared my parents' expectation that I would grow up to become a successful adult.

But during those formative years, I also learned about discrimination and the barriers I would face. I learned about racism by reading Richard Wright's *Black Boy* and *Native Son* at the age of nine. A year later, I witnessed discrimination in the form of segregation when I traveled with my father to Memphis to attend a national meeting of the Church of God in Christ.

By the time I read Langston Hughes' *A Dream Deferred* at age 12, I was already beginning to think I might become an agent for change.

I met one of the world's greatest champions for social justice, Dr. Martin Luther King, Jr., while pursuing a college education. I had been drafted in January 1954 and was serving at the Army hospital at the Presidio in San Francisco. I worked nights and pursued my undergraduate studies at San

Francisco State College during the day. I completed my two-year Army commitment in January 1956 and eventually took a part-time job as a prison guard at San Quentin and as a Yellow Cab driver on the night shift as I continued my education.

On June 27, 1956, I learned that Dr. King would be speaking that night at the NAACP national convention in San Francisco. King had generated national and international attention for his leadership of the Montgomery Bus Boycott. I was an admirer. I drove the cab to the conference site and worked my way in to hear him speak. When he completed his address, I waited patiently among the throng of other admirers, drew up close to him, and extended my hand.

"I'm Robert L. Green," I said. "I want to get to know you."

I pursued my Ph.D. studies diligently but I kept in contact with Dr. King and his team of advisors at the Southern Christian Leadership Conference (SCLC) by writing letters. I had obtained my doctorate in educational psychology in December 1962, and Michigan State University hired me in January 1963. This was all due to the power of literacy invested in me at a very young age by my family.

I was concerned about the education of black boys and girls. I spoke out against school book publishing policies that limited the expectations of young black children. At a 1963 conference of publishers of elementary school books at Michigan State, I asked executives how black children could have a positive vision of themselves and their future when they were not even represented in the Dick and Jane stories that introduced them to reading.

> Reading helped me realize my dreams and I continue to work to help us achieve the society of Dr. King's dream.

Dwight Follett, chairman of the Follett Corporation, a major academic book publisher, responded to the message. Despite his fear that he would lose business in Southern school districts, he decided to include black characters in elementary school readers. Later, a number of other national publishers followed his lead.

I was a member of the MSU faculty in the spring of 1965 when I arranged to bring Dr. King to Michigan State. Thousands filled an auditorium for the address. After the speech, as I rode with him to the airport, he said: "You ought to consider working with us in the South."

Subsequently, I met with MSU President John Hannah and obtained a leave of absence. I joined SCLC in September 1965 and reported directly to Dr. King. At that time, whites in the South denied all blacks the right to vote regardless of their education level; but officially, whites claimed they were disqualifying only those who could not read and write.

Initially, Dr. King wanted me to provide instruction in reading and writing to semi-literate blacks to enable them to pass pre-vote literacy tests. He also wanted me to help build bridges to other scholars who might be able to help the Civil Rights campaign.

"Activism must be combined with education," Dr. King said, signaling the importance of my involvement. It was a phrase he would frequently invoke.

Dr. King demonstrated his devotion to learning by creating the Citizenship Education Program (CEP) and he later appointed me to head CEP in September 1965. After returning to Michigan State, I wrote a grant proposal that generated funding in 1967 to launch the SCLC's literacy project, designed to promote adult education as well as student achievement. King was one of the most literate and one of the most well-read persons I've ever known.

As a young professor, I continued to be informed and empowered by books. For example, *Dark Ghetto: Dilemmas of Social Change*, a 1965 book by Kenneth B. Clark, motivated me to write my 1977 bestseller *The Urban Challenge—Poverty and Race*. Clark and King were close friends.

In the decades since, I have authored and co-authored numerous books, served as a college dean and university president, and provided consulting services to public school districts nationwide. Reading helped me realize my dreams and I continue to work to help us achieve the society of Dr. King's dream.

● ● ● ● ●

Robert L. Green, Ph.D., is a former president of the University of the District of Columbia and former dean of the College of Urban Development at Michigan State University. He is now a dean and professor emeritus at MSU. From 1965–1967, Dr. Green worked for Dr. Martin Luther King, Jr., as the education director of the Southern Christian Leadership Conference. The author of many books and articles, Dr. Green is co-author of *Expect the Most—Provide the Best*, a book that examines the impact of expectations and innovation on education. He has worked on school reform efforts in Memphis, Detroit, Las Vegas, and Portland, Oregon. In addition, he has provided staff development for many public school districts and he promotes literacy and high expectations for early learners nationwide.

Awele Makeba

My Storytelling Destiny

"*L* isten up baby, this is a story you won't hear in school," Daddy would begin as he wove stories from his repertoire of family lore and historical accounts of the African American Freedom Movement. He would also spin tall tales while driving down south from St. Louis, Missouri, to Meridian, Mississippi,

to visit Bigmama Alice, my great-grandmother, and other relatives. Daddy would bring his stories to life with sound effects, emotions, and attitude as well as movements and gestures (yes, while driving!). Mesmerized by the telling, I would ask, "Daddy is *THAT* true?" "Oh, yeah, baby, dat's TRUE!" he would say, grinning ear-to-ear, showing all 32 pearly whites in the rearview mirror. I'd smile back, my eyes twinkling with excitement. Mama would then swat Daddy's shoulder, laughing between her words, "Stop lying to that girl!" This was our storytelling ritual.

My mother introduced me to the first book that I fell in love with, a royal blue over-sized book of *Mother Goose Nursery Rhymes.* Mama would point to a rhyme and I would "read" it, and it wasn't long before I had memorized the rhymes through rhythm, repetition, and our daily reading ritual. I learned lots of words reading my *Mother Goose Nursery Rhymes* book over and over again before Kindergarten. Every week, mom and I would visit the public library to check out books and read to discover our favorites. By the time I entered first grade, I was reading; as a result, my first grade teacher used to record me reading stories for our classroom's listening center.

My mom was told more than once during her parent-teacher conferences: "Your daughter is very animated. She is a talker! She is always telling stories. Sometimes she is telling stories when she should be working on her assignment." Little did they know I was on the path to becoming a storyteller like my father and Grandma Ruth. Destiny had called and I had responded. I had accepted the quest.

Grandma Ruth read the family Bible and would tell me stories about her daily adventures, bringing to life the characters from the Bible as well as the folks she'd met on the bus, from her work, in her church—you name it. Her gift was recreating dialogue and making voices resonate in your mind long after the telling. She played with intonation and inflection and painted pictures with her words, taking you to the various settings while highlighting the most important point of the story with delicious details.

I got to hear all of this from the best seat in the house, Grandma Ruth's lap, my head nestled in her soft bosom. Oh, what a precious gift she passed on to me! She had longed to be in school when she was a child but, having to work in the fields, didn't make it past fourth grade. Still, like my father, she was a powerful storyteller, and she was my mentor; she gave me a vision of what was possible during storytelling. She modeled the tools of the teller and she, like my father, modeled her knowledge about the power of story. I'll never forget the first time that I saw her testify at church. "I got a testimony this morning," Grandma Ruth began, and then revealed how one person's story can guide us all through a storm to help us find our inner strength.

As an early reader, I soon discovered that I had friends in books, too—characters whom I could always depend on—characters who looked like me, sounded like me, and who experienced struggles similar to the African American families I knew. My storybook friends, like my real friends and family, exhibited resiliency, perseverance, pride, and the beauty of our culture. Eloise Greenfield's books mirrored back life that I knew starting with *She Come Bringing Me That Baby Girl*. These were my very thoughts when my little brother was born. I especially loved the Logan Family series given to us by Mildred Taylor. I could walk in the shoes of Cassie and experience her sense of agency. Sometimes I *was* Cassie.

> The oral tradition has taken me around the world to teach through the power of story.

The Logan family's history of struggle and resistance as *upstanders* (people who stand up against injustice) was the same history that my father used to teach me about and sometimes I would overhear Bigmama Alice, Granddaddy Joe, and my parents discussing when "children were not meant to be seen nor heard." They would whisper about voting rights, freedom fighters, church burnings, Goodman, Cheney, and Schwerner, the Student Nonviolent Coordinating Committee, Ella Baker, and Dr. Martin Luther King, Jr. The Cheney family were Bigmama Alice's neighbors. Father was right. Teachers didn't tell the significant stories that he had shared with me nor did they teach about the courageous foot soldiers who looked

Open a World of Possible: Real Stories About the Joy and Power of Reading © 2014 Scholastic

like me and who helped to advance democracy in the U.S. But I could read this history in children's literature and my dad, who was a thespian, took me to see plays that had become classics set in this historical context. It was performance as text.

The oral tradition has taken me around the world to teach through the power of story, share my cultural heritage, promote my love of good books, and bear witness to our common humanity.

I am Awele, daughter of Alice, granddaughter of two Ruths, great-granddaughter of Bigmama Alice and M'dear Corrine, and great great-granddaughter of Anna. It is my hope to find my best possible self as I teach through the power of story!

● ● ● ● ●

Awele (ah WAY lay) Makeba has mesmerized audiences all over the world from Mississippi to Alaska, from the Kennedy Center for the Performing Arts in Washington, D.C. to Hawaii in cultural centers, museums, universities, festivals, libraries, churches, prisons, juvenile halls, schools, and TED-Ed Talks. She has taught through the power of story in Russia, Australia, Austria, Canada, Costa Rica, Cuba, France, Russia, Taiwan, and Suriname on a U.S. Department of State Tour. She is featured in award-winning CDs, including *Tell That Tale Again, This Land Is Your Land, Trailblazers: African American in the California Gold Rush*, and *The Undiscovered Explorer: Imaging York*. She is the recipient of the 2014 District Leadership Award for her speaker series Race Matters: Putting Race on the Table in the Oakland Unified School District where she is a drama/literacy intervention specialist. For more information, go to www.awele.com.

Pat Mora

Bookjoy!

The sound of the desert wind carries me back to our rock house in El Paso, Texas. Conversations and teasing in English and Spanish were the braided music in our childhood home. Nighttime stories comforted my three siblings and me. Words soaked into us—moon, *luna*; star, *estrella*. In time, books extended our verbal experiences. Magic.

I wouldn't be me without books. Early on, I discovered their pleasure and power. All my reading was in English, though my aunt and grandmother read their prayer books in Spanish. Neither of my parents had the opportunity to go to college, but they invested in books. Among my favorites were the Childcraft series, particularly the poetry book.

When I was home sick, I'd pull down that orange volume and savor "Old King Cole," "Daffy-Down-Dilly," and "Lady-Bird, Lady-Bird." Opening other books, in time, I rode in elegant carriages, learned with Clara Barton, traveled to Russia, heard the wind on a faraway prairie, tasted sorghum molasses, and solved mysteries with Nancy Drew—all through black symbols on a white page. Such wonder.

Early in my life, books became a rich and dominant thread in my family fabric, my memories. Reading was part of my school memories, too—waiting in anticipation for a teacher to read aloud the next section of *"B" Is for Betsy*, memorizing poems the nuns assigned year after year, rhythms that are still part of me. Through reading, I'd discovered, and still discover, that sitting still at home or in a plane, I can shed my physical self, forget about me, and enter a place or ideas created by a fellow human I'll probably never meet. Reading expands me.

When my three children were little, I experienced the intimate joy of sharing a habit I loved—reading! How we reveled in Mother Goose and books by Beatrix Potter and Richard Scarry. Now, I watch my adult children when, with a smile, they hold their old, worn books. Each thinks, "This is mine. I loved it best." They savor book memories, the books that were/are their steady friends. That private family joy prompted me years ago to write my own children's books, to hand other children some reading pleasure. I imagined a young stranger opening one of my books. Now, my daughter, Libby, who writes with me, also visualizes an unknown reader. Libby and I laugh together as we revise and revise to create "bookjoy."

Because I'd grown up bilingual, I've reached out to children in English and

Open a World of Possible: Real Stories About the Joy and Power of Reading © 2014 Scholastic

Spanish. Slowly, I began to realize that not all our children were equally valued—many children didn't see the details of their daily lives affirmed on the page. I realized that growing up a reader, I'd never read about a family who spoke two or more languages, or who enjoyed cheese enchiladas on Friday night. What we called American children's literature wasn't a balanced sampling of wonderful voices and traditions, of our plurality. I discovered how parents who spoke many other languages hadn't had my extensive literacy experience in English; indeed, many felt ashamed of not speaking English. Many low-income parents, including English-speaking parents, didn't feel welcomed at schools, libraries, and museums nor had they been coached to support their children's reading habit.

My reading life has been long and rich. Reading helps me to understand my country and my world—our cultural, religious, and personal complexities.

In 1996, I founded a family literacy initiative to honor *all* children and to share bookjoy with them. It's often known as *Día*, which means "day" in Spanish. Día, this daily commitment, significantly altered my life and has, I hope, enriched the lives of many committed literacy supporters. By 2018, children of color will be the majority in our country. Together, all of us who value all our children can work together to create a diverse reading nation, proclaiming again and again that literacy is essential in a democracy.

> Together, all of us who value all our children can work together to create a diverse reading nation, proclaiming again and again that literacy is essential in a democracy.

I now have a *grand* baby, a granddaughter, and I'm savoring the opportunity to share stories and books with Bonny, to continue a cherished family tradition. I want Bonny and all our children to be anticipating the next story, their next book. All our children deserve *alegría en los libros*, bookjoy.

• • • • •

Pat Mora is the author of more than 40 books, and has published poetry books for adults, teens, and children. *Zing! Seven Creativity Practices for Educators and Students* is one of her books of nonfiction. Her more than 30 children's books include books in bilingual formats and Spanish editions. An educator and literacy advocate, Mora founded *Día, El día de los niños, El día de los libros*, a year-long family initiative that honors children and connects them with bookjoy. Annually, across the country, April book fiestas reach out creatively to all children of all cultures and languages.

Nell K. Duke

A Passion for Social Justice

By far, the important book in my life has been *Wild Violets* by Phyllis Green, a book I read over and over again in my elementary-school years. The protagonist of the story is a fourth-grade girl named Ruthie, described as follows:

> *Ruthie was probably the least important person in Miss Farmer's class. And she was surely the poorest and most funny-looking. She was too poor to have hot water and soap to wash her straight, straw-thick hair, too poor for toothpaste to brush her crooked teeth, too poor even to wear the milky-brown, thick stockings that were held up by garters and that all the other girls hated and tugged at . . . Most of the time Ruthie had no lunch to bring to school at all . . . Ruthie always pretended she was eating so Teacher wouldn't notice and become upset and write notes to her father. She had an old, wrinkled lunch bag she had taken from the wastebasket, and every lunch hour she got it out and wiggled it around to make everyone think she was eating, too.*

Reading about this child had a profound effect on me. It was not as though I hadn't been exposed to poverty. We weren't poor ourselves—though I wouldn't say we were entirely financially secure either—but the elementary school I attended drew, in part, from one of the poor neighborhoods in town. There were many students who got "hot lunch" for free. I remember students taunting one another that they got their clothes or shoes from Kmart; I remember some didn't appear to get new clothes or shoes from anywhere. Yet it was *Wild Violets* that really revealed poverty to me. Sometimes it takes the distance of a book to help you see what's right in front of you.

My concern with childhood poverty continued. In my dissertation, I examined the literacy environments and experiences offered to first-grade children in high-poverty versus wealthy school districts in the greater Boston area. Differences between the two were legion. Children in the high-poverty school districts had access to fewer books; the books were older and included a narrower range of types. The walls of high-poverty classrooms included less print, and teachers referred to that print less often. Children in high-poverty school districts had fewer opportunities to experience instruction that involved reading and writing about science and social studies topics, had fewer opportunities to write for an audience beyond the teacher, spent much more time completing worksheets, copying, and taking dictation, and had fewer opportunities to actually read books. In *Wild Violets*, Ruthie was assigned the role of the maid in the school play, while wealthier peers had more coveted parts. My elementary-age self felt the injustice of that acutely, and in my dissertation work, so many years later, I felt that injustice again.

> Our celebration of reading must involve the ongoing mission to give all children the opportunity to read and to become lifelong readers.

This anthology celebrates the joy and possibilities of reading. I absolutely support that. But part of the celebration must involve the ongoing mission to give all children the opportunity to read and to become lifelong readers. I wish that future for Ruthie, for Rayshon, for Roberto, and for everyone.

• • • • •

Nell K. Duke, Ed.D., is a professor of literacy, language, and culture and faculty affiliate in the combined program in education and psychology at the University of Michigan. She is also a member of the International Reading Association Literacy Research Panel. Duke received her bachelor's degree from Swarthmore College and her master's and doctoral degrees from Harvard University. Her award-winning research focuses on early literacy development, particularly among children living in poverty. Her specific areas of expertise include development of informational reading and writing in young children, comprehension development, and instruction in early schooling, and issues of equity in literacy education. Duke's books include *Beyond Bedtime Stories: A Parent's Guide to Promoting Reading, Writing, and Other Literacy Skills From Birth to 5, 2nd Edition*, and the forthcoming *Inside Information: Developing Powerful Readers and Writers of Informational Text Through Project-Based Instruction*.

Stephanie Harvey

First Lines and the Power of Books

"**B**orn at sea in the teeth of a gale, the sailor was a dog." Now that's a first line for you. Dickens' "It was the best of times, it was the worst of times" has nothing on Margaret Wise Brown's *The Sailor Dog*. "Scuppers" sailed from port to port, toting a hobo stick, exactly like the one I shouldered on warm summer evenings as I slipped off to my secret hideout on the northern shore of Nepco Lake in central Wisconsin where I grew up.

I love first lines. I'm not great at hanging out with a book for 50 pages to get into it. I like being roped in straight out of the gate. "Mashed potatoes are to give everybody enough." I'm quite confident that the very first line of the very first book I remember, Ruth Krauss's *A Hole Is to Dig,* is the reason I devour the Thanksgiving mashed potatoes and gravy before even tasting the turkey.

". . . if I ran the zoo," said young Gerald McGrew. "I'd make a few changes, that's what I'd do."

Dr. Seuss understood that it is easier to change things when we're in charge. The primary reason people want control may well be so they can make their own changes.

The opening lines I absorbed from my early reading seem to have influenced my outward life. I travel to exotic places, eat dessert first if I want, and work to change the status quo. The opening lines from my later reading seem to have shaped my inner life.

When I look back on my childhood I wonder how I managed to survive at all. It was, of course, a miserable childhood: the happy childhood is hardly worth your while. Worse than the ordinary miserable childhood is the miserable Irish childhood, and worse yet is the miserable Irish Catholic childhood.

Like many WWII-generation men, my father didn't look back. He didn't talk about his perennially out-of-work father or the impoverished childhood he endured as a result. Frank McCourt provided the insights that enabled me to understand my dad's Irish-Catholic heritage and his childhood rooted in poverty.

When he was nearly 13, my brother Jem got his arm badly broken at the elbow . . . When enough years had gone by to enable us to look back on them, we sometimes discussed the events leading to his accident. I maintain that the Ewells started it all, but Jem, who was four years my senior, said it started long before that. He said it began the summer Dill came to us, when Dill first gave us the idea of making Boo Radley come out.

Harper Lee taught me more about the clandestine life of the boy with Down Syndrome at the end of my block than any psychology class. By reading *To Kill a Mockingbird*, I came to understand that isolating people who are different builds fear and loathing. I also learned that inviting them in changes everything. Once we kids on the block got the nerve to break through that isolation and invite Davey to come out and play baseball, he turned out, just like Boo, to be the kindest, most special kid in the neighborhood.

Hanging out with books changes us. Books shape who we are and who we become. Too many kids today have limited access to books. The more impoverished the home, the fewer the books. Without books, kids might not run away with Scuppers, as I did, or learn, with Frank McCourt's help, to understand their families, or dream with Dr. Seuss of running things to change them. We need to flood schools with books. After receiving a treasure trove of donated books for her Title 1 classroom, Cheyenne, a Chicago fourth grader, wrote, "Thank you for the books. We really appreciate the books. Now that you have given us the books, people have been checking them out left and right and there are barely any left. People have been fighting over books, that's how serious it is."

Although I am a pacifist at heart, if you're going to fight over something, what could be more urgent and essential than a struggle for your share of books? Living with books creates endless possibilities. Let's make those possibilities real for all kids; let's get books into kids' hands and send them sailing with their own beloved first lines.

Hanging out with books changes us. Books shape who we are and who we become.

• • • • •

Stephanie Harvey has spent more than 40 years teaching and learning about reading and writing. An elementary and special education teacher for 15 years, she now works as a staff developer, educational consultant, and author. Harvey works around the world with educators, schools, and districts to implement progressive literacy practices. Her work focuses on comprehension instruction, informational text literacy, and inquiry-based learning. Her books and resources include *Strategies That Work, Comprehension and Collaboration, Nonfiction Matters,* The Comprehension Toolkit series, and the National Geographic Ladders series. Insatiably curious about student thinking, Harvey is a teacher first and foremost and continues to work in schools on a regular basis, savoring any time spent with kids.

Kimberly N. Parker

Black Boys Who Read

*T*hey wait at the door, hoodies turned up to block the cold from their faces, sweatpants bagging at their ankles over sneakers. One leans vertically against the doorjamb, looking through the window and impatiently turning at the locked door. Another sits, balanced precariously,

impossibly, on a basketball, rolling slowly back and forth in an irregular rhythm. As I barrel around the corner, they turn in some sort of unplanned symmetry towards me. I exhale in relief that eight of the ten have shown up on a Saturday morning, apologize to them for being late, and ask the question that I've been turning around in my own head for the week since we last met.

"So, what did you think of how it all ended?" And as their eyes light up and we all spill inside the classroom together, they can't unwrap their words fast enough as we pull together a circle of chairs, push aside desks, sip our collection of drinks and snacks, and dig into the fate of Bobby in Angela Johnson's *The First Part Last*.

Since I began teaching, I never believed the narratives that proliferate about young men of color and reading. Every single young black man I have known enjoyed reading once I took the time to get to know them and to figure out what they were interested in—sports, music, action, or nonfiction. They were, of course, more apt to stick with that reading if I also created a climate that allowed them time to settle in and read. And, if they could read in the company of their friends? Well, then, they might just keep reading forever. What they most wanted, overwhelmingly, was to read books that allowed them to either see themselves within texts or to dream themselves into the texts. Many had never read a book where the main character shared their racial or ethnic

Reading allows black boys the ability to dream, to think, to feel, to love, and to be free.

background, was multi-faceted, and came from a different social class. These characteristics they desired were the ones that I sought to get into their hands. It was not unreasonable for me to think that their lives would be reflected in the texts they were either required to read or that they opted to read on their own. It was not impossible for me to find those texts, to gather them together, and to talk about the connections books hold for all of us.

That is why they wait—as patiently as young people can wait on a Saturday morning—for me and this informal book club we've organized. It began as an initiative to give struggling readers some more practice with reading, but it quickly morphed into reading lots of culturally relevant texts that appealed to them, spending some time talking about the books, and building a literacy community to which—once they belonged—they retained membership long after I stopped being their official teacher. Over the years, I've convened different varieties of these book clubs, all with the same goals: to pull together black and brown boys to read high-quality books that allow them to see themselves in all of the nuanced, beautiful possibilities. That is what reading makes possible: reading allows black boys the ability to dream, to think, to feel, to love, and to be free.

● ● ● ● ●

Kimberly N. Parker, Ph.D., teaches English at Cambridge Rindge and Latin School in Cambridge, Massachusetts. Her teaching and learning interests focus on the reading experiences of young black men and how to build positive literacy environments for them within classrooms. Parker is also the current secondary representative-at-large for the National Council of Teachers of English.

Pam Allyn

How Reading Made Me Strong

*T*he first time I read *Anne of Green Gables* by Lucy Maud Montgomery,
I turned the last page, took a deep breath, and started it all over again.
I think I did that ten times before my mother pulled it from my hands and
put the second book in the series in its place. What a miracle! That the

adventure continued, to know that more would
come! While Anne's hair was bright red (or "auburn"
as she liked to hope) and mine was brown (or "ash
blond" as I liked to hope), I felt we were the same
inside. We both had that same fierceness that made
our emotions big and strong but our hearts also so
easily broken. Anne met her friend Diana and in an
instant, in her own storytelling, claimed Diana as her
"kindred spirit." Anne was a writer, a poet, a teller of
stories. Diana, of the shiny black hair and bright blue eyes, became a kindred
spirit because Anne told the story that made it so. Anne, an orphan when
she arrived on Prince Edward Island, needed to be strong, resilient, and
independent. But through her storytelling, she made the characters beloved
to one another and turned loneliness into community.

I also read every one of Louisa May Alcott's Little Women books and
C.S. Lewis's The Chronicles of Narnia many times over. I loved how Jo cut
off her hair to support her family, and how she found a space for herself in
her attic to write her stories while also being the best friend to her cherished
sister Beth who suffered so. I loved how Lucy was so curious, going through
the wardrobe door into the new world of Narnia, and finding her way all
alone. Yet also being a friend to Aslan, stroking his poor head even when he
was stripped of his glorious golden mane. All these girls were like mirrors
and windows: mirrors of myself as I was, sometimes lonely, sometimes fierce,
and windows into the worlds of girls I was longing to become: stronger,
fiercer, braver, yet also surrounded by love and friendship.

Many years later, I was reading aloud E.B. White's *Charlotte's Web* to a
group of girls in Kenya. By the age of 12, Diana had already led an extremely
hard life, growing up in a place where girls do not often go to high school,
where lack of access to literacy prevents girls from achieving their dreams.
When we got to the part where Fern stands up to her father, demanding he

Open a World of Possible: Real Stories About the Joy and Power of Reading © 2014 Scholastic

save the baby pig Wilbur, Diana leaned forward, rapt. She said, "I've never seen a girl stand up to a man like that before." Out of this response, I created the organization LitWorld which has initiated LitClubs all over the world to bring girls out of isolation and into safe networks of readers, where books put into a girl's hand change her life, as they did mine.

Anne, Jo, and Lucy opened up worlds of possibility for themselves and for me through their stories—the stories Anne told to Diana that forged their friendship, the stories Jo told to her sisters to keep them strong, and the stories Lucy and Mr. Tumnus told to each other: a relationship that would warm up cold and bitter Narnia and make magic possible, even in the most frozen places. That incredible opening of worlds of possibility continues today, as Fern speaks up to her father and shows my Diana in Nairobi an entirely different path for the future—so that from a very hard place of beginning, her heart and spirit, too, can soar into possibility.

> I created LitWorld to bring girls out of isolation and into safe networks of readers, where books put into a girl's hand change her life, as they did mine.

• • • • •

Pam Allyn is a literacy advocate and internationally renowned educational leader. She is the author of many books, including *Best Books for Boys* and *What to Read When*. She founded and leads LitWorld (www.litworld.org), a 501(c)(3) organization advocating for literacy as a human right that belongs to every child.

Rebecca Constantino

Reading, Our Beloved Companion

*S*olace. Escape. Adventure. Friendship. In a home where a single mom was raising five children, a sister had run away for a time, a brother was involved with drugs, as the youngest, I was often alone and frequently sad. Books, reading, and stories became my companion. I was very fortunate to be raised by a reader.

Print of all kind filled my house. Almost every room had a bookcase with books three deep. Books lined the stairs and trailed down the hallways. Magazines subscriptions were a staple, not a luxury. I had access to Judy Blume, Agatha Christie, and Shakespeare. As a young child, I curled up with *The New Yorker*, starting with the cartoons and graduating to "Goings On About Town." With multiple encyclopedia sets and decades worth of *National Geographics*, I traveled the world while sitting in my upstairs hallway. Often, I would grab my bike and a book and take off to a park to sit by the lake and read. From age seven to 14, I had a morning paper route. After delivering it all over the neighborhood, I would read the entire newspaper from front to back. Many of those mornings, I was already bleary-eyed because I had stayed up too late reading.

Reading created the person I am. Lifelong friendships were struck over a conversation on a bus about a book I was reading. Today, I still relate to people based on the books that they've read. Reading is my constant pleasure and escape. I never leave home without something to read.

Eventually, my reading path led me to graduate studies where my area of study was access to books among under-served children and school libraries. My research showed the utter lack of reading material among children living in poverty. Not by design but as a response to necessity, I started a nonprofit organization called Access Books that stocks school libraries in the greater Los Angeles area. The formula for this program is simple. Donors provide money to purchase books, volunteers refurbish the library and catalogue the books, and children have access to books they would not normally have based on the current funding and priorities in our nation.

One Saturday, at a school library we were refurbishing, I got to know nine-year-old Marcus a bit. Feisty, inquisitive, and a little domineering, he followed me around all day. He craved constant reassurance that he was doing things right. As with all our volunteers, Marcus took home a book. He attended a school with one of the most vibrant, involved, and in-tune principals I have ever encountered. The principal revealed to me that Marcus had a challenging life. His mother worked on the streets and the home was chaotic and violent. There was rampant drug use and itinerant father figures. Marcus was known for his outbursts at school. He had few friends and was withdrawn most days. The principal made an early pact with Marcus—when he felt stressed like he might "bust out of his body," he could come to the office and sit with a book. He was there a lot.

I was spending time in that school's office doing follow-up research and would see Marcus there often. I brought him more books. He started requesting *Clifford* so I found a set for him. He moved onto *Captain Underpants* but he was most enthralled with the Diary of a Wimpy Kid series. He did not have any room in his apartment, so he had his own little bookcase in the principal's office. One day, we started chatting and I asked him what he liked about reading, about books. He paused a while and responded, "Well, first off, these books are the only thing that I know are just mine. They don't belong to nobody else. I never had that feeling before." After a moment of silence he added, "I guess mostly, books make me laugh, they make me forget about stuff. I guess they just make me feel good."

I knew exactly what he meant.

Reading is my constant pleasure and escape. I never leave home without something to read.

Not long after that conversation, the principal let me know that the Department of Children and Family Services had notified the school that Marcus was to be removed from his home and placed in foster care. Scared and uncertain, he asked the social worker, "Do I get to take my books?"

From the outside, Marcus, an African American boy from Watts, and me, a white girl from the suburbs, seemed to have nothing in common. The truth, though, is that we are really a lot alike.

● ● ● ● ●

Rebecca Constantino, founder of Access Books, holds a Ph.D. in Language, Literacy, and Learning. She has published articles and books in the areas of literacy development, equity in education, urban schools, and cultural perspectives of language acquisition. Constantino has been involved in language and literacy development programs in Russia, South Africa, and Eastern Europe. While serving as a foster parent, she adopted two daughters and later hatched one son.

ReLeah Cossett Lent

Danger: Literature Thieves

I love words, and have since I was old enough to find magic in mere squiggles on a page. As I grew older, words became increasingly important to my development in every way—my intellectual and emotional growth, my widening perspective of people and places, my very sense of self. It came as no surprise that

I eventually became a book-thumping English teacher; for my part, I could hardly believe I was actually being paid to deal in words and, what's more, to share with students the transformational power of reading.

As a new teacher, I must admit that I often exhibited more naïveté than many of my middle school students. I would have said, for example, that reading was an inalienable right, a sort of subset of the pursuit of happiness. As a result, students who were heretofore not interested in reading became positively addicted to the mysterious worlds created by Piers Anthony or the real-world events in the lives of Judy Blume's teens. Eventually, many of these kids developed a hunger for words and, together, we sated our appetites at every opportunity. During this halcyon period, it was simply unthinkable that anyone would attempt to steal books from my students by burying them under a shroud of shame.

"Inappropriate, dark, vulgar, obscene." The slurs echoed from local newspaper articles and church pulpits, often with the accusers never having read the entire works on trial. What started as a complaint from one parent about Robert Cormier's *I Am the Cheese*, a brilliant young adult novel that prompted my seventh-graders to engage in deep thinking and thoughtful discussion, eventually became an internationally-publicized censorship battle. The offended parent was not satisfied when I offered her child an alternate selection; she insisted that no child should be allowed to read the novel, even students whose parents had given them permission, in writing, to do so. Like a nasty virus, the complaint spread to other books and other classrooms. Students were questioned by parents who feared they were being sullied by language or ideas in print, teachers were threatened and slandered, and books themselves became targets of ridicule and abuse.

In the end, more than 60 books were banned in Bay County, Florida, many of which had existed in the canon for years, such as *Hamlet* and *Great Expectations*. Finally, when headlines such as "Redneck Riviera Bans Shakespeare" began to have a big impact on the county's reputation and, thus, its tourism potential, the classics were reinstated. It took a lawsuit, however, to bring *I Am the Cheese* back to the classroom.

By then, the damage was done, and it was just as ugly as the destruction of a hard-cover copy of *I Am The Cheese* set aflame and photographed by the *Washington Post* as a dramatic illustration of the events taking place in our district. Sadly, most teachers from this small Florida town, chilled by the devastating effects of censorship, removed all of Cormier's books from their shelves and thought twice before allowing any young adult novel back into the curriculum. I wish I could say that such sweeping censorship is an anomaly, but that would be untrue. Even today, books such as Mark Twain's *Huckleberry Finn*, Toni Morrison's *The Bluest Eye*, John Steinbeck's *Of Mice and Men* and, amazingly, even Dav Pilkey's *Captain Underpants*, have been banned in schools.

No doubt my contribution to this uplifting anthology strikes a pessimistic note and for that I apologize, but I know firsthand that reading can be a two-edged sword. It can cut to the heart and transform lives, but it can also frighten some into acting as literature thieves—and too often these perpetrators get away with the crime. If we do, indeed, believe in the power of reading, we must also believe that each of us has an obligation to protect that power so that it remains available to every person who seeks it.

> If we do, indeed, believe in the power of reading, we must also believe that each of us has an obligation to protect that power so that it remains available to every person who seeks it.

● ● ● ● ●

Now an international consultant, ReLeah Cossett Lent began her career as a teacher before becoming a founding member of a literacy project at the University of Central Florida, where she implemented leadership teams and professional learning communities statewide. The author of nine books including *Common Core CPR, Overcoming Textbook Fatigue,* and *Literacy Learning Communities,* she has also authored numerous journal articles and blogs. Lent is currently chair of NCTE's Standing Committee Against Censorship, and her book on censorship, *Keep Them Reading,* is influencing district policies around the country. Additionally, her work with Jimmy Santiago Baca, award-winning poet and writer, led to a book and CD for reaching at-risk students. Lent is the recipient of both NCTE's and ALA's Intellectual Freedom Awards. She was also honored with the PEN/Newman's Own First Amendment Award in 1999. In 2013, she received Wisconsin's Intellectual Freedom Award and Florida Council of Teachers of English President's Award. You can find her at www.releahlent.com.

Erin Gruwell

A Legacy Lives On

Words. My life has always been about words. When I was younger, I read words voraciously—learning their power, their persuasion, their passion. As an adult, I use words diplomatically, determinately, and deliberately to teach, to write, and to inspire.

I have always enjoyed reading, but as a teacher, I was able to watch the transformative powers a book can have on my students. The book that changed my life and the lives of many of my students was *Anne Frank: The Diary of a Young Girl*. I remember being afraid that my students would not understand the book's power because many of them had never opened a book, much less read one in its entirety. At the age of 14, they hated reading and thought all books were written by "dead white guys." Unlike me, most never sat on their daddy's lap and read bedtime stories. Unlike me, they did not have bookshelves lining their walls. And unlike me, they did not make trips to the local library or a bustling book store. Unfortunately, many of my students did not have books in their home, or even worse, did not have a father present to read to them.

I wanted my students to find their voice within the pages of Anne's diary, and perhaps be inspired to write their own. When I first presented the book to the class, however, I was met with resistance. Cynical students asked me, "Why do I have to read books about people who don't look like me, or talk like me, or come from where I come from?" In their minds, Anne Frank didn't come from their 'hood, and lived in a country they couldn't even identify on a map. Stumbling for an answer, I told my students, "You are much more similar than you are different."

Listening to the concerns of my students, I began to wonder, "How does the life and diary of a young Jewish girl in the Nazi-occupied Netherlands connect with the lives of my struggling students?"

I eventually found that, although my students' lives and Anne's life were not mirror images of each other, the same hatred and violence that surrounded Anne also surrounded my students in the neighborhoods of Long Beach, California. While their city may not have been occupied by the Nazi Regime, they were living in an undeclared warzone filled with gang violence and death. Many of my students had seen friends die due to senseless violence, while others had friends who were in jail for murder. These horrible atrocities connected my classroom to Anne's attic, and my students found that they could use more than bullets and fists to express themselves. Anne helped my students find their words, and I followed her idea and had them fill the pages of their own journals with their experiences and their secrets. I had hoped that one day their stories would inspire others to stop the hate and embrace love. Without the help of Anne Frank's diary, I fear that my students may have become just another statistic in the Long Beach records, case numbers that become buried and forgotten with no voice to tell their stories, rather than the wonderful individuals that I know and love today as the Freedom Writers.

> Reading allowed each of us to reach our prospective students, and reading allowed a legacy to live on!

Recently, I was invited with my former students, the Freedom Writers, to teach lessons at the Anne Frank House to teachers from around the globe. Although we spoke different languages, came from different countries, and had different students—we all shared a passion for reading, and the love for a certain book. I discovered that Anne Frank's book is one of the most read books in the world, and no matter what language her story has been translated to, her words transcend gender, race, and economics. Anne's story connected us and was the catalyst for us to instill the love of reading in our students—whomever and wherever they may be. Anne reminded us all, that "in spite of everything, I truly believe that people are good at heart." Reading allowed each of us to reach our prospective students, and reading allowed a legacy to live on!

● ● ● ● ●

Erin Gruwell is a teacher, an education activist, and the founder of the Freedom Writers. By fostering an educational philosophy that values and promotes diversity, she has transformed the lives of many troubled teens. Inspired by Anne Frank, Gruwell and her students captured their collective journey in *The Freedom Writers Diary*, the #1 *New York Times* bestseller. Their inspiring story was adapted into a critically acclaimed film starring two-time Academy Award winner Hilary Swank. While Gruwell has been credited with giving her students a "second chance," it was perhaps she who changed the most during her tenure at Wilson High School. She decided to channel her classroom experiences toward a broader cause, and today her impact as a teacher extends well beyond Room 203. Gruwell founded the Freedom Writers Foundation where she and some of the original Freedom Writers currently teach teachers around the world how to implement her innovative lesson plans in their own classrooms.

Sue Pon

Immigrant Women: Reading Toward Hope

O akland, California, is one of the most culturally diverse cities in the world. As the coordinator of the Oakland Family Literacy program, I have the good fortune of working with English-learning families from around the world who are learning to become literate in American society. These families enrich

my life and continually teach me not to take my own literacy for granted.

I am humbled by our most recent immigrants, by their resilience and determination to learn even when they may have no formal education and their own native language is not based on the Roman alphabet. Here are the stories of three courageous women, related by their teachers:

Samara, Age 20, Yemen (as told to Victoria Carpenter)

It felt like a small hurricane when Samara arrived each morning; black *hijab* billowing, shoulders weighted with straps of bags and packs, her three-year-old in tow lugging her own small backpack. Much to my frustration, Samara

and her daughter habitually arrived to class late and left early. She'd settle her daughter at childcare then make her way through the classroom to an empty seat, seemingly oblivious to the disruption her amiable arrival was causing—the whole chaotic process to be repeated in reverse later when she left early.

Victoria Carpenter

It was hard to be too angry with Samara; she was such a warm and funny person. But I still asked her more than once if she could be on time, and to please stay for the entire class, pointing out that she was missing an hour of instruction each day. When this general beseeching went nowhere, I took her aside, hoping for a more serious conversation where I might glean some deeper insight into her antics. Perhaps together we could come up with a remedy. The following is Samara's story.

Samara lived with her brother. He forbade her to leave the house without a male relative as chaperone, let alone go to school. He threatened that if she disobeyed, she and her young daughter would be sent back to Yemen.

Each morning, just after her brother left for work, Samara gathered up her daughter, bags, and books and stealthily left the house. She'd walk three blocks to catch the first bus, then another few blocks to catch the second that took her within walking distance of our class in Oakland's Chinatown. An hour and a half later, she would do the trip in reverse, anxiety propelling her to get home before her brother returned for lunch. It took her 50 minutes each way.

From then on, it seemed a small miracle that Samara and her daughter would arrive at all.

Halimo, 50, Somalia (as told to Audrey Sakai)

Despite living in a refugee camp in Kenya for 21 years, Halimo is a dignified and beautiful woman—tall, striking, and elegant, her clothes flowing around her. A widow with six children, Halimo arrived in Oakland in March 2012 without knowing any other Somalian families here. Her children range in age and attend elementary school, high school, and community college. Halimo studied Arabic for five years in a mosque in Somalia but never learned to read or write her mother tongue, Somali.

Audrey Sakai

I've never seen anyone so eager to learn. From her first day in class, Halimo was "drinking it in." Even during Ramadan, she came to class every day, all day, despite being weak from fasting. Halimo travels one hour each way on the bus, crisscrossing Oakland, to take her children and herself to class.

During her first month in class, Halimo learned to identify letters and to say their sounds. She carefully wrote the alphabet, filling an entire notebook. The second month, Halimo manipulated word cards, matching words with pictures. After two months, Halimo strung both words and pictures together into a sentence. When Halimo read her sentence, she couldn't contain herself and I could feel her adrenaline. Her face beamed, "I did it! I can actually read!" Halimo remembers that moment in October 2013, feeling "oh, happy."

Rafiqah, Age 26, Yemen (as told to Wendi Olson)

Rafiqah's four children attended elementary school, but growing up in Yemen, she had never been to school herself. Now 26 and living in a troubled Oakland neighborhood, Rafiqah walked her children and baby stroller across the freeway overpass and gathered in my Family Literacy classroom to chat with the other moms before the first bell rang. When I walked in the door, Rafiqah's children would look up and study me with big eyes. Rafiqah had apple cheeks and a lively, sonorous voice that rose above the others.

Wendi Olson

But her animation disappeared when English lessons began. Throughout September and October, she scowled in frustration as she tried to learn her first alphabet. One day, Rafiqah slammed her palm on the desk and said, "Teacher! ABC!" Her self-advocacy snapped me to attention. From then on, we opened each class with the alphabet song until she had it down.

Rafiqah sat with a group of traditional women in black *abayas* from her rural Yemeni village, but she stood out with her splashy-patterned *hijabs*. She had a fiery personality. In February, while the class made Valentine's Day cards, she ripped her red heart in half. In this way, I learned that her husband had abandoned her with six children, returning to Yemen to take advantage of the four-wife law.

But on Wednesday, November 7, 2012, she was ebullient. She met me at the door of the classroom with a big grin and her first English sentence.

"Happy Obama!" she said.

I gave her a high-five. "Happy Obama!"

Later in the year, while reading a picture book about Supreme Court Justice Sonia Sotomayor, she pointed excitedly at an illustration of a courtroom. "Me," she said. "Job." In this way, I learned that she dreamed of becoming a lawyer. If anyone has the drive to do so, Rafiqah does.

These women are not just learning for themselves, they are also learning for their families and for their communities. Becoming literate in American society empowers these mothers to support and to advocate for their children's education. As active parents, they are becoming important partners in their children's schools. Some are even becoming school leaders, improving education for all children. Becoming literate in American society empowers them to pursue their families' dreams, to persevere, and to press forward toward hope.

● ● ● ● ●

Sue Pon coordinates the Oakland Family Literacy program. The program provides skill development instruction to parents in the Oakland Unified School District, empowering them to support their children's academic progress and to develop family engagement and leadership skills in full-service community schools. Publications include *Sharing English Together*, an instructional English as a Second Language (ESL) DVD/workbook series featuring the daily lives of Oakland families learning together.

Marcus Curry

Reading Makes All Things Possible

Emily Dickinson wrote, "I dwell in possibility." That's what reading has done for me. It has opened up a world of possibility, empowering me to shape my reality and to help others shape theirs.

I realized the power of words at a young age. My teachers always described me as imaginative and poetic—an "over-describer." Words were a gift and during the lonely years of teenage angst, words provided cathartic release.

The first book I remember is the Bible. Those rich, dramatic stories I discovered at church filled my mind with wonder and helped shape my worldview. The second book I distinctly remember is *The BFG* by Roald Dahl. I read it in the first grade, and immediately fell in love with storytelling. I began filling journals with imaginative stories.

At my performing arts high school, I developed an even greater appreciation for reading and writing. I learned that stories contain messages; they are oracles of wisdom and truth that can impact the way a person might live his or her life. I had never looked at stories that way. Once I learned how to peel back the layers of meaning, I was changed. I had discovered a world of allegory, satire, parody, and symbolism—my eyes were opened. I felt a calling to introduce others to the power of story—to help them experience the life-changing potential of literature.

As a sophomore at Temple University, I chose to become a Secondary English Education Major. I went from simply exploring literature to learning how to teach literature. With each stage of my relationship with story, I discovered a deeper connection. And with each turn of the page, from elementary school to college, I discovered even greater potential in books. When I became a high school English teacher, I witnessed the transformative power of literature. I saw students begin to think and process their lives differently as a result of the stories we studied. However, there was one group that I could not reach. This group of students had skin that looked like mine. They were African American students who could not relate to Shakespeare or Whitman. I regard Shakespeare and Whitman as geniuses, but their works simply weren't penetrating the minds of my black students.

I was teaching in the suburbs just outside of Philadelphia, and the school where I taught was very diverse. I had students from various cultures and socio-economic classes, but many of my African American students, particularly the males, were not interested in reading. After several conversations with these students, I was inspired to write a novel of my own. I reconnected with my inner storyteller. I wanted to write a novel that spoke to an aspect of the black experience, but I wanted the novel to be more than just high interest. I wanted it to be a story with both urban edge and the sophistication of a Toni Morrison novel. And I wanted to send a message—one that would be applicable to all students. My novel—*You Down With O.P.D.?*—is a fictional story about two inner-city teenage males who lack the resources to fulfill their dreams and aspirations until they are given that opportunity by their musical idol. This rap icon gives these two young men the principles of success: O.P.D., which stands for *Organization, Planning,* and *Discipline.* These young men go on a journey to discover the meaning and power of these three principles, and it changes their lives.

Once I had completed and self-published the novel, I knew I wanted to share it with others, so I joined forces with my wife, who was also a high school English teacher. She taught in inner-city Philadelphia, and many of the demographics and challenges she faced were very different from those I experienced in the suburbs. By working with her, I discovered another hidden treasure of literature. Up until that point, I had seen how reading good literature could help students academically, but I had never seen how reading could actually change a student's life.

> I felt a calling to introduce others to the power of story—to help them experience the life-changing potential of literature.

Many nights, my wife would come home exhausted and frustrated. She told me that she was trying to take a group of her students to Paris. Many of them had never even left their neighborhoods, and all of them lacked the resources to finance the trip. Planning a trip to Paris seemed nearly an impossible feat, but I saw the passion in my wife's eyes. I wanted to know how I could support such a noble cause, and then it hit me. "Why don't you have them read and discuss my book? It may give them motivation," I said. Little did I know that we would embark on a journey that would change these students and profoundly change us. This group of teenagers began to read and discuss my novel. They identified with the characters, and they were taught how to find the richness in the symbolism. I spoke with them, and I was moved by their personal stories of hardship. I understood the economic disparity that crushed their hopes and limited their dreams, and my wife and I decided to do something about it.

We formed the OPD Movement Inc., a nonprofit designed to spread a message about success. Literature changed these students' minds, touched their emotions, and ignited a passion within their hearts. They achieved their goal, raising thousands of dollars to go to Paris—a goal many had scoffed at.

Reading changes lives—anything is possible.

●　●　●　●　●

Marcus Curry is a former high school English teacher. He is an author, playwright, and spoken word artist. He received his bachelor's degree in Secondary English Education from Temple University, later attending Cabrini College where he obtained his M.Ed. with a concentration in Reading Instruction. He is the founder of Urban Parables LLC, an education publishing company and consultation firm formed by a team of educators with the purpose of producing literature that is academically enriching and socially progressive. He is the author of the novel *You Down with O.P.D.?* and the co-founder of the OPD Movement Inc. He currently works as an education consultant and leader of the OPD Program, a social educational program geared towards urban students and based in the Washington, D.C. area. He resides in Maryland with his wife Nafisah and their dog Roscoe. To find out more about the work Curry is doing, reach out to him at www.urbanparables.com or www.opdmovement.com.

Kristina Mundera

Open the Door to Reading

*H*earing hushed giggles coming from the other side of my fence, I looked up from my book to peer through the banana trees that filled my backyard. Three young girls were leaning over the barbed wire, arms draped over each other's shoulders, hands hiding their smiles, and eyes shining with hope. After several more giggles, the oldest finally plucked up her courage to speak.

"Maestra, could we come in and read your books? We'll be really quiet!"

Before inviting the girls into my one-room home, I considered for a moment how tired I was after my teaching day (which had included a long, mountainous hike to several rural schools). But, of course I would open the door—what teacher would turn away young children yearning to read? As we sat huddled on the cement floor poring over my small selection of children's books, I marveled that this might be the first time these girls had held a book in their hands.

Books have been such an integral part of my life, I can't imagine how many books I have read over the years. Stored away in my memory, I have a large collection of beloved books that I can access whenever I need them—books that inspire me to stretch toward living my values, challenge me to consider new perspectives, take me on exciting adventures, offer me useful information, and console me and validate who I am in the world. In addition to the books I hold in my memory, there are thousands of books whose titles I have forgotten, but whose content helped shape who I am today.

Who would I be today without these books? Without this love of reading?

When I turned 13, my mother gave me 13 beautiful hardbound children's books. Although this gift might seem odd for a child on the brink of adolescence, my mother knew me well: my passion for the art form of beautiful children's literature has only deepened with age. Several years later, as I prepared to work as a Peace Corps volunteer in Nicaragua, it seemed only natural to dedicate as much space as possible in my limited luggage for the Spanish translations of a few of my favorites.

The three girls who arrived unannounced at my house read through every book I had that first night. That didn't deter them, however, from returning the next evening, this time with cousins and friends in tow. Soon my little house was bursting almost every evening with children who sprawled happily across my floor, immersed in the miracle of reading. This was obviously a different experience from what they typically experienced at school: memorizing letters off the blackboard.

What started as a simple request to read eventually turned into a large community project, which is now moving well into its second decade. With funds for materials coming from family and friends in the States, we built a children's library, a playground and, several years later, a preschool with the volunteer labor of community parents and children alike. By the last construction project, I was back in California teaching in a Spanish immersion program. During school vacations, however, I'd hop on a plane and return to Pueblo Nuevo to support our amazing librarians in their work.

A few years ago, we decided the time was ripe to expand our work into the local schools. We wanted to create a similar program in which rural teachers in Nicaragua could check out classroom sets of books and move their reading instruction off the blackboard and into quality literature. Which books merited the investment of a full class set? Where were the stories that reflected and validated these children's identity?

> Books open new worlds of possibility that develop our intellect and inspire our imagination.

"Let's write our own books," I finally suggested. "We can take pictures here in the community to illustrate them." How easy it all sounded. Of course, that was before I knew anything about photography.

Now picture me a year later, shoes covered in mud, sliding down a slippery incline under the cloud forest canopy as I animatedly shout, "Here come the monkeys —run! Yes, like that! Remember, Diego, you're scared!" I throw myself into the mud, lift my camera and attempt to hold it still enough to capture the band of young children tumbling after me. We wipe the mud off our faces and laugh and laugh and laugh, before trying it all over again. By this point in the project, I had learned enough about photographing children to know that every image correctly captured is a treasure only to be found among a hundred or so mistakes.

While not all of the books were as challenging to photograph as those for our fiction series, *The Adventures of Deyla and Diego*, over the course of creating 20-plus titles, we experienced our fair share of adventures and difficulties. All of the hard work was worth it, though, the moment I saw our finished books in the hands of the first class of students. The hum of distracted first graders was replaced with silent excitement as Irma turned the pages of our book, *Where Is Diego?* We heard cries of, "Look, that's our bus," and "Hey, he looks like my cousin!" as each child read through individual copies of our guided reading titles. It struck me, as I watched the lesson unfold, that I had never seen this scene in Nicaragua before: every student had a book in his or her hands—something we typically take for granted here in the States.

The name for our nonprofit is Abren, which in Spanish means "they open." In English, the name stands for "A Book to Read Empowers Nicaraguans" and over the past 15 years, I've been blessed to witness how books and the love of reading can do just that. Books open new worlds of possibility that develop our intellect and inspire our imagination. All children deserve an intimate relationship with reading.

And that little girl who asked me to open the door to reading so many years ago? Her love of reading grew and grew and carried her all the way through her schooling and into college, where she is now studying to be a teacher. She student teaches at the library she helped build with her very own hands.

● ● ● ● ●

Kristina Mundera headed to Pueblo Nuevo, Nicaragua, in 1999 as a Peace Corps volunteer with the hope of being able to offer her new community as much as she knew she would receive in return. As it happened, the children's library project she started changed Mundera's life as well as the lives of the families it continues to serve. Abren's most recent project has been creating a series of children's books that joyfully reflect the culture of rural Nicaragua. For more information, go to www.abren.org.

Closing Thoughts

*W*ithin the pages of this book, you'll find 118 distinct voices from every region of the country, including Alaska and Hawaii— and across the sea to Great Britain as well. One author attends college; others tend to their grandchildren and read to them daily. Some write and illustrate the books that open hearts wide; others study or teach the comprehension strategies that open the "intimate conversation" of reading. Academic or artist, researcher or teacher, our magnificent authors share a deep, true love of reading.

All celebrate reading for enriching their lives; some thank reading for saving their lives. And all share a fervent wish that children around the world enjoy abundant access to books so that they, too, may "live many parallel lives" and dream what may be possible for their own.

In the midst of editing this anthology, I lost my beloved mother. She was 88 years old and so fortunate to have lived a long and fulfilling life. Still, no one is ever prepared to lose a parent. I found myself turning to books— specifically, to my favorite poets—for comfort: Pablo Neruda, Naomi Shihab Nye, Mary Oliver, William Stafford, and Walt Whitman. Each one gave me the words to frame my grief, to help me accept the unacceptable, to understand the unfathomable.

Our authors explain, in this rich and varied collection, what books and reading have given them: they write of pleasure and play, comfort and companionship, introspection and illumination. "The ability to read is humanity's legacy," suggests Eduardo Puig. We read of lives so different from our own and, yet, often discover that beyond the surface distinctions of ethnicity, culture, gender, and age, all of us, all of humanity, are "connected at the core."

We must read, Frank Bruni writes; our well-being depends on it:

"Books are personal, passionate. They stir emotions and spark thoughts in a manner all their own, and I'm convinced that the shattered world has less hope for repair if reading becomes an ever smaller part of it."

Reading is a miracle. Every day, we can open a book, enter a world of possible, and heal ourselves, renew ourselves, and rejoice that we're not alone. We have books, we have each other, we have hope.

—Lois Bridges

List of Authors